Sādhu Sādhu!

Sādhu Sādhu!

A Life of Bābā Śrī Tinkaḍi Gosvāmī

Binode Bihari Das Bābājī

Translated from Bengali
with an introduction and notes
by
Neal Delmonico, PhD

Recollections of Bābā by Neal Delmonico,
Joseph Knapp
and
Mark Tinghino

Blazing Sapphire Press
715 E. McPherson
Kirksville, Missouri 63501
2008

ISBN 0-9747968-8-3 (978-0-9747968-8-8) (Paperback)

Library of Congress Control Number: 2008921093

Published by:
Blazing Sapphire Press
715 E. McPherson
Kirksville, Missouri 63501

Available at:
Nitai's Bookstore
715 E. McPherson
Kirksville, Missouri, 63501
Phone: (660) 665-0273
http://www.nitaisbookstore.com
http://www.blazingsapphirepress.com
Email: neal@blazingsapphirepress.com

Contents

Publisher's Foreword ix

Translator's Introduction xiii

Saints and Hagiography xxxi

This Translation xxxix

Introduction (Comments by Mādhava Dās Bābā) xli

Blessing xlvii

Author's Introduction xlix

Author's Acknowledgments liii

I Prabhupāda's Life Story 1

Early Life 3

Pilgrimage to Holy Sites 15

Second Marriage 21

Intense Practice in Vṛndāvana 31

Prabhupāda's Final Days 49

II Prabhupāda's Sweet Nature 63

Various Supernatural Incidents and Traits 67

A Miraculous Event 67
Protecting with His Subtle Body 68
Acquiring by Wish Alone 70
A Novel Incident 70
Curing Disease by Compassionate Glance 71
Grace Through Dreams 71
Ability to Know Things From Far 71
Knowing Mental States by Supernatural Power 72
Kṛṣṇa's Qualities in His Bhakta 74
Compassionate 75
Compassionate Salvation from the Wombs of Ghosts . . . 77
Inoffensive to Others 79
Truthful to the Core 80
Equable 80
Nonviolence of Living Beings Towards Prabhupāda 81
Faultless 83
Generosity 87
Softheartedness 87
Purity 88
Being Without Possessions 88
Offering Help To All 88
Peaceful 89

Without Lust 89
Indifferent 89
Calm 90
Conquered the Six Vices 90
Moderation in Eating 92
Without Frenzy 92
Humility 92
Taciturn 94
Compassion 94
Friendliness 94
Poetic 94
Expert 94
Silent 94
The Actual True Guru (*Sad-guru*) 95
Guileless Behavior like a Child 96
Unaware of Contemporary Affairs 97
Vigilant Observation Even Though Unmanifest 97

III Prabhupāda's Sūcaka Kīrtanas **101**

Kīrtana One **103**

Kīrtana Two (Śrī Hṛdayānanda Dāsa Bābājī) **131**

IV Appendices **173**

Glossary of Terms and Names **175**

Bābā Tinkaḍi Gosvāmī

Publisher's Foreword

It is with great happiness and joy that we are able to offer another wonderful book to the public, nicely translated by Dr. Delmonico. And being on the life of our most blessed Gurudev, it is of special significance and blessing not only for students of our particular *rasik* path but also for all people of the world. Reading about the lives of saints is important in many spiritual and religious traditions. It helps us to open our eyes, minds and hearts to new possibilities. As we read and think about the saints, we become inspired spiritually, imbibing the grace of their attainments through a process of loving remembrance. In reading about their lives we also find instruction and consolation on our own journeys on the path. How did they attain the goal? What did they go through? What did they sacrifice along the way? With what advice do they leave us?

The great Vaiṣṇava saint presented here represents one of the last of his kind, perhaps the last of his era, for, as anyone can see, modernity is such that it can now hardly be escaped. With the influx of so much wealth into India and the resultant modernization of life there, it becomes harder and harder for the present generation of practitioners to devote their minds, bodies and souls, with diligence and concentration, to full time practice of the traditional path.

The distractions have increased. More and more wealthy people, wanting to buy entrance into heaven or an even more affluent and comfortable life while here on earth, give more and more wealth to the *sādhus* and saints in the hope of accruing their blessings. It is a miracle that the *sādhus* are left with any sanity at all. The noise, the pollution, the hustle and bustle and finally, yes, the competition. With the stakes higher now we see a lot of competition for students—the belief being that more students equal more power and wealth and therefore more prestige. It has even reached the point that some so-called holy people, self-proclaimed gurus and god-men, however well established they may be, now try to steal outright *āśramas* (monasteries), money, followers, land, and so forth from others.

The above might sound surprising to many who read this: What? In the holy land of India!? How can this happen there? The answer, however distasteful, is that it has been happening there for hundreds of years—yet with an increased level of audacity such that nowadays, it is unmistakable. And yet many people are still fooled—they are unwilling or unable to distinguish a real saint from a fraud, or, harder still, from a half-fraud. How can one see the true qualities of a person or what the real motivations are for what they do? Are they self-proclaimed and therefore self-involved, or are they selflessly serving according to the orders of the guru? Do they humbly follow the path set forth by the acts and instructions of the guru? Or have they become swept up by the business-like modernity, which is more like an illness than the needed medicine?

With the dynamic increase of land prices that has scourged the whole world, the stakes get higher and greed becomes more intense. No doubt it is a sad situation, but we are on the earth in a time that is not nurturing to any form of life including human life! There has never been a time on earth, at least in recorded history, free of strife, free of greed, free of dishonesty perpetrated on others. Since this is so and there does not seem to be much we can do about it, perhaps we should look instead into our own psyches, our own characters, and try to work on ourselves and become as much as we are able, living examples of wisdom, truth, devotion, compassion, joy and loving-kindness. That is the sub-text of this book!

So let us dive deeply into stories of the lives of the saints and especially into this account of the life of this saint with whom some of us have lived and whom we have served personally. This is a translation from Bengali of a disciple's collection of the biographical details of the life of Śrīmān Tinkaḍi Gosvāmī. While it is a sincere and honest work, it represents the views and experiences of only a few of Bābā Tinkaḍi's disciples, collected and arranged by Śrī Binode Bihari Das Bābā. Therefore, we have added some 'extra accounts' in the form of our own reminiscences of the times we spent in the presence of our blessed Gurudev. Perhaps, in addition, you will find in these accounts the seed of something holy, profound, and liberating. May that indescribable seed take root in your hearts, where, it is our hope, it will grow, flower and eventually fructify, filling your lives with the delightful sweetness of divine love.

> *gurur brahmā gurur viṣṇur gurur devo maheśvaraḥ*
> *gurur sākṣāt parabrahma tasmai śrīgurave namaḥ*

"The guru is Brahmā; the guru is Viṣṇu; the guru is the god Maheśvara. The guru is supreme brahman directly. Unto that guru we bow."

Jagadish Das
June 20, 2007
Gokula Dhāma,
Kirksville, Missouri

Translator's Introduction

Binode Bihari Das Bābājī's book on the life of Bābā Tinkaḍi Gosvāmī, which is translated here, is called in Bengali *Prabhupāda Śrī Śrī 108 Kiśorī-kiśorānanda Bābā Tinkaḍi Bābā Jīvana Caritra*. This is certainly a much longer name than the one we have given it in English: "Sādhu Sādhu: a Life of Bābā Tinkaḍi Gosvāmī." A literal translation of the original Bengali name would read something like this, "The Life and Deeds of Prabhupāda Śrī Śrī 108 Kiśorīkiśorānanda Bābā also known as Tinkaḍi Bābā." That is quite a mouthful and has hardly any meaning to most Western readers who are unfamiliar with the Caitanya Vaiṣṇava tradition, to which the saint described in this book belonged. "Prabhupāda" is a title of respect given to members of the Caitanya Vaiṣṇava community who are born into traditional Caitanyite families that trace their ancestry back to the original members of the community of followers of Śrī Caitanya (15-16th cents.). Such hereditary families of Vaiṣṇavas, commonly called Goswamis (in strict diacritical style, Gosvāmins or Gosvāmīs), have formed the backbone of the Caitanya tradition almost since its inception over five hundred years ago. The tradition's cherished mantras, texts, and practices have been developed, preserved and handed down in these families, generation after generation, and the members of those families have acted as the gurus or spiritual guides for the Caitanya tradition throughout its existence. *Prabhu* means "master" and to it is added *pāda* which means "foot." One does not, according to proper Vaiṣṇava etiquette, refer directly to one's master, or spiritual preceptor, but to his feet, that is, his lowest part. The word *prabhupāda* is thus an expression of the humility and respect with which one should regard one's spiritual guide and preceptor and it is also part of the training in humility the disciple must undergo. Humility, though not much understood or appreciated in the modern world, is considered an important virtue, perhaps *the* most important virtue in the Caitanya tradition. The saint who is the focus of this book was born into one of those hereditary families of Caitanya Vaiṣṇavas and thus is rightfully referred to by the title "Prabhupāda" by his disciples and others who wish to follow the proper etiquette and show him respect. What about his own humility, someone might ask? He had his own Prabhupādas, his own masters and teachers, before whom he humbled himself and under the guidance of whom he cultivated his own humility.

The business with the "Śrī Śrī 108" is another manifestation of Vaiṣṇava or Hindu etiquette. When referring to someone who is highly regarded or honored, one places the word "Śrī" (for women Śrīmatī) in front of that person's name as a kind of honorific prefix, meaning Sir or Revered. *Śrī* means "light, luster, radiance, splendor, glory, beauty, and grace." Thus, when placed before a person's name, it suggests that that person possesses those fine qualities and is thus worthy of one's respect and honor. Some people, not satisfied with the placement of just one "Śrī," which out of common politeness can be placed in front of anyone's name, wish to place a whole string of "Śrīs" before a name to indicate extraordinary reverence and high regard for the person named. The "108" in this formula means that the author wishes to place one hundred and eight "Śrīs" in front of the name of Tinkaḍi Bābā to indicate that he stands high above all others in grace, fortune, and reverence. One hundred and eight is an auspicious number in Indic culture. Why this is so is not entirely clear, but it has many extraordinary qualities[1] and it appears in many important contexts in the Hindu and Buddhist traditions. There are officially one hundred and eight *Upaniṣads*. Many of the gods and goddesses have hymns composed of one hundred and eight names. There are one hundred and eight beads on strings of meditation beads, and so forth.

Of his many names, two are represented in the Bengali title of this book. He was known as Kiśorīkiśorānanda Bābā. The first part of that name means "one who brings pleasure to the young lady (Rādhā) and the young man (Kṛṣṇa)," that is, one who is a source of joy for the main deities of the Caitanya tradition, Rādhā and Kṛṣṇa. Conversely, it can also mean "one whose only joy is found in the young lady and young man," an indication of his devotion to and love for Rādhā and Kṛṣṇa. This first name, Kiśorīkiśorānanda, was his given name; that is, it was

---

[1]It is an abundant number, a semiperfect number, and a tetranacci number. It is the hyperfactorial of 3 having the form: $1^1 \times 2^2 \times 3^3$.

the name given to him by his father, Śrī Harimohana Goswami, probably after consulting with astrologers, as is the general practice in India when a child is named. "Bābā" or "Bābājī" means "father" and is the title given to male members of the renunciant community of Caitanya Vaiṣṇavism. "Bābā" is the way a member of that community is generally addressed. Women as renunciants are often referred to as Mātājī, "mother."

His other name, "Tinkaḍi," is a nickname commemorating an odd little rite that his midwife performed at the time of his birth. After she cut his umbilical cord, she declared, "This is my son." His mother, Suradhuni Devī, had to buy him back from the midwife for three cowries (*kaḍi*), or three pennies. Thus, his name became Tinkaḍi (pronounced Teen-kardi or Teen-kurdi) "Three Pennies." The purpose of this rite was no doubt to protect the child. Since he was sold for three pennies, the impression was created, for any greedy beings, both natural and supernatural, visible and invisible, who might have been watching and coveting the new-born baby, that the child was not worth very much and that he should be of little or no interest to them. Tinkaḍi Gosvāmī was the eighth child of his parents. His six older brothers and one older sister all died in childhood. Thus, it was that his superstitious midwife and anxious mother sought to protect him in any way they could. This folk ritual is reminiscent of the way in which Śacīdevī, Śrī Caitanya's mother, named him Nimāi as an infant. Nimāi refers to the Nimba tree which has very bitter and unpleasant leaves. There, too, the idea was to make Caitanya unattractive to any kidnapers or evil spirits.

In addition to the two mentioned in the title of the Bengali version of this book, Tinkaḍi Bābā had several other names as well, reflecting some of his other qualities and practices. He was widely known in Vraja (the major religious center in India for worshipers of Kṛṣṇa) as Maunī Bābā, "Silent Father," because he maintained a vow of silence (*mauna*) during various stages of his religious cultivation. He was known as Ṭāṭa Bābā, "Burlap Father," because he only wore cloth made out of burlap. Even his shoes and bedding were made of burlap. He was known as Bānglā Bābā, "Bengali Father," because he was Bengali. He was known as Gosvāmī Bābā because he was a member of a respected Gosvāmī family. In addition to all these commonly known names, in the spiritual realm Bābā had a spiritual name and identity which was secret, known only to his closest disciples and companions.

Instead of translating the Bengali title we have given the English version of Binode Bihari Das Bābājī's book a different title, as I have already mentioned: "Sādhu Sādhu: a Life of Bābā Tinkaḍi Gosvāmī." A few words of explanation are necessary. The title is based on an event witnessed by Jagadish Das (Joseph Knapp) and written about in his essay in the appendix of this book recalling some of his experiences with Bābā. One time someone came to visit Bābā and when Bābā saw the person, he immediately said, "Sādhu Sādhu!" *Sādhu* means "holy or saintly man" (feminine form: *sādhvī*) It seems that Bābā saw in his visitor a special quality of goodness or holiness that made him exclaim, "Sādhu Sādhu," as soon as he saw him. We thought that those two words would be an appropriate title for a book that attempts to present the unusual goodness and holiness of Tinkaḍi Bābā himself. "Sādhu Sādhu" also means in Sanskrit something like "Well done! Well done!" That, too, seems appropriate when recounting the life of a great Vaiṣṇava practitioner like Tinkaḍi Bābā.

This book is part of a series of works that attempts to explore modern Caitanya Vaiṣṇavism through the lives and teachings of some of its well-known and respected saint-practitioners. The first book in this series was *The Life and Teachings of Krishna Das Baba of Radhakund* by Zakrent Christian (Karunamayi Das). In that work, the author sought to demonstrate that Śrī Krishna Das Baba fit the criteria of sainthood based on a certain vision of the nature of a saint in the Caitanya tradition. According to that vision a saint is a living, breathing embodiment of the important texts of the tradition. Not only do the saint's actions fully accord with the tradition's textual guidelines and expectations, the texts veritably pervade the consciousness of the saint and spring forth from his or her mouth at every available opportunity. As a result of this approach to sainthood, Zakrent Christian's book forms a valuable introduction not only to his beloved guru, as an example of lived experience within the tradition, but also to the fundamental texts of the Caitanya tradition within certain of its communities. This approach to the study of religion as a mode of textual reception or reading has captured the attention of some scholars of religion of late,[2] That approach to the study of religion seems promising, especially with respect to Caitanya Vaiṣṇavism and some of the other Indic religious traditions. A similar approach which focuses on the lives of the saints as data for understanding a religious tradition is found in many of the works of Dr. O.B.L. Kapoor which are in the process of being re-edited and republished by Blazing Sapphire Press. One of his shorter works, *Experiences in Bhakti: the Science Celes-*

[2]Most notably Gavin Flood and Oliver Davies in their forthcoming *Religion as Reading: Text, Ritual, Asceticism.*

tial, has already become available.

In the immediate future we intend to publish an English translation of a life of Siddha Manohara Dāsa Bābājī by one of his disciples, Navadvīpa Dāsa Bābājī. Siddha Manohara Dāsa Bābājī was a great practitioner of private worship (*bhajana*) and a *śikṣā* or instructing guru of Bābā Tinkaḍi Gosvāmī. Along with the story of his life and an account of his practices we will include in the book one of his original works, the *Śrī Vaidagdha-vilāsa*, "The Play of Cleverness." Beyond that we hope in the future to present accounts of great saint-practitioners like Śrī Vijayakṛṣṇa Gosvāmī, Śrī Rāma Dāsa Bābājī, Śrī Hṛdayānanda Dāsa Bābājī, and others. Through the medium of biography, or more properly hagiography, we hope that a more life-like image and understanding of modern Caitanya Vaiṣṇavism will emerge than one gets solely by studying its classical texts.

Some engaged in the academic study of religion have begun in recent years to realize the importance of hagiography for understanding a religious tradition. Rupert Snell pointed out in his introduction to one of the few works devoted to the exploration of hagiography in India:

> Such 'biographies' typically contain elements of the fantastic such as miracles and a variety of chronological impossibilities offensive to the historical basis of objective research principles; such ostensibly 'biographical' writing has often, in consequence, been dismissed out of hand as a tedious impediment to verifiable historiography. More recent research on this literature, however, sees it as addressing and revealing facets of belief and attitude which, though at some remove from historical actuality, lie at the very heart of the traditions that they represent; and indeed this literature allows us to understand more fully not only the nature of the traditions being studied but also the mechanics whereby they propagate themselves.[3]

It is with the hope of approaching a fuller understanding of the core beliefs and practices of the Caitanya tradition as it exists today that we intend to present and discuss the hagiographies of many of the important saint-practitioners of this tradition. Additionally, we hope that by

[3]Rupert Snell, "Introduction: Themes in Indian Hagiography," in *According to Tradition: Hagiographical Writing in India*, p. 1. (Wiesbaden: Harrassowitz Verlag, 1994.)

presenting these hagiographies we may contribute to a better general understanding of the nature and roles of saints and their hagiographies in modern Indic religious movements and traditions. As Snell concludes in the same essay:

> The hagiographical traditions discussed here are varied in respect of time, place, language, religion, register, and purpose. Of the many connections between them, the formulae through which the narratives are told are particularly evident: miracle stories (including miraculous births, comparable to the *svayambhū* origins of temple deities), dream interventions, precocious erudition, conquests in debate with established scholars, conversions, adventurous journeys, credence-stretching longevity, formulaic sacred numbers and other such themes occur time and again, inviting recourse to a system of motif classification such as is applied to folk narrative and oral epic. Some hagiographies are naive and predictable panegyrics; others act as informal commentary on the primary writings of *bhaktas*; still others play a central part in the formulation and transmission of sectarian theology and communal identity. In all such categories, the genre of hagiography offers fertile ground for many different aspects of scholarly research in the history of Indian culture and religion.[4]

At the present, I am unaware of any system of motif classification developed out of Indic hagiographical writings.[5] William J. Jackson has produced an interesting set of twelve motifs on the basis of his study of South Indian saints which will be discussed later in connection with the present hagiography. Apart from that it appears that little progress has been made since Snell's essay appeared in a collection of essays on Indian hagiography some fifteen years ago.

The present work by Binode Bihari Das Bābājī takes a less textual approach than Zakrent Christian's work on Śrī Krishna Das Baba does. The textual approach is still present to some degree, however, especially in some of the later sections of the biography where Binode Bābā tries to

[4]ibid., 12-13.

[5]There are, of course, a considerable number of hagiographic motifs in the motif index which have been selected out for India in Jonas Balys and Stith Thompson's *The Oral Tales of India* and in Thompson and Warren Roberts' *Types of Indic Oral Tales*.

demonstrate that Tinkaḍi Goswami had all of the qualities that the scriptures say true Vaiṣṇavas should have. The implication is that Tinkaḍi Gosvāmī embodied or proved the validity of the scriptural texts. In fact, it often works both ways. The scriptural texts authenticate the saint and the saint in turn authenticates the scriptural texts; that is, he demonstrates their truth in the events, experiences, and qualities of his own life and character. This tension between lived religious experience and the textual tradition has been an important and enduring dialectic in the history of the Caitanya Vaiṣṇavism. One can see it at the beginning of the tradition in the relationship between Śrī Caitanya and his learned disciple Sanātana Gosvāmin. Sanātana, with the help of his younger brother Rūpa and nephew Jīva, was charged with the responsibility of justifying and authenticating in scripture the ecstatic experiences and religious madness of Śrī Caitanya. In turn, Śrī Caitanya no doubt represented for Sanātana and his helpers the embodied fulfillment of those ancient sacred texts, the clear evidence that the claims found in scripture were true.

Binode Bābā in his book places greater stress on events of a supernatural or miraculous nature in Tinkaḍi Bābā's life as evidence of his saint-hood. Numerous anecdotes are presented in which Tinkaḍi Bābā knows things that are happening far away or visits in his spiritual or astral body disciples who are sick or injured in the hospital and helps them to heal. Many times dreams are involved, in which Bābā appears and speaks or in which some deity appears to give instruction and guidance to various disciples on some matter. These stories, gathered from various of Bābā's disciples, apparently represent just a small sampling. Another couple of Tinkaḍi Bābā's disciples have collected together such stories about Tinkaḍi in large numbers. The point of these stories is to demonstrate that Bābā in his state of "perfection" or "accomplishment" (*siddhatva*) had acquired many miraculous abilities and powers, called *siddhis*, as patent evidence of his great achievement. This is certainly one approach to the question of saintliness in Caitanya Vaiṣṇavism and in other South Asian religious traditions.

There is something, however, even more fundamental in Binode Bābā's presentation of the life of Tinkaḍi Bābā that also tells us something of his vision of the nature of the saint in Caitanya Vaiṣṇavism. That is Tinkaḍi Bābā's single-minded, whole-hearted, can't-be-swayed-from-it, enthusiastic, and, yes, almost maniacal pursuit of his spiritual goals. We learn from Binode's account that Tinkaḍi Bābā was a distracted and frivolous child; he was not interested in anything but playing. When it came time to go to school he would often hide out somewhere to avoid having to go. This trait is often a feature of Indian biography and hagiography, and culturally it is understood as a sign of precociousness, intelligence, and future promise. Something, however, changed in him when he underwent his *brāhmaṇa* initiation at roughly the age of nine, and that change was later reinforced and strengthened when he received his Vaiṣṇava initiation from his father. Tinkaḍi Gosvāmī then left behind the frivolity of his childhood and some sort of spiritual awakening occurred in him that became the object of his pursuit for the rest of his life. It drew him away from home to the sites of pilgrimage in the Himalayas and eventually to Vraja, the heartland of Kṛṣṇa worship. It caused him to regard his household life as a dark well from which he must escape. Something in him was no longer satisfied with the sights, sounds and homely pleasures of ordinary, everyday life. He was consumed with a burning passion for something greater and with the troubling sense that human life had a greater purpose than just begetting children and making money so he could eat good food, smoke good tobacco, ride in fine palanquins, and wear the finest cloth. This yearning for intimacy with the divine rattled him, unsettled his mind and caused him to run away from home on several occasions. It was, indeed, the driving force behind his spiritual cultivation and many would say the prime cause of his eventual success.

The process by which Tinkaḍi Bābā achieved his success is never very clearly presented in Binode Bābā's book, which is rather odd. If, as he says in his introduction, one of his goals was to provide those striving for *bhakti* with a model for its practice, then more should have been said about how Tinkaḍi Bābā actually practiced Caitanya Vaiṣṇavism. We hear of his organizing seven-day long, ceremonial readings of the *Bhāgavata Purāṇa*, of his holding festive feasts, open to all, to distribute grace-food (*prasāda*), and of his organizing non-stop *kīrtanas* or musical presentations of songs featuring the holy names, qualities, forms, and activities of Rādhā and Kṛṣṇa. Tinkaḍi Bābā's practice is mostly referred to simply as *bhajana* or "private worship," but what exactly that is is never clearly spelled out. We hear of him rising very early and we hear of him "remembering" his mantras.

Those of us who knew Tinkaḍi Bābā personally, who stayed with him for some time, know something more about his daily practices. He used to rise very early (around one or two in the morning) and begin *japa* or recitation of Kṛṣṇa's names in the form of the mantra known as the Mahāmantra, or the Great Incantation.[6]

The combination of recitation of mantra (*mantra-japa*) and remembering the divine activities (*līlā-smaraṇa*) is generally what is meant by *bhajana* or private worship. Tinkaḍi Bābā's practice was to repeat the names of Kṛṣṇa three hundred thousand times a day, a process that took him from ten to twelve hours to complete, during which he observed a vow of silence.[7] That is to say, until he had completed his daily *japa* he would not speak to anyone or respond to questions except in case of emergency. During this period of *japa* he also "remembered" the divine activities (*līlā-smaraṇa*) of Rādhā and Kṛṣṇa in Vraja,[8] the practice taught him by his instructing guru, Śrī Manohara Das Bābājī. This was the core of his daily practice. This core practice would be punctuated or interrupted at various times throughout the day by other practices and rituals, such as the morning greeting ceremony (*maṅgala ārati*) of the sacred images which he attended (about an hour and a half before sunrise), remembering his initiation mantras (around sunrise), lunch (or the honoring of grace-food, the holy remnants of food offered to the sacred images, around one in the afternoon), group reading of *bhakti* texts (around three or four in the afternoon), the evening greeting ceremony of the sacred images (around six or seven in the evening), the evening *kīrtana* (after the evening greeting) and finally dinner (again honoring grace-food around nine or ten at night). In this way his day was filled with recollection of the names and activities of Rādhā and Kṛṣṇa.

The question now arises, "what does this sort of practice or cultiva-

---

[6]The Mahāmantra:

Hare Kṛṣṇa Hare Kṛṣṇa
Kṛṣṇa Kṛṣṇa Hare Hare
Hare Rāma Hare Rāma
Rāma Rāma Hare Hare

This mantra is found in several places in the Hindu scriptures. It is found, for instance, in a short apocryphal Upaniṣad called the *Kali-santaraṇa Upaniṣad* ("Crossing Over in the Age of Kali") where it is called the *tāraka-brahma* mantra or name. That means "the mantra composed of sacred speech (*brahma*) that carries one beyond the material world." There it appears in the reverse order, with the third and fourth quarters given first and the first and second quarters given last. It also appears in the *Brahmāṇḍa Purāṇa* in the order given above.

[7]Three hundred thousand names is rounded to going one hundred and ninety-two times around a string of Vaiṣṇava chanting beads, much like a rosary, which contains one hundred and eight beads, repeating one complete Mahāmantra on each bead. Each mantra contains thirty-two syllables amounting to sixteen names. Thus, 16 x 108 x 192 = 331,776.

[8]Vraja is the idyllic, pastoral paradise in which Kṛṣṇa lives eternally with his parents, friends and cowherd girl lovers.

tion lead to?" The Caitanya tradition divides *bhakti* into two or three distinct aspects. Śrī Rūpa Gosvāmin in his *Bhakti-rasāmṛta-sindhu* or "Ocean of the Nectar of the Flavors of Devotion," which is considered one of the most authoritative accounts of *bhakti* for the tradition, says, "That bhakti [as defined in general terms in the previous chapter] is said to be threefold: *bhakti* as practice, *bhakti* as feeling, and *bhakti* as love."[9] *Bhakti* as practice includes as an essential part *bhajana* or private worship as described above. In addition to that there is public worship which includes participation in *kīrtana* (singing and sometimes dancing), rites connected with the worship of sacred images (ritual greetings and offerings), and readings from sacred texts. The other two aspects of *bhakti,* feeling and love, are considered aspects of *bhakti* as goal. Thus, the word *bhakti* is used to mean both practice and goal. *Bhakti* as feeling or *bhāva* is defined by Rūpa Gosvāmin:

> *Bhakti* as feeling (*bhāva*) is said to be a particular kind of pure being or existence which is like a ray of the sun of divine love and which by its illumination softens the heart."[10]

Bhakti as feeling is closely connected with *bhakti* as love or divine love (*preman*), being here described as "a ray of the sun of divine love." *Bhakti* as feeling is thus the first stage in the appearance of divine love. Just as the first rays of the sun in the morning give one warmth and relief from the chill and darkness of the night, *bhakti* as feeling warms one up and illumines one with the first glimmering or awakening of love for Kṛṣṇa. This is in part what is meant when it is said that *bhakti* as feeling softens the heart. Beyond that, in native Indian psychology, powerful emotions are thought to soften the mind or heart, leaving behind them lasting impressions, like markings left in wax after it has hardened again, that then become part of the surviving mind-scape of the persons who underwent them. The impressions left by *bhakti* are considered different from those left by ordinary powerful emotions in that they have a transcendent source in the presence of this ray of pure being or goodness

---

[9]Śrī Rūpa Gosvāmin, *Bhakti-rasāmṛtra-sindhu*, 1.2.1: सा भक्तिः साधनं भावः प्रेमा चेति त्रिधोदिता।

[10]ibid., 1.3.1:

> 'सुद्धसत्त्वविशेषात्मा प्रेमसूर्यांशुसाम्यभाक्।
> रुचिभिश्चित्तमासृण्यकृदसौ भाव उच्यते॥

(*śuddha-sattva-viśeṣātmā*) in the individual.[11]

How is the presence of *bhakti* as feeling or *bhāva* known? Rūpa cites from an unidentified *tantra* which describes the effects of this divine presence.

> The first stage of divine love is called *bhāva* (*bhakti* as feeling). In it occur in small measure the physical manifestations (*sāttvika*): tears, horripilation, and so forth.[12]

The physical manifestations referred to here are the classical *sāttvikas*, autonomic physical manifestations of powerful internal emotions. There are eight given in the standard lists found in the texts on drama and literary criticism. They are: being stunned or immobilized, perspiration, horripilation, cracking of the voice, shuddering, loss or change of color, tears, and fainting.[13] These appear in small measure in persons who have reached the level of *bhakti* as feeling. Naturally, they occur in full measure in people who have reached the level of *bhakti* as love. During

---

[11]This thing of pure being or goodness is rather mysterious in Śrī Rūpa's text. His nephew Śrī Jīva commenting on this verse is more specific and detailed. He defines *śuddha-sattva-viśeṣātmā* as a self-revealing operation of the internal or essential power (*svarūpa-śakti*) of Bhagavān called the *saṃvit* or the power of awareness, and denies that it is an operation of the illusory power of this world, *māyā*. Śrī jīva informs us that he discusses this operation at more length in the second treatise of his six-treatise work called the *Bhāgavata-sandarbha* and in the second chapter of his *Vaiṣṇava-toṣaṇī*, his commentary on the *Bhāgavata Purāṇa*. He then cites a famous verse from the *Viṣṇu Purāṇa* that describes the three essential or inherent powers of Bhagavān: ह्लादिनी सन्धिनी संवित्त्वय्येका सर्वसंस्थितौ। ह्लादताप-करी मिश्रा त्वयि नो गुणवर्जिते॥, "Pleasure-giving, together-holding, and consciousness-informing are main powers in you, who are the support of all. The joyful, miserable, and mixed are not in you who are free from the material strands (*guṇa*)." (1.12.69-70) Śrī Jīva then argues that in accordance with the meaning of that verse, one should understand that this *śuddha-sattva-viśeṣātmā* is the core portion of the consciousness-informing power (*saṃvit*) inherently or intimately connected with the core operation (*sāra-vṛtti*) of the great power called the "pleasure-giving power" (*hlādinī-śakti*). Thus it combines two powers: consciousness-informing and pleasure-giving. The point of specifying "core" here is to suggest the idea that it is the bare essentials of those two powers that compose *bhakti* as feeling (*bhāva*). The more developed, enhanced, and fully articulated versions of this *śuddha-sattva-viśeṣa* are found in Kṛṣṇa's greatest *bhaktas* like Rādhikā and others in the form of the great emotion (*mahābhāva*) and the rest.

[12]ibid., 1.3.2:

> प्रेम्णस्तु प्रथमावस्था भाव इत्यभिधीयते।
> सात्त्विकाः स्वल्पमात्राः स्युरत्राश्रुपुलकादयः॥

[13]ibid., 2.3.16.

the period when I was getting to know Tinkaḍi Bābā, and later when I lived with him and his entourage for a time, I was told often and by several different people that Bābā had experienced all of those physical effects, sometimes just one or two at a time and sometimes all eight at the same time. I never saw symptoms personally, however—unless I did, but simply failed to recognize them. I was also rarely in a position to observe him closely under circumstances in which they might have been present in him.

Another verse that Rūpa cites from the *Padma Purāṇa* connects intense and repeated meditation, such as one practices in *bhajana*, with the experience of those physical effects:

> After meditating repeatedly on the lotus-like feet of Bhagavān [Śrī Kṛṣṇa], the eyes [of a King Ambarīṣa] who was undergoing slight transformation became tearful.[14]

Here we see represented the transition from *bhakti* as practice to *bhakti* as result or experience. A strong connection is forged between intense and repeated meditational practice and the softening of the heart that is indicated in this verse by tearful eyes. The tearful eyes represent a relatively mild manifestation of the *sāttvikas* as compared with the outpouring of profuse tears and intense weeping connected with the experience of divine love. This again suggests that *bhakti* as feeling is the seed or first stage of the development of *bhakti* as love. Is there, though, some causal relationship between meditating and the development of *bhakti* as feeling, as this text implies?

According to Śrī Rūpa, whose considered opinion became for succeeding generations the authoritative statement of the views of the Caitanya tradition, that special element of pure being (*śuddha-sattva-viśeṣātman*) appears from outside or beyond the natural elements or constituents of the person in whom it appears and becomes an essential part of that person's mental operations. Rūpa says:

> After appearing among the mental operations it becomes of their essential nature [that is, it becomes one with them].

[14]ibid., 1.3.3:

> ध्यायं ध्यायं भगवतः पादाम्बुजयुगं तदा।
> ईषद्विक्रियमाणात्मा सार्द्रदृष्टिरभूदसौ॥

> Though by nature self-revealing it appears like something that needs to be revealed [an object of illumination instead of illumination, itself]. Though that attraction (*rati*) is essentially relish itself, it acts like the cause of a relishing that has Kṛṣṇa and the others as its objects.[15]

As I suggested before in another introductory essay, this idea of the infusion of a divine power or presence into the hearts and minds of practitioners can be usefully understood as a kind of possession experience.[16] One in that situation is pushed beyond self-control, into a state that is much appreciated and praised by members of the Caitanya tradition. One weeps, shudders, one's hair stands on end, one's voice cracks and one faints, all uncontrollably. India is full of religions that feature possession experiences that operate on all levels of society, ranging from simpler folk religions to the more complex religions of the upper classes. Why should Caitanya Vaiṣṇavism be any different? Yet, there are differences among all these various expressions of possession religion. India's vast religious panorama is a brilliant example of a unity-in-diversity or in the terms of the Caitanyite tradition inconceivable difference-and-nondifference. Thus, rather than possession by a goddess or a god, Caitanya Vaiṣṇava practitioners are possessed by a divine power, a power formally described as belonging to Bhagavān's essential being and as bearing the core part of the divine pleasure-giving power inherently connected with the core part of the consciousness-informing power. Thus, two capacities are bestowed on the recipient of this power: the capacity to know and the capacity to please. The capacity to know is the capacity to know both the true nature of the divine being and one's own true nature in relationship with that divine being. The capacity to please is the capacity to give pleasure or joy to the divine being and thereby secondarily taste pleasure oneself. This is *bhakti* as goal in the view of the Caitanya Vaiṣṇava tradition. Most importantly, though, *bhakti* is understood fundamentally as a type of knowledge or

---

[15]ibid., 1.3.4-5:

> आविर्भूय मनोवृत्तौ व्रजन्ती तत्स्वरूपताम्।
> स्वयम्प्रकाशरूपापि भासमाना प्रकाश्यवत्॥
> वस्तुतः स्वयमास्वादस्वरूपैव रतिस्त्वसौ।
> कृष्णादिकरमकास्वादहेतुत्वं प्रतिपद्यते॥

[16]See my introduction to Zakrent Christian's *The Life and Teachings of Krishna Das Baba of Radhakund*, xi-xii.

consciousness.[17]

Śrī Rūpa defines *bhakti* as divine love as a development or intensification of *bhakti* as feeling. He says:

> *Bhakti* as feeling (*bhāva*) when intensified, causing its possessor's heart to become completely softened and marked by an abundance of possessiveness, the wise call divine love (*preman*).[18]

Bhakti as divine love is thus an intensification of *bhakti* as feeling which is its core. Nothing new is infused into a person with the appearance of divine love. Divine love builds or grows upon the core that was already present by the infusion of the element of pure being that marked the transition between *bhakti* as practice and *bhakti* as feeling. A significant new development is the sense of possessiveness or *mamatā* (lit. "mine-ness") with respect to the divine being, Kṛṣṇa. The experience of intimacy is thus heightened here. It goes almost without saying that the expression of the eight *sāttvikas* is more frequent and more intense in *bhakti* as divine love. That is the significance of the complete softening or melting of the heart. The experience of *bhakti* as divine love is what is meant by "accomplishment" or *siddhi* and this distinguishes the saint or *siddha*, the accomplished one, from all others.

There is perhaps one more element of the state of "accomplishment" that requires discussion. In a rather extraordinary section of his *Ocean*

[17] Baladeva Vidyābhūṣaṇa argues that *bhakti* is a type of knowledge in his *Siddhānta-ratna*, 1.32: भक्तिरपि ज्ञानविशेषो भवतीति ज्ञानत्वसामान्यात् तमेवेति विद्यैवेति च व्यपदेशः।, "Bhakti, also, is a type of knowledge, because it shares the general quality of being knowledge. It is thus called knowledge in those passages: 'Having known him one passes over death. There is no other path for progressing [to liberation]' (*Śvetāśvara Upaniṣad*, 3.8) and 'But knowledge alone is the cause of liberation because scripture ascertains it' (*Brahma-sūtra*, 3.3.48)." A more complete statement of his argument, drawing from para. 1.31, is as follows: The Lord says in the *Bhāgavata* (11.20.6) that he has taught three yogas out of a desire for the highest good for human beings: the yoga of knowledge, the yoga of action, and the yoga of *bhakti*. However, the yoga of action is not a direct cause of the highest good but assists the other two by cleansing the minds of the practitioners. Thus, when knowledge alone is said to be the only direct cause of the highest good (as in the two passages cited above), it must mean that *bhakti*, too, is a type of knowledge. Otherwise, the Lord's statement in the *Bhāgavata* would be falsified.

[18] Rūpa, ibid., 1.4.1:

> सम्यङ्मसृणितस्वान्तो ममत्वातिशयाङ्कितः।
> भावः स एव सान्द्रात्मा बुधैः प्रेमा निगद्यते॥

of the Nectar of the Flavors of Devotion, Śrī Rūpa Gosvāmin, after listing and providing examples of the sixty-four "limbs" or forms of *bhakti* as practice, singles out the final five forms for special attention. Those five forms of *bhakti* as practice are: service of the sacred images, listening to the *Bhāgavata Purāṇa*, associating with *bhaktas* of Kṛṣṇa, repeating the holy names, and residing in the holy land of Vraja. These five forms, says Śrī Rūpa, have a special vigor or power:

> In this group of five there is an amazing and hard-to-comprehend power. Put faith far aside for the moment. Even a tiny connection with those five brings about the birth of *bhāva*, *bhakti* as feeling, in those who have good hearts (*sad-dhī*).[19]

Those five forms of *bhakti* as practice, says Rūpa, work even without faith or also even, it would seem, without foreknowledge. Just as one is burned by fire, whether one has faith in its power to burn or any knowledge of fire's capacity to burn, so is the performance of those five forms of *bhakti* as practice effective without any faith or knowledge. And what is it that they do? They bring about *bhakti* as feeling. There is a qualification here and of course much is made of it in later Caitanya Vaiṣṇava discourse. This power works for those who have "good hearts" (*sad-dhī*). Śrī Jīva glosses this term with the phrase, *niraparādha-citta*, "those whose minds are free of any offense." Thus, two kinds of people without faith are envisioned here: those who lack faith but are innocent and those who lack faith but are opposed or inimically disposed towards Kṛṣṇa. Śrī Rūpa claims that even a tiny amount of contact with the five forms of *bhakti* as practice mentioned above will produce in innocent people *bhakti* as feeling. Naturally, it is thought that when performed *with* faith those five practices are even more powerfully effective. Those five forms of practice were the mainstay of Bābā Tinkaḍi Gosvāmī's religious cultivation (*sādhana*).

As if this claim were not enough, Śrī Rūpa goes even further in his next verse. Here is what he says:

---

[19]ibid., 1.2.238:

दुरूहाद्भुतवीर्येऽस्मिन् श्रद्धा दूरेऽस्तु पञ्चके।
यत्र स्वल्पोऽपि सम्बन्धः सद्धियां भावजन्मने॥

> Supernatural objects have an inconceivable power like this which can manifest *bhakti* as feeling *and* its object [Kṛṣṇa] simultaneously.[20]

By supernatural objects, Śrī Rūpa means, because of the context, the five forms of *bhakti* as practice. In addition to manifesting *bhakti* as feeling, those forms make the object of those feelings appear as well, and the object of those feelings is Śrī Kṛṣṇa. Thus, it is not just the appearance of *bhakti* as feeling that constitutes "accomplishment" in the view of the Caitanya Vaiṣṇava tradition. It is also having a direct or visionary experience of Śrī Kṛṣṇa and/or Śrī Rādhikā, Kṛṣṇa's loving divine consort. The experience of divine love and of the divine beloved simultaneously are what make someone a saint in this tradition.

To the core set of five practices Bābā Tinkaḍi Gosvāmī added a few more. The most important of those were his observation of vows of silence (*mauna*), his rejection of all cloth except for burlap, and most of all, his practice of "remembering" the sacred sports or divine *līlā* of Rādhā and Kṛṣṇa. His practice of silence was aimed at supporting his wish to chant a certain large number of holy names a day. He would practice silence until that number of repetitions of the holy names had been completed. The practice of silence thus gave him a space within which he was free from outside interruptions and distractions, and he could concentrate all his attention on his private worship. His rejection of all cloth except for burlap was a discipline he imposed on himself in response to his own enjoyment of fine cloth and the other finer things in life as a young man growing up in the privileged Gosvāmī caste. Even his bedding and his shoes had to be made of burlap. Though his practices of silence and personal austerity were ancillary to the core practices mentioned above, helping him with his concentration and his cultivation of detachment, the practice of "remembering" (*līlā-smaraṇa*) became a central feature of his religious cultivation.

According to Śrī Rūpa Gosvāmin, "remembering" the divine sports is the central practice of a kind of *bhakti* as practice called passion-motivated or *rāgānugā bhakti*. The five forms of *bhakti* as practice mentioned

---

[20]ibid., 1.2.244:

> अलौकिकपदार्थानामचिन्त्या शक्तिरीदृशी ।
> भावं तद्विषयञ्चापि या सहैव प्रकाशयेत्॥

above are considered to belong to the other type of *bhakti* as practice called rule- or injunction-motivated *bhakti*, *vaidhi-bhakti*. In passion-motivated *bhakti* one undertakes the practice of *bhakti* out of a strong desire, even a greed, to draw close to Kṛṣṇa in the ways the people of Vraja are. One's motivation to practice is not based on being enjoined to practice by scripture or being convinced of it by reason. This strong desire or greed generally arises when one hears stories about Kṛṣṇa that feature his loving interactions with his close friends, family, and lovers in Vraja. Here is what Śrī Rūpa says about this passion-motivated practice:

> The sole possessors of passionate *bhakti* for Kṛṣṇa are the people of Vraja. One who strongly desires to attain feelings like theirs [for Kṛṣṇa] is qualified for this passion-motivated *bhakti*. If, when the sweetness of their various sentiments for Kṛṣṇa is heard of, the mind no longer depends on scripture or argument for its motivation, this is a characteristic of the rise of the strong desire or greed for that. ... Remembering Kṛṣṇa and some person [in the eternal sport] who is dear to him [to Kṛṣṇa] whom one finds appealing and being engaged by their stories, one [motivated by desire to have that kind of passion] should always reside in Vraja. Service in this practice should be performed, following the examples of the people of Vraja, with the practitioner's body and the accomplished body by one wishing to attain those sentiments.[21]

From Binode Bābā's description of Bābā Tinkaḍi Gosvāmī's life we see the extraordinarily intense desire or greed he had from quite early on to attain that kind of love for Kṛṣṇa. The desire so unsettled him that he ran

[21] ibid., 1.2.291-2, 294-5:

रागात्मिकैकनिष्ठा ये व्रजवासिजनादयः।
तेषां भावाप्तये लुब्धो भवेदत्राधिकारवान्॥
तत्तद्भावादिमाधुर्ये श्रुते धीर्यदपेक्षते।
नात्र शास्त्रं न युक्तिञ्च तल्लोभोत्पत्तिलक्षणम्॥
...
कृष्णं स्मरन् जनञ्चास्य प्रेष्ठं निजसमीहितम्।
तत्तत्कथारतश्चासौ कुर्याद्वासं व्रजे सदा॥
सेवा साधकरूपेण सिद्धरूपेण चात्र हि।
तद्भावलिप्सुना कार्या व्रजलोकानुसारतः॥

away to Vṛndāvana without telling anyone and later on to Nīlācala (Jagannātha Purī). In Vṛndāvana he heard about and then met the great accomplished master of the "remembering" practice, Siddha Śrī Manohara Dāsa Bābājī. At their first meeting Siddha Bābā recognized that Tinkaḍi Gosvāmī was not yet ready for the practice and sent him home. Eventually, though, after Tinkaḍi Bābā had formally left home and had gained the consent of his wife, Siddha Bābā became Tinkaḍi Bābā's instructing teacher (*śikṣā-guru*) and taught him the details of the practice. After Siddha Bābā trained him Bābā Tinkaḍi went off to practice wholeheartedly and with his characteristic intensity in various scarcely populated and hard to reach places around the region of Vraja. After many years of such practice he achieved success, it it believed.

Śrī Rūpa is careful to point out that the practice of "remembering" does not exclude or replace the other practices that are described as forms of *vaidhi-bhakti*.[22] Those practices, especially the chief five forms, support and strengthen the practice of "remembering." Śrī Rūpa's use of the word *smaran*, "remembering," here points to a practice in which the practitioner meditates on and visualizes the activities of Kṛṣṇa and his companions as they are described in the main *bhakti* scriptures. Eventually, a number of specialized texts were written by members of the Caitanya tradition to describe the daily activities or "sports" of Kṛṣṇa and his companions for the purpose of supporting this remembering-visualization practice. When Śrī Rūpa wrote those words, however, none of those texts existed. In addition, his reference to the two forms or bodies, the accomplished form and the practitioner's form, indicates that not only was the practitioner to visualize the divine activities of Kṛṣṇa, the practitioner was also meant to participate in those activities in an imagined form suitable for the kind of role the practitioner wishes to play in those activities. This is referred to here as the "accomplished" body (*siddha-rūpa*). The practitioner's body (*sādhaka-rūpa*) is the ordinary, physical body with which the practitioner performs the other forms of *bhakti* as practice.

The addition of the "accomplished" body, the identity and description of which is generally given by one's initiation guru, radically transforms all the other forms of practice. The practices themselves remain the same to outside observers, but they have a new *raison d' être*, a new unifying logic and goal. This is because they are performed from the

[22]ibid., 1.2.296: "Hearing, loudly repeating, and so forth which were described under *vaidhi-bhakti* are understood by the wise to apply equally here."

core of a new identity. That new identity is the one connected with the accomplished body and it is the identity of someone who is an insider rather than an outsider. The practitioner's body and identity is that of the outsider. In the terms used by the tradition, it rests on the external or *bahiraṅga* power of the supreme deity. It is the body and identity that is subject to the laws of nature. Practice or worship based on this external body and identity approach the object of worship as an "other," that "highly exceptional and extremely impressive 'Other'" spoken of by van der Leeuw.[23] The accomplished body and identity rest on the internal or *antaraṅga* power. The accomplished identity transforms the object of one's worship into an intimate friend or relative and one's worship no longer consists of an attempt to propitiate or win over but to please and make happy. Offerings lose their sacrificial nature and become expressions of a sharing initiated out of love and closeness. The addition of recollection and its attendant body and identity thus overlay the practices, giving them new colorings and meanings. Bābā Tinkaḍi Gosvāmī seemed to feel most at home and alive in that altered, intimate landscape created by recollection. This description is but a brief peek at some of the religious practices and cultivations that occupied him for the last forty or so years of his life.

Saints and Hagiography

Let us return to a discussion of the place of the saint and of hagiography in this and other religious traditions. Anyone who has much knowledge of the great religions of the world knows something of the importance of the saint, especially if one understands "saint" in its broadest possible sense as any person who directly interacts with some form of divine being or presence. The scriptures of the various religious traditions are filled with stories about such persons. There is Adam and Eve who were cared for and then cast out of the garden by Yahweh (or rather the Elohim), Noah who was warned by the same deity of an impending flood, Abraham who was "called" by Yahweh, Moses who was given guidance and the laws, and countless others from the Hebrew scriptures. From the Christian scriptures there is Jesus, of course, and his many disciples or followers. From the Islamic tradition there is Muhammad himself whose Koran is said to record the history of his interaction

[23]Gerardus van der Leeuw, *Religion in Essence and Manifestation*, Vol. One, 23. (Gloucester, Mass.: Peter Smith, 1967)

with Allah. That text is enlarged by the Hadith in which Muhammad gives teachings and examples in the context of specific occasions in his life. Similarly, the major text of the Vaiṣṇava tradition, the *Bhāgavata,* is filled with people and their stories in relationship to Viṣṇu/Kṛṣṇa. From these examples it should be clear that personal stories bring home and make vividly present to an audience a religious orientation or worldview or teaching in ways that mere didactic presentations or enumerations of laws and codes of conduct cannot. As John Stratton Hawley has noted: "The great religions did not gain their hold on us by precepts alone. Within each religion a powerful body of tradition emphasizes not codes but stories, not precepts but personalities, not lectures but lives."[24] One often finds that teachings or laws are easily forgotten, but the stories about persons, real or mythic, that occasion them or that in some way exemplify them, either positively or negatively, are not so easily forgotten.

The case of the *Bhāgavata Purāṇa* is of special interest. The *Purāṇa* as we have it today appears to be the product of gradual enlargement over the centuries. At some point, for instance, it was "framed" by another, outer set of stories relating to the period after the great war of the *Mahābhārata.* By its own admission the actual *Purāṇa* begins with the Third Book which is when the first redactor of the work, Śukadeva, arrives on the scene. He learned the *Purāṇa* from his father, Vyāsa, the putative author of the text. The first two books and the Twelfth Book appear thus to be later additions, perhaps as late as the 10th or 11th centuries C.E., They show a certain sophistication, especially in the concept of *rasa,* that is missing from the "inner" sections of the *Purāṇa.* Rasa does not become a major idea in Sanskrit literary criticism until Ānandavardhana and his work the *Dhvanyāloka* (*Illumination of Suggestion*) in the 9th century C.E. Thus, though closed, the *Purāṇa* presents a quality of openness and potential expansibility. Even the name *bhāgavata,* which means "things or people related to Bhagavān (the supreme lord)," suggests an openness and the possibility of expansion. The term *bhāgavata* might be applied to any thing or person considered to be related in some way to Bhagavān. Thus, the stories of the saints of the eighteenth, nineteenth, and twentieth centuries might well be considered extensions of the *Bhāgavata* in its larger sense. A twenty-first century version of the *Bhāgavata* might be expected to include stories of the saints who lived in more recent times. The creation of hagiographical accounts of the lives

[24]John Stratton Hawley, editor, *Saints and Virtues,* xi. (Berkeley: University of California Press, 1987)

of the latter day saints, therefore, continues the process of scriptural development observable in the structure of the earlier texts.

This points to the peculiar relationship mentioned before between a religious tradition and its texts. It might be described as a bidirectional form of textualization. On the one hand the person or saint is textualized by being inscribed by, or becoming a textual embodiment of, the received sacred texts of the tradition. The saint thus becomes recognized as saint by being portrayed as an embodiment or living instantiation of the sacred texts. That is one direction of this process of textualization. In the other direction the saint is transformed into text through the creation of his or her own hagiography and thus, now embodied as text, becomes part of that received textual tradition that is passed on into the future to inscribe or become embodied in future saints. Text becomes embodied as saint and saint becomes encoded as text. In this way religious traditions move forward peering both backwards and forwards at the same time. If a tradition becomes blind in either direction it either ceases to be the same tradition or it ceases to be a living tradition.

At the beginning of this section I expanded the meaning of the word saint to cover any person related to a supreme being or deity in some way and hagiography would then be the narrative of that person. This is not how we usually understand the word saint or hagiography. Saints are a small sub-group, often quite exclusive, of people who are related to a supreme being in some way. Some people are not regarded as related to the divine in favorable ways and thus would not be considered saints in most traditions. Their narratives are meant to be taken as warnings of paths to be avoided, paths not to be tread. Even then, not everyone who is favorably related to the divine is considered to be a saint. The question then becomes, "what is it that makes a saint?" We have already seen some of the possible answers to that question. A saint, for instance, is someone who embodies the scriptures of a religious tradition in a ideal way. A saint thus becomes a model for the followers of a religious tradition. Not only that, the scriptures and the saints are mutually authenticating. The scriptures are authenticated in the saint and the saint is authenticated by embodying the scriptures. Another way of establishing a saint is to discover in a person miraculous powers or abilities. This is the method primarily used in this hagiography by Binode Bihari Das Bābājī. Unlike Karunamayi Das in his hagiography of his gurudeva, Śrī Kṛṣṇadāsa Bābā of Rādhākuṇḍa, Binode Bihari Das refers to scripture sparingly. Instead, he has collected stories that tell of Bābā Tinkaḍi Gosvāmiī's miraculous feats or supernormal knowledge. Someone who is "accomplished" (*siddha*) in the Caitanya tradition is believed to acquire all kinds of miraculous abilities, a belief shared by many religious traditions with respect to their saints. A variation on this way of establishing sainthood is to identify saints on the basis of virtues observed in their actions, words or characters. Binode Bihari Das Bābājī has also applied this method in the sixth chapter of this work where basing himself on a few passages of scripture he systematically, virtue by virtue, discovers all the virtues said to develop in a true *bhakta* of Kṛṣṇa in Bābā Tinkaḍi Gosvāmī. Hawley has given us some more examples of this way of distinguishing saints in his essay "Morality Beyond Morality in the Lives of Three Hindu Saints" in the book, *Saints and Virtues*.[25] We shall look at that in more detail in the following paragraphs. Finally, there is the attempt to discern sainthood by discovering a certain pattern in the lives of saints. William J. Jackson has given us a good example of that in his work on the great South Indian saint-songwriter, Tyāgarāja. We shall look at that pattern and see how well it fits with the way Binode Bihari Das Bābā has presented the life of Bābā Tinkaḍi.

In *Tyāgarāja: Life and Lyrics*[26] and in an essay entitled "A Life Becomes a Legend: Śrī Tyāgarāja as Exemplar" in the *Journal of the American Academy of Religion*,[27] William J. Jackson presents twelve motifs that "display the growth of hagiographical material associated with Tyāgarāja and the fulfillment of archetypes already known to south Indians at the time of Tyāgarāja's birth."[28] Although this system of motifs was developed in connection with the singer-saints of South India, it can be applied with some minor alteration to saints all around India, even to saints who were not necessarily singer-songwriters. In fact, in laying out and supporting his motifs, Jackson himself refers to many saints from all over India and points out that each motif is not invariably a part of every saint's life. Let us see how well they apply to the life of Bābā Tinkaḍi Gosvāmī as presented by Binode Bihari Das Bābājī.

Jackson refers to the first of his motifs as the "miracle of origins," by which he means that there is some kind of dream in which the future saint's parents are informed of the coming of the gifted child. While such may have been the case for Tyāgarāja and countless other saints, Binode Bābā has not mentioned any dream in Bābā Tinkaḍi's case. He

[25]See the bibliography.

[26]William J. Jackson, *Tyāgarāja: Life and Lyrics*. (Madras: Oxford University Press, 1991)

[27]William J. Jackson, "A Life Becomes a Legend: Śrī Tyāgarāja as Exemplar," in the *Journal of the American Academy of Religion*, Vol. LX, no. 4 (Winter, 1992), 717-736.

[28]ibid., 725.

has pointed to the birth of Bābā on the full moon day of the month of Māgha when the atmosphere was full of singing of the names of Kṛṣṇa. Such a birth is not exactly miraculous, but it is certainly very auspicious and as the author surely wants us to understand the time of his birth was an indication of the future interest and passions of the fortunate baby. Perhaps we are also to understand that the very survival of Tinkaḍi Bābā was miraculous since all of his elder brothers and sisters perished in childhood. Jackson's second motif is "initiation and aid from a *sannyāsin*." For Tyāgarāja this refers to a holy man who revived him when he was very ill as a child. For Bābā Tinkaḍi, this probably does not apply. He was initiated by his father, Śrī Harimohan Gosvāmī; however, he does seem to have undergone a major transformation when that occurred. Instead of wanting always to play, he becomes deeply interested in spiritual topics and begins to study the *Bhagavad-gītā* seriously. One might also say that Bābā Tinkaḍi was aided by Siddha Manohara Dāsa Bābājī when he recognized that Bābā was not yet ready for renunciation and sent him home to his wife. The third motif is "learning from an extraordinary guru." Certainly, Bābā's relationship with Siddha Manohara Dāsa Bābājī accords with this motif.

Jackson's fourth motif is "trial and vision." This motif corresponds to Bābā Tinkaḍi's giving himself over to intense practice for an unspecified number of years. This would amount to his "trial" period and then, after years of intense practice, his visions of Vallabhācārya, who gives him a *mantra* to help him control his mind and of Vallabhācāya's son Viṭṭhalanātha, who gives him his blessing, and finally, and most importantly, his vision of Śrī Rādhikā who tells him: "Your wishes have been fulfilled. There is much for you to accomplish still. When the time is right you will see me again." The fifth of the Jackson's motifs is "contempt of court." There is nothing in Binode Bābā's account that corresponds to this as far as I can tell, but one does get the sense that Tinkaḍi Bābā was completely a-political and had no interest in politics. Perhaps this was the point of Binode's section on Bābā's lack of awareness concerning contemporary affairs.[29] Jackson's sixth motif is "endangered musician is rescued." Bābā Tinkaḍi was not a musician per se, but he did fall into difficulty when he became lost at sunset in a lonely forest while on pilgrimage by himself. According to Binode Bābā's account he met a man carrying a lantern who led him to a near by deserted temple and then was fed by a young village woman.[30] Naturally, we are meant

[29]See page 97 and following.
[30]See pages 20-22.

to infer that these were Kṛṣṇa and Rādhā who were moved to save their beloved devotee.

Motif number seven is "a loss of divine images." I cannot think of anything in Binode's account that corresponds to this motif. Again, all motifs need not be found in all saints. The eighth motif is "miraculous recovery or auspicious discovery" often related to "a body of water." Here again, there is nothing that is specially suggestive of this motif in Binode Bābā's account. In the case of Tyāgarāja, he found his sacred images, which had been stolen by his wicked brother (motif seven) in the Kāveri after receiving some kind of inspiration to search there. In the case of Bābā Tinkaḍi, while nothing dear to him was lost, he was often given precious things, especially sacred images. Indeed whole *āśramas* and temples were either given to him or placed in his care. An excellent example is the *āśrama*-temple at Manipur Ghat in Navadvīpa that was given to him by Fruit-eating Bābā (Phalāhārī Bābā) because the latter wanted to go to Vraja to spend his final days. Another example is found in the way an ancient pair of sacred images of Rādhā and Kṛṣṇa was given to Bābā by the widow of their former caretaker on the basis of a dream she had. Those images became the Rādhāvallabha images that are the center of worship at Bābā's *āśrama* at Manipur Ghat.

Jackson's ninth motif is "the power of music is made manifest." Once again, Bābā Tinkaḍi was not a musician or song writer. Nevertheless, he had a kind of music, too. It was the recitation (*japa*) and singing (*kīrtana*) of the holy names. Binode Bābā recounts many instances in the life of Tinkaḍi Bābā that demonstrate the power of those practices and of the seven-day recitation of the *Bhāgavata Purāṇa*.

The tenth motif is "the Lord responds to song." If Bābā Tinkaḍi's song was his unceasing recitation of the holy names, then one could say that his hagiographic corpus of stories demonstrates this motif, too. Although Binode Bābā makes no reference to it in his account, a common feature of the stories told about Bābā Tinkaḍi is that in the privacy of his private worship, Śrī Rādhā and Kṛṣṇa used to come visit him and converse with him. Many of his close companions have reported hearing him carry on lively conversations, punctuated sometimes by laughing and sometimes by weeping, with someone when he was alone in his hut or room. I myself have heard such half-conversations from outside his room, though I must admit that I could not follow what was being said. Others are more sure of their interpretations of the meaning of these conversations. Rāma is said to have appeared to Tyāgarāja on numerous occasions to give him comfort and to show his approval of the saint's songs. If these stories fulfill this motif in the case of Tyāgarāja, then I suppose the many reports of Bābā's private interactions with Rādhā and Kṛṣṇa do as well.

Jackson's eleventh motif is "the musician is an *aṃśa*," that is, an incarnation of a part or portion of a divine being. Binode Bābā says nothing of the sort in his hagiography of Tinkaḍi Bābā. Śrī Hṛdayānanda Dās Bābājī, however, provides some hints along those lines in his song of praise (*sūcaka-kīrtana*) of Tinkaḍi Bābā which is translated in the appendix of this book. Śrī Hṛdayānanda Bābā suggests that like his own guru, Śrī Rāmadāsa Bābājī, Tinkaḍi Bābā came to earth to provide examples of how the religion of Śrī Caitanya should be practiced. Śrī Rāmadāsa Bābājī exemplified congregational singing (*saṅkīrtana*) in its perfection and Bābā Tinkaḍi exemplified *bhajana* or private worship. No specific divine being is mentioned as Bābā Tinkaḍi's source, though perhaps Śrī Hṛdayānanda Dāsa Bābājī had one in mind. At any rate, Bābā Tinkaḍi's hagiographical corpus of stories and accounts is still young and relatively undeveloped. There is still plenty of time for his followers to draw more bold lines of identification. It might be worth pointing out here that sometimes a saint is not regarded as a mere part or portion of a divine being but as the divine being him- or herself. Such is the case of Prabhu Jagadbandhu Sundara who was thought by his followers to be another incarnation of Śrī Caitanya Mahāprabhu. Śrī Caitanya himself was regarded as a full incarnation of Śrī Kṛṣṇa in a particular mood.

Finally, the twelfth motif according to Jackson is "foreknowledge of death." Binode Bābā does not specifically indicate that Tinkaḍi Bābā knew the time of his death, but he suggests that such may have been the case through his account of the dream that Bābā's son, Śrī Vṛndāvanacandra Gosvāmī, had: Bābā appears to him and orders him to return home immediately. That dream occurs, according to Binode Bābā, the day before Bābā departed from life. Taken as a whole, then, it appears that the system of motifs that William J. Jackson has described does indeed capture many of the important features typical of Indian hagiography and applies relatively well to even the relatively underdeveloped hagiography of Bābā Tinkaḍi Gosvāmī, especially if we do not limit his hagiography to only what Binode Bābā has described in this account. If we take into account some of the stories in the broader corpus of hagiographical stories circulating about him, then Bābā Tinkaḍi substantiates most of the motifs.

There are other ways that writers of hagiography demonstrate the holiness of a saint besides incorporating or "discovering" the motifs of typical saintly lives in the lives of their chosen saints. Binode Bābā, taking his cue from a passage of the *Caitanya-caritāmṛta* of Kṛṣṇadāsa Kavirāja,[31] discovers the roots of Bābā Tinkaḍi's saintliness in the twenty-six virtues he displayed in his life. Thus he takes each virtue one by one, twenty-six virtues in all, and gives an event or practice from Bābā's life that exemplifies that virtue. The presence of those virtues define him as a true Vaiṣṇava, a model Vaiṣṇava, and in addition those virtues are understood as developing in him as a result of his *bhakti* for Śrī Kṛṣṇa. As John S. Hawley wrote at the end of an essay interpreting the lives of three (or four?) *bhakti* saints (Mīrā Bai, Narasī Mehtā, and Pīpā and Sītā) on the basis of the hagiographical classic, the *Bhakta-māl* ("Garland of Devotees," 16th cent. C.E.) of Nābhājī:

> Indeed, as John Carman has pointed out, the virtues these saints exhibit are aspects of the divine character itself. According to the vision of God that is dominant in the tradition of Vaiṣṇava *bhakti*, God quells all fear, shows incalculable generosity, and serves his devotees at every turn. It is therefore no surprise that those who worship him should manifest these virtues, both individually and collectively, and that such qualities of life are genuinely fostered nowhere else but in the community of devotion.[32]

Hawley only discusses three virtues: fearlessness, generosity, and service, but one can make a strong case for the centrality of those three virtues in the Vaiṣṇava tradition and perhaps in Indian culture as a whole. The other twenty-six virtues mentioned in the *Caitanya-caritāmṛta* can be understood without too much stretching as ancillary to one or another of those three central virtues.

---

[31]Kṛṣṇadāsa Kavirāja, *Caitanya-caritāmṛta*, 2.22.43-47. The passage lists twenty-six virtues, but the very first verse of the passage says that the virtues of Kṛṣṇa appear in his *bhaktas* and the commentator, Dr. Radhagovinda Nath, adds that of the sixty-four virtues of Kṛṣṇa only twenty-nine appear in Kṛṣṇa's *bhaktas* and those in small measure. The list of twenty-nine, however, does not match the list of twenty-six given by Kṛṣṇadāsa Kavirāja. Kṛṣṇadāsa leaves the door open, however, by saying he is not able to mention all of the virtues of *bhaktas* and he is only giving a glimpse of some of them.

[32]John S. Hawley, "Morality Beyond Morality in the Lives of Three Hindu Saints," in *Saints and Virtues*, 72. (Berkeley: University of California Press, 1987)

This Translation

In translating Binode Bihari's Bengali text into English I have tried to stay as close to the literal meaning as possible without doing too much damage to English syntax. Sometimes this has been challenging because Binode Bābā's linguistic range in Bengali is not very large. While on the one hand, this made his book easy to translate, on the other I found him using the same stock phrases and structures over and over again. To reduplicate that in English would have made the translation rather tedious and clumsy. An example that springs immediately to mind is his use of the verb *lāgā* which means "to strike or hit." When used with another verb, however, it has the meaning "to strike out" on an endeavor or more simply "to begin" some action. Prabhupāda began to do this; Prabhupāda began to do that. In the beginning of my work on this book, I faithfully translated the construction in just that way. Eventually, however, I realized how cumbersome that construction was becoming in English. In addition, it occurred to me that even in Bengali it seemed to lack force in several cases. Someone as a result of that construction is described as "beginning" an action that in fact that person was already engaged in performing. As a result, when I went over the translation again to polish it and edit it, I wound up removing many of those "beginnings." I do not think that much has been lost as a result. Nevertheless, many of those "beginnings" still remain, enough to give readers some sense of what the original was like.

Apart from these stylistic oddities, there is one other complaint I have about Binode Bābā's book. That has to do with the almost complete absence of chronology. Very few dates are cited in the book. It would have been grand to know when it was that Bābā Tinkaḍi did this or that and at what age this or that happened. How long was it, for instance, that Bābā underwent intense practice before some results began to show? When did he leave household life? When was it that he studied with Siddha Manohara Dāsa Bābājī and for how long? When did he become a *bābā*? When did he have the stroke that left him partially paralyzed? This complete lack of chronology is rather deplorable, but perhaps it was beyond Binode Bābā's control. He seems to suggest that that was the case in his own introduction to the work. Still, it would have made this biography much more like a conventional life.

As is my usual practice, I have added notes to the text in anticipation of any questions that readers unfamiliar with this tradition might have while reading the work. There is also a glossary at the end defining some of the main concepts and ideas encountered in the text and its tradition. A select bibliography contains works that have been used in producing this translation, its introduction, and notes. The bibliography also includes other works that might be useful for further reading on this tradition.

There are two extra texts included in the appendices of this book. They are poems written in introduction and praise of Bābā Tinkaḍi by his disciples and/or admirers. The authorship of the first is unclear. It may be by Binode Bihari Das Bābājī himself. However, the authorship of the first is uncertain. Bhakti poets usually include a self-reference in their final lines, and "Dīna Caitanyadāsa," (humble servant of Caitanya) appears in that spot. It may be the name of an unknown disciple, but it may be Binode Bihārī's own self-deprecating signature line. The second poem is by Śrī Hṛdayānanda Dāsa Bābājī Mahārāja, who was close to Tinkaḍi Bābā when he was alive. The poem was passed to me in manuscript form by two of Hṛdayānanda Bābā's American disciples. It appears here for the first time in print with my translation. Sadly, Hṛdayānanda Bābā passed into eternal sport while this book was being worked on. I deeply regret that he was not able to see it in print. I hope that I have done his thought and sentiments justice in my translation.

In addition, the recollections of three of Bābā Tinkaḍi's American disciples have been included in the appendix. Each of the recollections presents a distinct perspective on Bābā, mellowed and matured over the years since those disciples were in his presence. The hope is that viewing Bābā through all of these different lens will provide a fuller, more well-rounded image and understanding of this quite extraordinary man.

Introduction (Comments by Mādhava Dās Bābājī)

From his grace comes the grace of Bhagavān,
From his displeasure there is no other recourse;
Meditating on and extolling his fame three times a day,
I praise the blessed lotus-like feet of my guru.[33]

This ornament of the community of Vaiṣṇavas, this highest goose (*paramahaṃsa*)[34] of Bhagavān's servants, this ornament of Vraja, Śrī Śrī Tinkaḍi Gosvāmī Mahārāja, is well known to all in Vraja and Nadīyā. To the people of Vraja he is known by the names, Tinkaḍi Bābā, Mauni Bābā, Ṭāṭa Bābā, and so forth. In Bengal he is known by the names, Prabhupāda,[35] Gosvāmī Bābā and so forth. The *Śrī Bhāgavata* says:

---

[33]Viśvanātha Cakravartin, *Gurvaṣṭaka Stotra*, 8:

यस्य प्रसादाद्भगवत्प्रसादो यस्याप्रसादान्न गतिः कुतोऽपि।
ध्यायं स्तुवंस्तस्य यशस्त्रिसन्ध्यं वन्दे गुरोः श्रीचरणारविन्दम्॥

[34]Goose or *haṃsa* has a special significance for the people of India as a symbol of high spiritual awakening and insight. This meaning is especially connected with the form *parama-haṃsa* or highest goose. *Haṃsa* is often mistranslated as "swan."

[35]The title"Prabhupāda" is usually reserved for those exemplary *bhaktas* born into highly respected families of Goswamis, families who trace their guru-lineages and their ancestry back to the close companions of Śrī Caitanya Mahāprabhu. *Prabhu* means "master." *Pāda* meaning "foot." The *pāda* is added as a sign of special respect for the members of those ancient families of hereditary Caitanya Vaiṣṇavas. Members of the Caitanya tradition believe that one is born into such families only after lifetimes of *bhakti* practice and cultivation. One does not refer to such persons directly, but instead to that person's feet, that person's lowest part. It is the survival of an old form of etiquette from traditional Indian society.

He should not be called a teacher,
He should not be called a relative,
He should not be called a father,
She should not be called a mother,
That should not be called divine,
Nor should he be called a husband,
Who cannot cause a person
to be released from impending death.[36]

In other words, one who is unable to save a living being, who is beginninglessly turned away from God, from the wheel of material existence in the form of the stream of births and deaths, such a person even though he gives initiation and instruction is not a teacher; even though he acts beneficially is not a relative; even though he and she supports one and bears one in her womb are not a father and a mother; even though he grants one wished-for results is not a deity; and even though he takes one's hand in marriage is not a husband. Therefore, only one who bestows on one the means to liberation from the bonds of becoming is a teacher. *Nara-tanu bhajaner mūla*: "the human body is the very root of worship." Those whose lives are exemplary are the ones to be remembered. One such shining example, Prabhupāda Tin Kaḍi Gosvāmī, descendant of the most respectable *ācāryas*, appeared in the first part of the twentieth century.

It has been said in the *Caitanya-caritāmṛta*: "Whoever has been born as a human being in the land of Bhārata should perfect his own life and help others."[37] And again: "If one does not practice it oneself, teaching *dharma* does not work. This conclusion is sung in the *Gītā* and *Bhāgavata*."[38] The significance of this has been reflected in the entirety of Prabhupāda's religious life. Through his own deep absorption in worship, love, and the holy names, he pointed out the path to the attainment of service to Gaura and Govinda for living beings lost in the Age of

[36] *Bhāgavata Purāṇa.*, 5.5.18:

गुरुर्न स स्यात्स्वजनो न स स्यात्
पिता न स स्याज्जननी न सा स्यात्।
दैवं न तत्स्यान्न पतिश्च स स्यान्
न मोचयेद्यः समुपेतमृत्युम्॥

[37] Kṛṣṇadāsa Kavirāja, *Caitanya-caritāmṛtra*, 1.9.39: *bhārata bhūmite manuṣya janma haila yār, janma sārtha kari kara para upakāra.*

[38] ibid., 1.3.19: *āpane nā kaile dharma śikhāna nā yāy, ei ta siddhānta gītā bhāgavate gāy.*

Kali as well as for practitioners. His example is extremely rare in this day and age. Prabhupāda's worthy servant, Binode Bihari Dasa Bābājī Mahārāja, collecting various events from the Prabhupāda's early life briefly and from his life of worship in greater detail, has created a beautiful biography. The honorable author wrote a little while earlier another book (*Obstacles to the Gradual Development of Bhakti*)[39] and became famous throughout Vraja. Therefore, I hope that this offering of *bhakti* in the form of his biography of Prabhupāda will also become well regarded everywhere.

On this book or on Prabhupāda, there is nothing in particular that needs to be said. All those practitioners who want to attain the undivided love-service of Gaura and Govinda must certainly become intent upon three things: (1) worshiping the dust of the lotus-like feet of Śrī Rādhārāṇī, (2) living in Vraja, and (3) association with great souls who are expert in meditating on the Divine Couple (Rādhā and Kṛṣṇa). Without these three things, there is no way to taste the limitless sweetness of the *rasa* and beauty of Śyāmasundara. In the words of the Gosvāmins:

> Without worshiping the dust
> Of the lotus-like feet of Rādhā,
> Without resorting to Vṛndā's paths
> That bear the imprints of her feet,
> Without conversing with people
> Whose minds are steeped in her feelings,
> Whence comes immersion
> in the *rasa* of the ocean of Śyāma?[40]

It goes without saying that this example—worship in the service of Rādhā, intense devotion to private worship (*bhajana*) and association with the great—existed in embodied form in Prabhupāda.

In the Śrī *Caitanya-candrāmṛta* it is said:

---

[39] The Bengali title of the book is: *Bhakti-krama vikāśer Antarāya.*

[40] Raghunātha Dāsa Gosvāmin, *Svasaṅkalpa-prakāśa-stotra,* 1:

> अनाराध्य राधापदाम्बुजरेणुं
> अनाश्रित्य वृन्दाटवीं तत्पदाङ्काम्।
> असम्भाष्य तद्भावगम्भीरचित्तान्
> कुतो श्यामसिन्धो रसस्यावगाहः॥

> As much as a person, rich in merit,
> May possess of *bhakti* to the lotus-like feet of Gaura,
> That much into that person's heart flows
> nectar from the lotus-like feet of Rādhā.[41]

In other words, as much *bhakti* as someone offers to Gaurasundara, one later attains in loving *bhakti* to the feet of Śrī Rādhārāṇī. Faith in Gaura is the life-breath of the worship of Gauḍīya Vaiṣṇavas. A descendent of an *ācārya* once asked Prabhupāda why he was showing so much grace to the residents of Vraja, but did not go to Navadvīpa. In response Prabhupāda said: "The way that ordinary people know about Gaura and Nityānanda in Bengal is not found to that degree in Vraja. Gaura and Nityānanda are the objects of worship for this age. To spread their story and worship in Vraja, Rādhārāṇī has retained me." By this statement Prabhupāda's deep love for Gaura and Nitāi was revealed. Beyond that, he breathed his last breath uttering the holy name in the holy land of Navadvīpa. Therefore, he was an unwavering beacon of faith in Gaura as well.

> I seek shelter with him,
> that one ancient person,
> an ocean of compassion,
> who, to teach the process
> of *bhakti* to himself
> along with renunciation and wisdom,
> assumed the form of Śrī Kṛṣṇacaitanya.[42]

The *Śrīmad Bhāgavata* and talks about Hari were Prabhupāda's life and soul. Wherever he was in Vraja, he would organize a seven-day

---

[41] Prabodhānanda Sarasvatī, *Caitanya-candrāmṛta*, 88:

> यथा यथा गौरपदारविन्दे विन्देत भक्तिं कृतपुण्यराशिः।
> तथा तथोत्सर्पति हृद्यकस्माद्राधापदाम्भोजसुधाम्बुराशिः॥

[42] Kavi Karṇapūra, *Caitanya-candrodaya-naa.taka*, 6.78:

> वैराग्यविद्यानिजभक्तियोग-
> शिक्षार्थमेकः पुरुषः पुराणः।
> श्रीकृष्णचैतन्यशरीरधारी
> कृपाम्बुदिर्यस्तमहं प्रपद्ये॥

recitation of the *Śrīmad Bhāgavata* and bestow grace upon even the lowest of living beings, ghosts, ghouls, even serpents and other fierce creatures. His highest ideals were: "The holy name is independent and self-luminous," "feeling lower than a blade of grass, one should repeat the holy names," and serving the Vaiṣṇavas.

The native residents of Vraja say: "We have seen many saints in Vraja, but never anyone near as compassionate as Tinkaḍī Bābā." From this statement one can perceive what sort of compassionate and well-wishing soul Prabhupāda was. Therefore, this biography of Prabhupāda, being respected on all levels, will give pleasure to all and bring to all the greatest assistance. This I wish from the Supreme Lord.

Enough with prolixity.

Mādhava (Khaṇḍavāsī),
A semblance of a servant
sheltered at the feet of Prabhupāda

Blessing

29 Bhādra (August-September), 1394 (1988).

The account of the life and deeds of that vast ocean of greatness, the most worshipable Śrīla Śrīyukta 108 Tinkaḍi Goswāmīpāda Mahodaya, which a recipient of his grace, Śrīmān Binode Bihārī Dāsjī, has written, contains Prabhupāda's goings and comings to and from places like the holy abodes Navadvīpa, Śrī Vraja, Śrī Nīlācala and his birthplace Śrī Manoharpur, in order to spread divine love. He has collected the occurrences from those various places and put them in writing. In that endeavor, his enthusiasm, strenuous effort, and skill are being introduced. In connection with Prabhupāda's life, even though some of the incidents that occurred during his residence in Vraja are known to me, events in other places are not. All of them have been mentioned in this account. By reading this biography Prabhupāda's disciples will obtain the highest joy and I hope that all the *bhaktas* living in the world will also find pleasure by reading it. All of the amazing incidents that occurred during Prabhupāda's residence in Vraja are true. In his company I had the good fortune of visiting many of the villages of Vraja and had an opportunity of going to and staying in many extremely hard-to-reach places. In all those places he sponsored seven-day recitations of the *Śrīmad Bhāgavata* through various reciters. He was extremely affectionate towards me and showed me his grace. He used to keep me in his company. All those very private incidents Prabhupāda himself revealed to me, like the incident at Premasarovara which is mentioned in this book.

When his passing was at hand, I was extremely saddened and heartbroken. Reading this biography about him, I felt his direct companionship again and was gratified. May Śrīmān Binode Bihari attain loving *bhakti* to the blessed feet of Śrī Mahāprabhu and Śrī Śrī Rādhavallabha. This is my prayer.

A humble follower of Guru and Vaiṣṇavas,
Priyācaraṇa Dāsa,
Bhāgavata Bhavana,
Cākleśvara, Govardhana

Author's Introduction

Many practitioners come to the holy land, Śrī Vṛndāvana, with intense longing and enthusiasm for worship in order to obtain the lotus feet of Śrī Śrī Yugala-kiśora (the Divine Young Couple). In the first stage the intense enthusiasm many have for private worship (*bhajana*) is clearly noticed and they nourish the hope of obtaining the lotus feet of the Divine Couple in this life. But, after doing private worship for a long time, a kind of hopelessness of the nature, "I have not achieved anything," arrives and covers the mind of the practitioner. As a result the practitioner's enthusiasm for private worship gradually becomes weak. Then the practitioner thinks: "When I have done so much private worship and not achieved anything, I doubt that anything will be accomplished in this life." This line of thinking gradually takes root and as a result a laxity in private worship arises. Then, with his mind becoming attracted to worldly things, the practitioner moves far away from his destination.

If some student knows with conviction that he will not be able to pass a coming test, then he will certainly become lax in his studies. That student will then think: "Since I will not be able to pass this time, what is the point of my studying?" In just that same way, if someone nourishes the mental attitude, "In this birth, I will not be able to obtain the lotus feet of the Divine Couple and who knows how many more births will be needed," there certainly will be a laxness in that person's private worship. And if the firm belief stays in one's mind that "Rādhārāṇī will certainly show me her grace in this birth," then one's enthusiasm for private worship and longing will gradually increase. This belief is an absolute necessity for the attainment of the lotus feet of the Lord.

In order for that belief to become strong one needs an example. One needs the life stories of those who have obtained the grace of Rādhārāṇī in this birth. How did they do private worship? What was their detachment like? What was their freedom from worldly desire like? How did they lead their lives? How many kinds of obstacles and challenges did they have to pass through? If one raises these kinds of examples before practitioners, they will no longer fall prey to hopelessness. If laxness comes into one's private worship, by observing those examples one will try to keep one's mental strength unbroken. With this intention, I became enthusiastic about writing the biography of Prabhupāda Śrī Śrī 108 Tinkaḍi Goswami Mahārāja.

Not a great deal is known in connection with Prabhupāda's life. He never told anyone about his life. Those who were in his age group during his previous stage (the householder stage) have gone on to the next world. As a result, I was not able to write about his life in detail. Still, listening to those who were his companions and to Prabhupāda's own statements, I gathered the materials for this work.

By the causeless grace of Prabhupāda, I had, for a short while, the good fortune of his companionship. Whatever I saw over the course of that very short space of time and whatever I heard from him directly, I have gathered together as materials for this book and have endeavored to write it down.

Prabhupāda's life can be divided into three parts. The first part extends from his childhood to his leaving home. The period from the time of his leaving home until he attained the grace of the Divine Couple and traveled from the holy land of Vṛndāvana to Nīlācala makes up the second part. The third part covers the period from his going to Nīlācala until the wrapping up of his earthly sport in Navadvīpa.

Since I did not know many of the details of his life in the first part, it is covered briefly. In the second part I learned about the incidents of Prabhupāda's life from my guru-brothers and from those who were with him at the time and have tried to apply that information accurately. In the third part, since by Prabhupāda's causeless grace I attained his deep affection and proximity until the wrapping up of his earthly sport, I have tried to write about it in greater detail.

I am not a writer. I have no understanding of literature. Still, at the urging of my Śrī Gurudeva I became interested in giving little glimpses of his life. If mistakes and confusions are found anywhere in this work, I trust that my generous readers, understanding me to be extremely inexperienced, will correct my shortcomings.

If in the reading of this book, a practitioner's enthusiasm for private worship is increased even a little and some light is shed on the path of private worship, then I consider my efforts successful.

Binode Bihari Das

Author's Acknowledgments

I am deeply indebted to my Guru-mother Ṭhākurāṇī[43] who told me of many of the incidents from Prabhupāda's household life before he left home. I am grateful to my senior guru-brother, Śrī Sudāmā Dāsa Bābājī Mahārāja, of the Nityānanda Dhāma *āśrama* in Cākleśvara at Govardhana for telling me about many of the incidents in Prabhupāda's life and for giving me special assistance in the publication of this book. I am also bound by gratitude to my guru-brother, Śrī Mādhava Dāsa Bābājī (Khaṇḍavāsī), who reviewed all of the subjects discussed in this book. May most compassionate Rādhārāṇī make him fulfilled by shining the light of pure *bhakti* in his heart. Śrī Kāśī Prasāda Biyānī has born the entire cost of printing this book [the Bengali version]. May compassionate Rādhārāṇī illumine his heart with the light of *bhakti*. And to all the others who have enriched this book by telling me of various incidents in Prabhupāda's life I make known my special gratitude.

Binode Bihari Das

[43]This refers to Prabhupāda Tinkaḍi's second wife, Sarasvatī Devī, to whom the Bengali version of the book is also dedicated.

Part I

Prabhupāda's Life Story

Early Life

Jaya Śrī Gurudeva!

Victory to the Blessed Guru!

Nearly thirty years ago[44] at a place named Ādibadrī in Vraja a practitioner (*sādhaka*) was sitting, leaning against the wall of a small room near a temple. He had matted hair and his body was well-shaped. While he submerged his mind in thinking of *yugala-kiśora* (the youthful couple, Rādhā and Kṛṣṇa) he from time to time became drowsy. Suddenly, his drowsiness broke and he began to chastise himself for it. One could not tell how late it was. There was no way of telling what time it was at all inside the room. It seemed to be after midnight. The practitioner with shuffling steps went out of the room. Then, observing the positions of the stars in the clear sky, he tried to determine the time. He decided to take his bath and then sit down again for private worship (*bhajana*).[45] In front of him was dense forest. As soon as the *sādhaka* took hold of a water pot and stepped forward, he noticed two shining eyes splitting the dark night in front of him. They were just like two bright stars! It was probably some ferocious forest animal. The animal was not standing very far away. The practitioner fixed his gaze on the animal and tried to determine what kind of animal it was. In those circumstances, the practitioner was unable to determine what it was and remained standing there, unsure of what to do. Thinking to himself that valuable time was being wasted, the practitioner became restless. Then, in order to scare the animal away, he shook his pot and made a sound like "hūsh hūsh." The creature, not even slightly frightened, remained standing just

[44]The book was written in 1987. This incident took place around 1957, therefore.

[45]See the glossary for an account of what this typically is.

as it was before. After spending sometime in this impasse, the animal jumped across the path of the practitioner and quickly disappeared into the forest. At that moment he saw stripes on the body of the animal. The practitioner realized then that it had been a tiger!

Who was that practitioner whom even a ferocious tiger, standing just in front of him, gave up as food and left? Who was that practitioner who, though seeing death in the form of a hungry tiger standing before him, did not feel fear? That practitioner had attained such a treasure that even a ferocious tiger forgot his violent nature. He had attained such a state of fearlessness that even when confronted with a dangerous tiger he was unperturbed.

He was known in Vraja and among those born in Vraja, who especially thought of him as one of their very own, as Tinkaḍi (Three Cowry)[46] Bābā or Mauni (Silent) Bābā.

There is a village named Manoharpur (Mind-enchanting Town) in the administrative district (*ghāṭāla*) of Mahakumār in the district of Medinipur in West Bengal. Its qualities are just like its name. Truly, the beauty of that village steals everyone's hearts. Nature adorned that village in an expert way with many kinds of trees, flowers, and ponds. Therefore, perhaps, the village was named Manoharpur.

Several generations of Vaiṣṇavas in the lineage of Mother Jāhnavā Ṭhākurāṇī, the indistinguishable power (*śakti*) of Nityānanda Prabhu,[47] passed their lives in this village. Śrī Śrī 108[48] Prabhupāda Tinkaḍi Go-

---

[46]A cowry or small conch-like shell was used in Bengal as a medium of monetary exchange. It was equivalent to a penny. "Three Penny" was a name given to Bābā as a baby. It was part of a system of village superstition which sought to deflect evil attention from loved ones by giving them nick-names indicating insignificance or lack of value. The story connected with the name Tinkaḍi, sometimes written Tinkuḍi or Tinkoḍi, is given later in this chapter. The name stuck with Bābā for the rest of his life.

[47]Mā Jāhnavā or Jāhnavī was one of the two wives of Caitanya's companion Nityānanda Prabhu. She later, after the passing of her husband, became a major figure and leader in the movement inspired by Caitanya. As his wife she is referred to as his "power" and she is regarded in the tradition as inseparable or indistinguishable in terms of spiritual power and illumination from her husband, Nityānanda.

[48]This is a way of showing respect in Caitanya Vaiṣṇavism and other related religious traditions arising from Hinduism. The addition of "Śrī" before a name means that the speaker considers the person so named to be blessed by Śrī, the goddess of good fortune. Unhappy with just one or two "Śrīs," some want to pile up a hundred and eight "Śrīs" before the names of people they highly respect. That is what is meant by "108." I have followed Binode Bihari Dāsa's practice here.

swami was born in that village. His father's name was Harimohan Goswami and his mother's name was Suradhunī Devī.

It was the full moon day of Māgha in Bengali year 1313 [1907 c.e.]. In all directions *saṅkīrtana*[49] of the holy names and other auspicious rites were being performed. The house of Harimohan Goswami was also filled with the joy of *saṅkīrtana* of the holy names. In the house were sacred images named Gaura[50] and Balarāma[51] that were nearly five hundred years old. In the courtyard of the temple the *saṅkīrtana* of the names of Hari was in progress. Many Vaiṣṇavas, too, made auspicious appearances at the house of Harimohan Goswami. On such an auspicious day, at such an auspicious time, a male child was born, lighting up the lap of Suradhunī Devī, wife of Harimohan Goswami. Harimohan Goswami's joy knew no bounds. With great pleasure he began to serve the Vaiṣṇavas.

That was Suradhunī Devī's eighth child. Before him six sons and one daughter had died. In the birth house the mid-wife cut the child's umbilical cord and took him on her lap. Then she said: "this son is mine." Suradhunī Devī gave the mid-wife three cowries (*tin kaḍi*) and bought her son back. Therefore, the son became hers and the son's name became Tinkaḍi.

Harimohan Gosvami named his son Kiśorī-kiśorānanda.[52] He was a very beautiful baby. Gradually, in due course, he learned to walk and became very mischievous. At the slightest inattentiveness of his mother the child scattered and broke pots and lamps and drove his mother to distraction. From time to time, his mother became upset at the misbehavior of her child and would tie him up. All of the neighbors in the area loved that child. With or without cause the neighboring mothers would come and caress him.[53]

In this way five years quickly passed. By the laws of fate, suddenly

---

[49]See the glossary for a detailed discussion of this religious practice.

[50]A popular name of Caitanya meaning "golden," descriptive of his light complexion.

[51]Balarāma was Kṛṣṇa's older brother in his Vṛndāvana sport. He is believed to have become Nityānanda Prabhu in the Caitanya sport. Thus, the images worshiped in the house of Bābā's father were a variation of Caitanya and Nityānanda images worshiped commonly among Caitanya Vaiṣṇavas.

[52]According to this account, Bābā's given name was Kiśorī-kiśorānanda, "Joy of Kiśorī (Rādhā) and Kiśora (Kṛṣṇa)."

[53]This childhood naughtiness is, of course, reminiscent of both Kṛṣṇa and Caitanya. Mischievousness in a child is considered a good sign in Hindu society, a sign of the child's lively intelligence and future promise, especially so among boys.

one day, darkness descended on the house of Harimohan Goswami. After only a few days of illness Suradhunī Devī passed on to the next world. At the loss of his wife Harimohan Goswami was deeply troubled. Above all, the biggest problem for him then was who will now take care of his child. Many recommended to the Goswami that he marry a second time, but he was not at all in agreement with the idea of marrying a second time. He owned a little bit of land, but not enough to maintain his household. From time to time he had to visit the households of his disciples. From what little he received as gifts from them, he ran his household.[54] In this situation who would take care of his child?

Harimohan Goswami was worried. However, one of his distant cousins was extremely affectionate towards the Goswami's son. Seeing the Goswami so worried, she said to him: "Why are you worrying? I will take care of your child. Give your child over to me. From today you should think that this child is mine not yours." Hearing these words, the Goswami became completely free from worry. He said: "You've done a good thing, sister. You have saved me; from today I entrust this child to you," From that time on the Dhāimā[55] began to raise Tinkaḍi.

That child, only five years of age, was the very life of Dhāimā. Her house was four or five miles away from Manoharpur in a town called Rāṇīcak. In order to take care of the boy Tinkaḍi, she had to move to Manoharpur. Harimohan Goswami was generally off visiting his disciples' houses. After ten days, fifteen days and sometimes even a month he would return to the house. Goswamiji entrusted the care of his son to Dhāimā and was able to go back and forth to and from his disciples' houses without anxiety.

The boy was very capricious. If he wasn't watched every minute he would disappear somewhere. When Dhāimā did not see the boy for a while, she became agitated and began to search for him. After much

---

[54]Harimohan Goswami was what is referred to as a caste Goswami, or *jāti-gosvāmin*. He and his ancestors supported themselves and their families by acting as gurus for a community of disciples. In many cases such families have been acting as gurus for other families for many generations. They give initiation and spiritual guidance to the members of those families and the disciples give gifts in return. This relationship required Harimohan to visit more or less regularly the houses of his disciples. It was the primary way that Harimohan Goswami supported himself and his family.

[55]*Dhāimā* means "wet-nurse." It is not clear from the account whether Tinkaḍi was still nursing at five years old or not. Nor do we learn whether she had other children and was even able to nurse him. So it is not clear whether she was indeed a wet-nurse for Tinkaḍi. She may have just been a foster-mother which is another meaning of the word. We don't even learn her name from this account. She is just referred to as Dhāimā.

searching, she would catch him and bring him back. She always and in all places had to watch him; otherwise, where this mischievous boy was and what he was doing was difficult to keep track of. For Dhāimā it was an extraordinary responsibility. If one did not give him whatever he wanted, whenever he wanted it, he would cry, roll around in the dirt on the ground, and make a big fuss. It was a good deal of trouble for Dhāimā. In this way, though, through her care and his father's affection, the boy Tinkaḍi was well cared for.

In time, chalk was placed in his hand for his education,[56] and he was enrolled in school. But it was a great problem sending him to school, for he did not want to go to school at all. How much caressing and begging was necessary to send Tinkaḍi to school! In the evening Dhāimā would sit and teach the boy. He learned to read very quickly, but he still did not want to study at all. With much coaxing Dhāimā repeatedly read many kinds of stories to him and made him practice his reading. How many times after sitting down to study he said, "I'm hungry! I'm tired!" and so forth. In this way the education of the boy Tinkaḍi progressed.

As much as his age increased, the boy's capriciousness also increased. All the time it was only play and more play. If he even heard the word "study" it was as if the sky had broken and fallen on his head. Getting him to study at school was a huge problem. Just before it was time to go to school the boy would disappear. His anxious foster mother would search for him at this house and that house and bring him back. After that, so much coaxing and begging was required to get him to go to school. Some mornings she wasn't able to find Tinkaḍi at all. After the time for school had passed he would show up. For example, one day just before it was time to go to school he disappeared. Dhāimā after much searching returned to the house without finding him. At that moment she happened to glance up at a tree and saw that he had climbed it and was sitting there. After a great deal of Dhāimā's begging, he felt sorry for her and came down from the tree. Another day she was again unable to find Tinkaḍi when it was time to go to school. When she went to take care of some work in the house she found him hiding under the bed.

In this way Tinkaḍi gradually became older. After a while the time for his brahminical initiation (*upanayana*) arrived. When Tinkaḍi was about the age of nine, Harimohan Goswami performed the sacrament of

---

[56] This refers to the ritual placing of chalk in the hand of a boy six or seven years old as a sign of the commencement of his education.

brāhmaṇa initiation and gave him [Vaiṣṇava] mantra initiation (*dīkṣā*) as well. When the day of the initiation arrived an amazing transformation occurred in Tinkaḍi. When his head had been shaved and he had put on the saffron cloth, a wonderfully profound state of feeling was noticeable in him. Nearly all of the Vaiṣṇavas who had come inferred that this boy was not an ordinary boy. Through him many blessings will come to the world. They all gave him their blessings from the core of their hearts. Saying to Dhāimā: "[Please give] alms, Mother!" he accepted his first alms from her.

After his initiation Tinkaḍi's capriciousness for the most part diminished. Every day in the morning he wanted to read one chapter of the *Gītā*. It was as if the *Gītā* was his whole life. When it was time to go to school he would take a copy of the *Gītā* with him. At school when it was time to practice reading he would read the *Gītā* instead of the other books. At the time he showed a special attraction for *saṅkīrtana* of the holy names, too. Every day he wanted to perform *kīrtana* in the evening in front of the Gaura and Balarāma images worshiped in his house. When *kīrtana* was being performed, from time to time special emotional states were seen in the boy Tinkaḍi.

Gradually Tinkaḍi left boyhood behind and entered his teenage years. In his teenage years, his body developed in an marvelous way. His eyes became deep-set, his chest more defined, and a special beauty appeared on all of his limbs with the arrival of fresh youth. His verbal expressions and ability to speak were also amazing. He used to please everyone with his beautiful expressions. During this period, since he had become so inattentive towards learning, his education ended.

His father Harimohan Goswami became concerned about his son's future. They owned a little bit of land, but it was not enough to support a family on. Therefore, the Goswami thought that if he introduced his son among some of his disciples, in the future he would be able to support himself in the profession of guru. Thinking in this way, he began to take his son with him to the houses of his disciples. Just taking him to the houses of disciples was not enough, however. He also needed to have some knowledge of scripture. Just becoming a guru does not work. Therefore, Harimohan Goswami began to teach his son the *Bhāgavata*, the *Caitanya-caritāmṛta*, the *Caitanya-bhāgavata* and so forth.[57] Though

[57]These are all important scriptural texts for the Caitanya tradition. The *Bhāgavata Purāṇa*, in Sanskrit, is one of the most complete treatments of the story of Kṛṣṇa and the philosophy that forms the foundation of Vaiṣṇavism. The other two works focus specif-

his son had no enthusiasm for study in general, for the study of all those texts on *bhakti* he was extremely enthusiastic. In time, following the system of the family gurus, he began to have a few disciples of his own. When he was at home Prabhupāda Tinkaḍi Goswami would recite every day the *Bhāgavata, Caitanya-caritāmṛta* and other *bhakti* texts in front of the sacred images, Śrī Gaura and Balarāma. From time to time he would go with his father, and sometimes alone, to the houses of disciples.

In time, Prabhupāda Tinkaḍi Goswami turned into a young man. His father Harimohan Goswami then began to worry about his son's marriage. He received information about a young lady with all the right qualities. In a village near Manoharpur named Khāñjāpur lived Gopīnāth Goswami. He had a seven year old daughter named Śītalā Sundarī. Her nature and her figure were quite beautiful. Her father, too, had begun to worry about finding his daughter a good match. Harimohan Goswami one day made a proposal to Gopīnāth Goswami. Gopīnāth Goswami could not control his joy. He, too, in his mind had nourished the wish to offer his daughter to Tinkaḍi Goswami. He joyfully accepted the proposal of Harimohan Goswami. On an auspicious day, at an auspicious hour, the marriage of Prabhupāda Tinkaḍi Goswami with Śītalā Sundarī, the daughter of Gopīnāth Goswami of Khāñjāpur, was performed. Gopīnāth Goswami with tears in his eyes sent his daughter to the house of her father-in-law.

In the village of Manoharpur at the house of Harimohan Goswami, the new bride's arrival was auspicious. No one's joy knew any limits. Seeing the young, capricious girl-bride Harimohan Goswami was lost in happiness. In this way, in the midst of so much happiness a year passed. Suddenly, by the laws of fate, on to this golden household fell the shadow of great sadness. Prabhupāda's father, after only a few days of illness, left his perishable body and set out for eternal sport. Prabhupāda was then only sixteen years of age. Without his father and without his mother, Prabhupāda's heart was stricken with sadness. He felt himself completely helpless. All of his neighbors began to console him. Gradually, Prabhupāda regained his mental strength and began to take

---

ically on the life and teachings of Śrī Caitanya, who was believed by his followers to be the most recent and revealing of the descents (*avatāra*) of Kṛṣṇa. The *Caitanya-caritāmṛta* is by Kṛṣṇadāsa Kavirāja in Bengali with numerous citations from Sanskrit works and the *Caitanya-bhāgavata* is by Vṛndāvana Dāsa Ṭhākura who had access to many of Caitanya's closest companions for materials on his life and teachings.

care of the responsibilities of his household. In this way, a few years passed in the midst of a mental state burdened with sadness.

Though indeed Prabhupāda Tinkaḍi Goswami passed his married life in this way, still day after day it seemed more and more as if his mind had disappeared somewhere in the thought of higher truths. Prabhupāda had heard when he was a child, "Churning curds in the early morning makes the butter come out good. Worship of Kṛṣṇa when one is young brings success when one grows old." This saying troubled his mind again and again. The most valuable time of his life was passing by. If worship of Kṛṣṇa does not happen now, when will it? As more days go by, bondage to worldly life will increase. If someone waits, sitting on the shore of the sea thinking: "when the waves of the sea calm down I will take my bath," one is not likely to ever get his bath. In the same way, if someone waits thinking: "when the waves of the troubles of worldly life become calm I will worship Kṛṣṇa," then one's worship will not likely ever happen. In such thoughts, the joys of worldly life started to lessen for Prabhupāda and his passion for worship began to increase.

At that time Prabhupāda was very fashionable. He always wore *dhotis* and *kurtas* of the finest cotton. He never wore ordinary or soiled clothes. He also used to smoke, using a very beautiful hookah and along with it the finest tobacco from Vishnupur. When he had to go somewhere he would not forget to take his hookah and Vishnupur tobacco with him. When going to a disciple's house he used to take a *brāhmaṇa* cook with him. When going from one village to another his disciples used to carry Prabhupāda in a palanquin.

After passing a few years in this manner a son was born lighting up the lap of his wife, Śītalā Sundarī. The birth of a son should have been a joyful matter for Prabhupāda. But in his heart there was no joy. It was as if his joy had disappeared somewhere. He began again to think that the most valuable time of his life was passing and that his bondage to worldly life was increasing day by day. When will I offer my body, mind, and life-breath to the lotus feet of Śrī Govinda and wholeheartedly do private worship (*bhajana*)? This kind of thought lessened his joy in worldly life. From time to time Prabhupāda visited Navadvīpa and Nīlācala.

At that time there arose an uncontrollable desire in his heart. He thought: "I have made many disciples, but if I am to explain scripture, a little knowledge of Sanskrit is necessary. Thinking like this, he began for some time to study with some *paṇḍita* in Navadvīpa. But worrying about his household life and thinking about the Lord created interruptions in his study. His studying never happened again. He returned to Manoharpur. On account of his responsibilities, he remained in household life, but his mind again and again ran away to Vṛndāvana. It was as if some invisible power were beckoning him. Because of the uncontrollable force of his mind, one day, without telling anyone, he actually started out for Vṛndāvana.

After reaching Vṛndāvana his joy knew no bounds when he saw the places where Śrī Kṛṣṇa's sports occurred. After visiting those places he practically forgot all about his home and deciding that he wanted to live permanently in Vraja, he began to pray to the feet of compassionate Śrī Rādhārāṇī: "O Compassionate Kiśorī, don't throw me back into the dark well of worldly life. Mistress, don't allow me to go from Vraja to any other place." While praying in this way he arrived at Mount Govardhana. There he heard from people that at Govindakuṇḍa lived a perfected great-soul (*siddha-mahātmā*). His name was Śrī Śrī 108 Manohara Dāsa Bābājī Mahārāja. Prabhupāda with great excitement and little delay went running to Govindakuṇḍa wishing to meet the perfected *bābā*.

The perfected *bābā*, when he saw Prabhupāda, offered him a full eight-limbed, stick-like prostration.[58] Prabhupāda was completely unprepared for that and objected. The perfected *bābā* said: "Why not? You are a descendant of the great teachers (*ācārya*). You are a world-guru. If I do not offer prostration to you, to whom should I offer it?" After that the *bābā* with great respect offered him a seat and made arrangements for his stay.

One day Prabhupāda asked him: "Mahārāja, what must one do to attain *bhakti*?" The perfected *bābā* replied with astonishment: "What kind of question is that? *Bhakti* is one of your household belongings and you are asking: how does one get *bhakti*?" After spending a few days in many question-and-answer discussions of private worship (*bhajana*), Prabhupāda informed the *bābā* of his wish not to return to his house any

[58]This is the most complete form of prostration. Eight limbs or parts of the body touch the earth as one lays out full-length on the ground. Since one has to lay one's body out full-length one looks rather like a stick lying on the ground. Thus, it is called "stick-like," (*daṇḍavat*). Siddha Manohardāsa Bābā offered this prostration to Prabhupāda because he was honoring him as one of the descendents of the great teachers (*ācārya*) or companions of Śrī Caitanya.

more. In response, the perfected *bābā* said: "What kind of talk is that? Haven't you cherished the desire to become a big scholar?" At this statement of the *bābā*, Prabhupāda was particularly surprised and he began to wonder how the perfected *bābā* knew his inner desires. Because of that incident his faith in the perfected *bābā* became even stronger.

Then the perfected *bābā* gave Prabhupāda an order: "Return to your house. This in not your time. You still have much work to do yet. Through you many things beneficial to the world will come to pass. When the time is right your desire to live in Vṛndāvana will be fulfilled." Prabhupāda with a pained heart remained silent for a little while and then said: "But I have no money for a ticket. How will I go?" The perfected *bābā* said: "Don't worry. You go to Vṛndāvana. Ticket money has been sent from home for you there." Prabhupāda had no other recourse; he left Govindakuṇḍa at the order of the perfected *bābā* and went to the house of a relative in Vṛndāvana. There he learned that indeed a money order had arrived from home for his return trip. Prabhupāda took the money and started towards home.

Though Prabhupāda had returned to his house, his detachment from worldly life began gradually to increase. He had one son whom he named Vṛndāvana[candra]. When the child was only three months old, Prabhupāda's wife Śītalā Sundarī left aside her body and went to the next world, after only a few days of illness. At this, Prabhupāda lost his faith entirely in worldly life. Worldly life for him began to feel like a prison full of misery. Here there is nothing called happiness, only the essence of misery. Becoming deluded by the illusion of this false worldly life a human being neglectfully loses such a rare birth as a human. Seeing the impermanence of this kind of worldly existence, his mind became even more indifferent towards it. However that may be, now his major worry was: who will take care of this nursing child? His neighbors and friends all encouraged Prabhupāda to marry a second time. He made it known that he was deeply against that proposal. Even so, his childhood friend Yāminī Kumāra Banerjee Mahāśaya encouraged him with special vigor. He said: "Goswami, if you do not marry now who will care for this poor motherless child? Besides that, you yourself are still young. If there is no wife in the house, who will look after you?"

Prabhupāda was then twenty-eight years old. He was not at all in agreement with his friend's proposal, but he was especially worried about his child. Then Prabhupāda's own former *dhāimā* said to him: "You do not have to worry about this child. In the same way that I raised you, I will raise this son of yours." When Dhāimā said this Prabhupāda became freed from his anxiety.

Pilgrimage to Holy Sites

With the appearance of intense detachment from household life at the loss of his first wife, Prabhupāda Tinkaḍi Gosvāmin decided to tour all of India's holy places of pilgrimage. One day, he took with him a *bhakta* named Jānakī Hāita from the village of Sāgarpur, which is south of Manoharpur, and started out for the northern regions. With Jānakī Hāita he first went to Haridwar. He visited many of the important places in Haridwar, but he felt no peace of mind. After staying a few days in Haridwar he went on to Rishikesh. At Rishikesh, seeing the babbling Gaṅgā flowing from the foothills of the Himālayas, Prabhupāda felt some peace. After staying for a few days at Rishikesh they started out for Kedārnāth and Badarikāshram.[59] At that time traveling to Kedārnāth and Badarikāshram was not as easy as it is today. One had to travel by foot and so Prabhupāda started out on foot.

Deep emotions for the Himālayas, the place of austerities, filled Prabhupāda's mind. It was as if some unknown divine being were beckoning him, saying: "Come, come. Come home, o child, who has forgotten your true nature. Having fallen into the grip of *māyā* from time without beginning, how many agonies you have suffered. Now, come home. Here there is no sadness; here there is enduring peace. Here there is no darkness. Here, illumined by divine beings, there is enduring bliss. Here, there is enduring satisfaction. Don't cast your gaze again behind

[59]These are two important pilgrimage sites that are high in the Himalaya mountains. They are inaccessible for part of the year because of snow. This pilgrimage would have taken place sometime in the late 1930s. Even today it is a strenuous journey. Back then it must have been especially difficult. Kedārnāth is a temple of Śiva and Badarikāshram or Badrināth is a place of austerities in which some Hindus believe Vyāsa the divider of the Vedas and author of all the *Purāṇas* and the *Mahābhārata* is still living. By accessing some of the maps of the Himalayas available online, one can follow Bābā's route as he visited these sites. The *MSN Encarta* maps seem particularly useful in this regard.

you at *māyā*. Coming here you will be filled with bliss." In Prabhupāda's hand was his string of beads for reciting the holy names.[60] The holy names were flowing in a tireless current. Crossing peak after peak Prabhupāda arrived at Devaprayāg.

Seeing the beauty of Devaprayāg, Prabhupāda was overwhelmed. On one side was the Bhāgīrathī (Gaṅgā) and on the other, the stream of the Alakānandā came down and joined it. It was surrounded on all sides by mountain peaks. Prabhupāda, after finishing his bathing rites at the point where the Bhāgīrathī and the Alakānandā joined, sat on a fine rock nearby and repeated the holy names, absorbed in their ceaseless flow, his mind in deep meditation. Suddenly, he was startled by the call of Jānakī Hāita: "Gõsāi! [Goswami] Let's go. Let's start out now."

Again they moved up the path. They travelled along a narrow mountain path, sometimes with their faces turned down and sometimes with their faces turned up. At the end of the day, they spent the night at some tiny mountain village in an abandoned hut. When morning arrived, after finishing their baths, they took again to the path. In this way, viewing the profound natural beauty of the Himālayas, the land of asceticism, they headed on towards Rudraprayāg. The path was mostly deserted. From time to time some mountain tribals came along herding flocks of sheep. Sometimes, perhaps they met a few saintly *mahātmās* with matted hair. Or, somewhere on the bank of the Alakānandā in a narrow cave they saw some saintly *mahātmā*. Seeing their attachment to worship in the thoroughly solitary reaches of the Himālayas, Prabhupāda's mind became even more detached. How much longer until he too would cut the bonds of this illusory worldly life and in a thorough, whole-hearted way take shelter at the feet of Śrī Govinda? This kind of thought made his mind indifferent to worldly existence. In this way, after crossing through many splendid surroundings they arrived at Rudraprayāg.

After bathing at the place where the Mandākinī and the Alakānandā meet, they stayed for a few days before starting out for Kedārnāth. When he started his journey to the holy places, Prabhupāda brought some money with him to pay for expenses on the road. With that they travelled along, sometimes eating cooked meals and sometimes just fruit and raw vegetables. Traveling onwards in this way Prabhupāda came

---

[60]Caitanya Vaiṣṇavas repeat the holy names of Kṛṣṇa on a set of 108 beads generally made from the sacred basil (*tulasī*) plant. The beads are used to keep a count of how many names are recited in a day.

to Gupta Kāshi. There he visited Bābā Bholanāth[61] and set out to see Tricukī[Trijugī] Nārāyaṇ.[62] There, the climb was extremely difficult. All the mountain peaks seemed to kiss the sky. In the distance, there was snow on the peaks. Prabhupāda tolerated the many troubles and arrived at Tricukī Nārāyaṇ. After seeing the sacred image of Tricukī Nārāyaṇ, he went on to visit Kedārnāth. There, the climb was even more difficult than before. The path was not level anywhere. It was only climbing and more climbing. Many other *sādhus* and pilgrims had also started out on that path to visit Kedārnāth. When Prabhupāda arrived at Kedārnāth the sun was just setting. It was very cold and there was snow in all directions. Prabhupāda visited the sacred image of Kedārnāth and spent the night in a hostel for pilgrims. In his mind, though, he still was not satisfied. The next day Prabhupāda got up from bed and decided to begin the journey to see Badarikāshram. From Kedārnāth they first went to Gaurikund and bathed in the hot springs there. Then they went to Sonprayāg[63] and by way of Gupta Kāshi, they started for Badarikāshram. In this way after passing through many places they reached Yogīmath [Joshīmath]. After resting there for a couple of days they proceeded on to Vishnuprayāg and from there, after overcoming many difficulties, they finally arrived at Badarikāshram.

There the beauty of the place was so attractive to the mind. The Alakānandā flowed gurgling along in front of the temple. Behind the temple was Mount Nara and in front, Mount Nārāyaṇa. To the south of Nara was the extremely high, snow-covered Mount Nīlakaṇṭha. In the light of the sun the mind-pleasing beauty increased. Prabhupāda after viewing Badrīnārāyaṇa took his bath in the hot springs there. After resting for a few days, they started out to visit the cave of Vyāsadeva. In that cave Kṛṣṇadvaipāyana Vedavyāsa wrote the *Śrīmad Bhāgavata*.[64] Prabhupāda after visiting the cave of Vyāsa went to see Bhīmapul. When the five Pāṇḍavas arrived at this place on their journey to heaven they were unable to cross the fast-moving river there. Bhīma created a bridge over it with a massive stone. Therefore, the place's name is Bridge of Bhīma (Bhīma-pula). Prabhupāda visited Bhīmapul and returned to Badrīnārāyaṇa. Even after visiting all those places Prabhupāda did not

[61] An image of Śiva.

[62] A famous image of Nārāyaṇa or Viṣṇu.

[63] At the confluence of the Mandākinī and the Son-gaṅgā and where the path splits for Tricukī Nārāyaṇ. They must be retracing their steps at this point because they had to pass through Sonprayāg and Gaurikund on the way to Kedārnāth.

[64] The *Bhāgavata Purāṇa* is believed by Caitanya Vaiṣṇavas to have been written 5,000 years ago, just after the departure from earth of Kṛṣṇa.

feel even the most ordinary peace. After this, he decided to return to Haridwar. In this way, after traveling on the trail for many long days and passing through many adventures he returned with his friend Jānakī Hāita to Haridwar.

From Haridwar he began another pilgrimage. From Haridwar he went to visit Kurukshetra,[65] Pushkar[66] and so forth and arrived finally in Ayodhyā.[67] From there he visited Kāshi,[68] Prayāg,[69] Gayā[70] and so forth and then, after a long time away, he returned again to his own home.

Prabhupāda had returned after traveling around to the holy sites. Receiving this news, many of his disciples from the surrounding towns and villages came to Manoharpur to escort him to their homes. Prabhupāda then spent some days immersed in the joy of *saṅkīrtana* at his disciples' houses. Meanwhile, all of Prabhupāda's friends began to beg him insistently to marry again. Prabhupāda was extremely averse to this, but he did not outwardly reveal it. In secret he left his house again desiring this time to visit the holy sites in eastern India.

Prabhupāda first went to the holy place of the goddess, Kāmarūpa Kāmākṣyā. After viewing the goddess Kāmākṣyā he started out for Paraśurāma Kuṇḍa. The way was unfamiliar. Prabhupāda proceeded by inquiring again and again.

One day while he was traveling on the path evening came. It was a forest path and there was no sign anywhere of human habitation. Wearied, exhausted, and hungry, Prabhupāda became worried. He continued moving down that dense forest path. Gradually the darkness be-

[65]The place where the great war described in the *Mahābhārata* is said to have taken place and where the *Bhagavad-gītā* was spoken by Kṛṣṇa to Arjuna.

[66]Pushkar is a pilgrimage site in Rajasthan, an ancient town with many temples and a sacred lake. It seems a bit out of the way for Bābā, as after Haridwar he seems to have been making his way down the Ganges towards Bengal.

[67]The sacred epicenter of the Rāma narrative.

[68]The ancient city of Vārāṇasī mentioned in the Upaniṣads and *Mahābhārata*. It is a center for traditional learning and a place pious Hindus visit for sacred baths and at the end of their lives in expectation of death.

[69]A sacred city where the Ganges and the Yamunā meet. The famous Kumbha Melā, a gathering of pilgrims and holy men and women, takes place every twelve years at Prayāga and millions of people bath in the confluence at that time, a time thought to be particularly auspicious for bath.

[70]A sacred place dear to the followers of Śrī Caitanya as the site of his conversion to Vaiṣṇavism. Śrī Caitanya is also associated with the cities of Kāshi and Prayāg visited earlier.

came even more thick. Prabhupāda now became agitated and began to worry about a way out. Suddenly, it was as if a ray of hope shined down. Someone carrying a lantern was coming towards him. The person, seeing Prabhupāda in that lonely spot, was extremely surprised, and what he said in the language of the villages was something like this: "Traveller, you have lost your way. If you stay here you will find yourself in the belly of a ferocious tiger. Come. I will show you a place where you can spend the night."

After saying this, the man guided him a little further along and pointed him to an ancient temple. He then warned him that he should not go outside in the night. Prabhupāda took a few steps towards the temple and then looked behind him; he was greatly surprised to see that there was no sign of that man. Nevertheless, he decided to spend the night in a room of that broken down temple. Prabhupāda was by then extremely hungry and he helplessly began to do *japa* on his *harināma* beads. After a while he heard a *jhum-jhum* sound outside, like the sound of ankle bells. Prabhupāda's ears perked up and he began to listen carefully to try to determine what that sound belonged to. It sounded to him like the sound of the ankle bells of a woman. Indeed, a woman with some food on a plate entered into Prabhupāda's room. That woman asked Prabhupāda in a village dialect to eat some food. Prabhupāda thought to himself that there must be a human settlement nearby and that she brought the food from there, knowing that there was a guest in the vicinity. He was by then very troubled by hunger. Without giving it any more thought he ate the food. After giving Prabhupāda the food, that woman without saying anything more departed, accompanied by that *jhum-jhum* sound. Some doubt entered Prabhupāda's mind and suddenly after peeking outside, he was astonished to find that there was no trace of the woman. He thought to himself that this was certainly the goddess Kāmākṣyā who came and gave him grace-food (*prasāda*).[71] Thinking in this way, his chest became soaked with his tears. Then, after experiencing extraordinary tastes while eating the grace-food, he expressed his salutation at her feet again and again and made this request: "O Goddess, you have shown me such grace, Mother. Let me attain *bhakti* for Kṛṣṇa and make this human birth of mine most fortunate." After honoring [eating with respect] the grace-food, he began chanting the holy names and when sleep overtook him he did not know. When he awoke he saw that night had ended. The birds in the trees loudly announced

[71] *Prasāda* or grace-food is food offered to a sacred image. It is later consumed by the votaries of that image as a form of the image's grace.

the rising of the sun. When he awoke from sleep, he felt much more healthy and strong than before. In this way, he passed through a series of various visions and adventures and visited many of the great holy sites of eastern India.

There was another incident from this period. While Prabhupāda was traveling, at some point he came to the home of some great saint. Coming near him Prabhupāda was infused with his power. He stayed there a few days and served him. One day the saint said: "You have served me a great deal. What do you want?"

Prabhupāda replied: "I want pure *bhakti* to the lotus feet of the Divine Couple."

The holy man said: "I will not be able to give you that. Go to Vṛndāvana. There, your desired objective will be fulfilled. Still, you have given me so much service. I want to give you a little something in return. Do you want anything else?"

Then Prabhupāda said: "See, Mahārāja. I am from a family of gurus. Receiving gifts as a guru is our custom. Moreover, I do not have that much of an education. Therefore, I don't have any real knowledge of scripture. In order to properly reply to the questions of one's students, knowing the arguments of scripture is necessary. Please give me your grace so that I will be able to understand the deep meanings of scripture."

The holy man gave his blessing to Prabhupāda and said: "Go. From now on all the arguments of scripture will appear within you." A little while after that Prabhupāda started out for his home.

Prabhupāda traveled around to so many holy sites but still did not find even the smallest amount of peace. Gradually, his indifference towards household life increased. After returning to Manoharpur and spending some time at the houses of his disciples and at Navadvīpa he departed again on a journey to the holy places of South India. After wandering around to all the holy sites in South India starting with Ramesvaram, Kanyākumārika and so forth, he returned once more to his home in Manoharpur.

Second Marriage

Prabhupāda now focused his mind on spreading the holy name in the towns and villages. He did not like staying at home. He began to spend more of his days in *saṅkirtana* of the holy names among his disciples, moving from one village to another. He did not want to return home because, when he did, all of his friends would beg him to get married again. In such a manner he one day became extremely detached and determining that he would never return to his home again, he went to Vṛndāvana. There he went to the *siddha bābā* (Manohara Das Bābājī) at Govindakuṇḍa and began to stay with him there. After staying there for a few days, however, Prabhupāda began to be troubled by the impulses of sexual desire. Siddha Bābā knew everything. One day he said to Prabhupāda: "Goswami, you should return to your home."

Prabhupāda became extremely sad and said: "Mahārāja, I do not want to return to the cycle of *māyā* again. Please give me shelter and make me successful."

Siddha Bābā replied: "If you merely say that, Goswami, what good will it do? You have even now some remaining *karma* to experience. Apart from that, there are many necessary things that you must first achieve. I tell you: return home and marry again. After that, when the time is right Rādhārāṇi will draw you back here. Don't worry. Your desired goal *will* be achieved."

With no other choice Prabhupāda stayed a few more days and then returned home.

At Prabhupāda's return all of the villagers were overjoyed. His friend Yāminī Banerji and many who were older than he now pressed Prabhupāda again to marry. By the order of Siddha Bābā and the requests of all the villagers Prabhupāda agreed to marry again.

On an auspicious day, at an auspicious time, Prabhupāda's second marriage, with Sarasvatī Devī, the twelve-year old daughter of Āśutoṣa Haḍa who lived in a village near Manoharpur, was performed. His age then was probably thirty-two or thirty-three. Everyone thought that this time his mind would become drawn into worldly life. But that did not happen. His indifference to household life remained unflagging like before.

After only three years had passed in his second marriage, his household life felt another fierce blow. His nanny whom he dearly loved died after a brief illness of only a few days. At this Prabhupāda was deeply moved. Seeing at every step that worldly existence is impermanent, he lost all faith in happiness derived from worldly existence. Now, he spent more time each day applying his mind to thinking about the Lord. At that time, Prabhupāda used to wake up in the third *ghaṭikā*[72] of the night and sit to do private worship (*bhajana*) and he would remain seated [on his meditation seat] until eleven in the morning doing private worship.

In one way, his worship was not accomplished by staying at home. He needed to pull living beings, scorched by the three miseries[73] and devoured by *māyā*, out of their sufferings. In order to free living beings from their suffering, he had to leave his house, especially to spread the holy names from village to village. At that time at whatever house he stayed in he encouraged the unbroken [continuous] *saṅkīrtana* of the holy names. Then, being attracted to Prabhupāda's firmness in practice and his discussions of Hari, people came in groups and began to receive initiation from him. The number of his disciples began to increase day by day. Whichever house he went to, there many *bhaktas* would come. As a result, householders who were poor were often not bold enough to invite him to their houses.[74]

One young son of a poor householder, drawn by the influence of Prabhupāda, revealed his enthusiasm to receive initiation from him. Hearing that, the young man's father burst out in anger. He scolded his

[72]The third 24 minute period of the night. The period of night begins according to Indian custom at 11:42 pm. Thus, Goswami Tinkaḍi rose seventy-two minutes after the beginning of night, or around 1:00 am.

[73]The three miseries or sufferings shared by all living beings are those caused by their own bodies or minds (*ādhyātmika*), those caused by other living beings (*ādhibhautika*) and those caused by natural calamities (ādhidaivika).

[74]Householders are bound in Hinduism to feed and serve any guests who come to their homes. When Prabhupāda arrived, many guests would come also to see him and it was the responsibility of the householder to feed them.

son: "Sure! Into this little shamble of a house he is bringing an elephant. Into this little hovel he is bringing an elephant. He will break it down, pulverize it, and utterly destroy it. What business have we with that sort of guru? In two days, he will empty our house. Our guru should be like us. He will come here and then take out his own flat rice brought from his own house and eat. When he leaves I will trick him and give him just two *paisa*, and he will take it and leave. What business have we with this kind of big guru?" Without any recourse that young man was forced to give up his desire to receive initiation from Prabhupāda.

With the coming of many disciples, however, many amazing incidents also occurred. One time a young *brāhmaṇa* received initiation from Prabhupāda. That *brāhmaṇa*'s mother expressed her great dissatisfaction: "Great! Wonderful, son! We are *brāhmaṇas*. That fellow is of a lower caste. Therefore, Bābā,[75] why in the end have you gone and become a member of a lower caste?"[76]

Day after day Prabhupāda's influence began to increase. When he went from one disciple's house to another disciple's house, his disciples would gather together into groups and go along with him performing *saṅkīrtana* of the holy names. At that time, although he was indifferent to worldly, household life and his private worship was intense, he still was unable to give up the hookah. Prabhupāda thought to himself: "This, too, is a chain." Thinking like this he made up his mind to give up smoking. One day a person named Śrīdhara, who was specially well-known to him, asked for Prabhupāda's hookah. Prabhupāda then offered it and all of his smoking paraphernalia to Śrīdhara and said: "Śrīdhara, you should not return these things to me. Take them away from me. I will never smoke again." Saying this, he gave everything over and was free. After that Prabhupāda never smoked again. At that time he no longer wore expensive clothing like he did before. He only wore a simple cotton *dhoti* and a loose cotton waistcoat.

When he went to the houses of his disciples, he would not stay in anyone's house. Instead, he would build a small hut of leaves, branches,

---

[75]Here just a term of affection used by a mother addressing her son. This does not refer to a Vaiṣṇava renunciant in this context.

[76]As far as I know, Tinkaḍi Goswami was also a *brāhmaṇa*. Within the *bāhmaṇa* community, however, there are different social rankings. Some *brāhmaṇas* generally referring to themselves as *kulīna*, "of high or eminent descent," think of themselves as superior in rank and ritual purity to other *brāhmaṇas*. This is most likely what this young man's mother had in mind here.

and bamboo in some uninhabited place nearby and do his private worship inside it. When he was doing his private worship, sometimes from outside the hut one would hear him shouting and sometimes weeping. He did not under any condition fail to perform his regular private worship. In the third period (*ghaṭikā*) of the night he would take his bath, enter his hut, and sit for private worship. Only in the afternoon would he read the *bhakti* scriptures and in the evening take part in *saṅkīrtana* of the holy names. Sometimes, during the *saṅkīrtana* of the holy names he would dance so wildly and shout so loudly that many seeing him in this unusual condition, would become frightened.

At this time Prabhupāda, suffering feelings of separation from the Lord, went to Nīlācala.[77] After arriving there, he decided that he would do his private worship in Nīlācala permanently, making up his mind never again to return to his house. Residing there, he started to do private worship with great resolve, to visit the sacred image of Jagannātha and to spread the holy names. At that time, many Bauls, becoming enchanted by his heart-touching talks about Hari, chose Prabhupāda as their guru and were blessed. Six months passed in this way. Meanwhile, back home, Prabhupāda's wife, Sarasvatī Devī, was crying and in great distress. Troubled by her tears a fellow who was specially well-known to Prabhupāda named Hari Jānā from the village of Galāgeche near to Manoharpur took Sarasvatī Devī with him and went to Nīlācala looking for Prabhupāda. There, troubled by Sarasvatī Devī's crying, Prabhupāda returned once again to Manoharpur.

Even if he returned home, though, what could happen? For Prabhupāda the household often felt like a waterless well. He returned to spending his days like before in the bliss of *saṅkīrtana* at the houses of his disciples. During that period he became the father of two daughters. After spending a while in this manner Prabhupāda's desire arose to leave Manoharpur and live permanently in Navadvīpa. After that, without much delay he went to Navadvīpa along with his family.

In Navadvīpa there was no place for Prabhupāda to live. At that time there was a *bābā*, who used to eat only fruit, doing private worship at Navadvīpa's Maṇipur Ghāṭ (quay). He had great faith in Prabhupāda. The fruit-eating *bābā* developed a desire to go to Vṛndāvana for a while to do private worship there. Therefore, he handed over his *āśrama* to Prabhupāda and went off to Vṛndāvana. From then on Prabhupāda

---

[77]Jagannātha Purī on the coast of Orissa.

and his family lived there. After the fruit-eating *bābā*'s departure for Vṛndāvana, Prabhupāda took care of the *bābā's* temple.

At that time there was a Goswami living in Telipāḍā who had old sacred images of the Young Divine Couple.[78] Their name was Śrī Śrī Rādhā-Mādhava. After the passing of that Goswami, his wife decided to sell those Rādhā-Mādhava images to some rich Śeṭh[79] from Kolkātā, because it was impossible for her to keep up their service. One night the sacred images gave that old Goswami lady an order in a dream, according to which she was to give the sacred images to Prabhupāda Tinkaḍi Goswami. After receiving that dream order, the old Goswami lady came to Prabhupāda the next morning with tears in her eyes and, telling him the whole story of the dream, made known to him her desire to give the images she served to him. Prabhupāda with great pleasure accepted her offer and considered himself blessed. In time, after establishing the extremely beautiful Śrī Śrī Rādhā and Mādhava and along with them a sacred image of Śrīman Mahāprabhu he considered himself most fortunate. After their establishment, the name of the images was changed to Śrī Śrī Rādhāvallabha. Since then those images have been served beautifully in the Śrī Śrī Rādhāvallabha temple on Navadvīpa's Maṇipur Ghāṭ Road. Gradually, with the increase of the number of his disciples, the expenses for the service of those images and of Prabhupāda were assumed by his disciples. At that time, there was no Nāṭa-mandira [audience hall situated just before the image room] in front of the temple of Rādhāvallabha. After the sacred images were established, the disciple-*bhaktas*, joining together, repaired the temple, constructed a tin roof, and built an audience hall.

Even after coming to Navadvīpa, Prabhupāda did not stay in populated places. He used to spend his days on the bank of the Ganges, under a tree, absorbed in private worship. When gradually more and more people started to come to see him, he went to the Bāblā forest on the far bank of the Ganges and engaged in private worship for a few days there. Not even the least bit of attachment was seen in Prabhupāda who, it seems, was born with detachment. Even though he had a wife, a son, two daughters and many disciples, Prabhupāda was always free of attachment. In this period, too, he used to visit Vṛndāvana from time to time, spend a few days there and then return to Navadvīpa.

---

[78] *Yugala-kiśora*, "the Young Couple" or "Youthful Pair." This refers to Śrī Rādhā and Kṛṣṇa understood as a young couple in love.

[79] Same as *śreṣṭhī*: a merchant, banker, or wealthy man.

At this time, Prabhupāda became particularly close to Rāmadāsa Bābājī Mahārāja.[80] Bābājī used to look upon Prabhupāda with special faith. Seeing Prabhupāda he would show extreme humility. Prabhupāda was very embarrassed by this. In later times, Prabhupāda expressed his embarrassment in this way: "Even though I tried many times, I was not able to give my prostrated obeisance to Bābājī first. I tried very hard, but whenever I would go to prostrate before him, I found that he had already prostrated before me." Bābājī Mahārāja's humility and personal example were particularly powerful influences on Prabhupāda's mind.

In Navadvīpa Prabhupāda passed his days in discussions of Hari and in *saṅkīrtana*. He engaged his son through his first wife, Vṛndāvana [Candra] Goswami, in the study of Sanskrit. At that time Prabhupāda visited Manoharpur from time to time. Once, in Manoharpur, he established the performance of a four-month-long great rite of worship (*mahāyajña*) consisting of the uninterrupted singing of the holy names.[81] A little while after that, Prabhupāda desired to establish a Navakuñja (Nine *kuñjas*, bowers or garden cottages) and have the uninterrupted great rite of the holy names performed in them. This would mean establishing nine garden or bower cottages in nine places [in Manoharpur] and carrying out simultaneously the uninterrupted singing of the holy names in each of those nine cottages. Prabhupāda was worried because he thought it would be very expensive. When the *bhaktas* came to know of Prabhupāda's desire they decided conjointly to meet the costs of that performance of the nine bowers. Before too long the uninterrupted great rite of the holy names in the nine bower cottages began. Many people started to come to Manoharpur from the surrounding towns and villages to see this unusual ritual performance. Some of the villagers assisted the performance of the rite by bringing rice, pulses (*dāl*), and vegetables according to their ability. It was as if a market place of love (*prema*) had

[80]Śrī Rāmadāsa Bābājī was an influential member of the followers of Śrī Rādhāramaṇacaraṇa Dāsa Bābāji who founded a sub-tradition within Caitanya Vaiṣṇavism known for their characteristic *kīrtana* song: *Bhaja Nitāi Gaur Rādhe Śyām; Japa Hare Kṛṣṇa Hare Rāma,* "Worship Nityānanda Prabhu and Śrī Gaurāṅga [Caitanya] and [you will attain] Rādhā and Śyāma [Kṛṣṇa]. Repeat [on beads] Hare Kṛṣṇa, Hare Rāma [i.e., the Mahāmantra]." Śrī Rāmadāsa Bābājī was a superb singer of spontaneous *kīrtana* and is considered a great saint.

[81]The word used here is *mahā-yajña* which can mean "great or large sacrifice." This was not a sacrifice in the sense of offering into the fire an animal or some possessions for the sake of a deity. Here *yajña* has a meaning closer to its the meaning of its verbal root $\sqrt{yaj}$: to worship, adore, honor, praise. It refers here to a religious ritual directed at worshiping or honoring Kṛṣṇa by singing nonstop his holy names.

opened in Manoharpur. Seeing this amazing ritual performance everyone was enchanted. As the news spread from village to village more people came every day and from farther and farther places to float on this tide of the love of the holy name.

After this ritual performance had gone on in this way for many days, the day for its conclusion was determined. The images of Śrī Śrī Gaura and Balarāma were decorated and a litter was beautifully adorned to carry them out in procession. In the *āśrama* at Manoharpur there was a forest of people that day. Prabhupāda asked one *bhakta* to supply lots of sweets and black pepper molasses. And, since the parade would last for four or five hours, he also asked him to have *Sarbat*[82] made and brought as well, in case people became thirsty. Then the procession began. A large *saṅkīrtana* party was formed equipped with drums, hand cymbals, and gongs and the sounds of *saṅkīrtana* filled the air and led the way. After that came the sacred images of Śrī Śrī Gaura and Balarāma on the decorated litter and countless people followed them overwhelmed by love. One felt as if Nitāi and Gaura were truly leading the way followed by *bhaktas* who were fascinated by them. In the minds of all those who saw that beautiful procession the image of the Moon of Nadiyā, Śrī Gaurasundara[83] of a few hundred years before was awakened. It was really as if Gaurasundara was moving along in the bliss of *saṅkīrtana* followed by the residents of Nadiyā[84] who were fascinated by him. The sounds of that *saṅkīrtana* travelled far and infused the minds of the people with deep emotions.

Back at the *āśrama* huge preparations for the big celebration were underway. Thousands of *bhaktas* would receive grace-food (*prasāda*). The cooks were working tirelessly. The *saṅkīrtana* party, after performing *saṅkīrtana* throughout the town returned around two o'clock in the afternoon with the images of Gaura and Balarāma. Along with them came countless people enthralled by divine love. Prabhupāda gave the order to Bhāgavata Dādā (one of the special recipients of his grace) to begin *kīrtana*. Bhāgavata Dādā began an especially enchanting *kīrtana*:

> Gaura came home; my Nitāi came home.
> Mother Śacī came running
> and took Gaura on her lap.[85]

---

[82]A cooling drink made from rose essence and sugar syrup.

[83]Śrī Caitanya.

[84]Navadvīpa, the home town of Śrī Caitanya.

[85]Source unknown: *gaura elo ghare āmār nitāi elo ghare; dheye giye śacīmātā gaura nilo kole.*

He sang this song. Dancing and performing this *kīrtana*, Bhāgavata Dādā drenched everyone in Gaura's love. After performing *kīrtana* in this way for an hour, the end of the festival was announced. Everyone was exhausted from the procession. Meanwhile, the cooking for the celebration was almost done. After the food had been offered to the sacred images, the meal began. There was no need of invitation. As soon as one sat, grace-food was served. Hundreds and hundreds of people after satisfying themselves with grace-food, departed for their homes and again hundreds and hundreds more sat to honor grace-food. Where so many people came from, who can say? The distribution of grace-food continued on ceaselessly. The sun was about to set. Meanwhile, the supply of grace-food was also almost exhausted, but even then the number of people coming for grace-food did not diminish. The servers became especially worried. What to do now? At that very moment the sky became covered with clouds and darkness spread in all directions. In a short while a torrential downpour of rain started. The rain seemed like it would not stop. After raining in this way for more than an hour, nature became peaceful. The arrival of people also stopped and everyone who was left was fully satisfied with the remaining grace-food.

Prabhupāda's mind, however, in any circumstance kept returning to the holy abode of Vṛndāvana. He began to wonder how long it would be before he became free from the bondage to impermanent worldly existence, made up of *māyā*, and with his body, mind and words would find shelter at the lotus-feet of the Young Divine Couple. In time, he arranged the marriage of his son Vṛndāvana Goswami. And after offering his first daughter in marriage into the hands of Anil Kumar Banerjee, the son of his childhood friend Jamini Kumar Banerjee, he became for the most part free of worry.

Now, thinking of a way to leave home, he expressed his feelings one day to his wife Sarasvatī Devī: "Look, worldly life is impermanent and without real happiness. For so long we have practiced this householding way of life. Have we attained the highest goal by means of it? Among all the different kinds of duties human beings have to perform the most important duty is worship of God. Having attained this rare human birth, if one does not worship the Lord then birth as an animal would have been better. If enjoying pleasure is the primary objective of life then what is the point of having a human birth? In an animal birth one can enjoy as much pleasures as one wishes. Therefore, I don't think we should delay any longer. You are my partner in *dharma*, my helper in reaching the supreme goal. Help me now. Please give me your permission. I want to go to Vṛndāvana. I want to spend what remains of my life engaging this stool, urine, and worm-infested body in the service of the Young Divine Couple. Don't feel any kind of sadness. I have left behind countless progeny to look after you. They will take care of you." At Prabhupāda's distressed entreaty Sarasvatī Devī with tearful eyes made her assent known and thus indeed became his helper in reaching the highest goal. After that Prabhupāda indeed, without telling anyone, tore apart the netting of the *māyā* of worldly existence and started out for the holy land of Vṛndāvana. He left at home one daughter unmarried.

Intense Practice in Vṛndāvana

Now Prabhupāda Tinkaḍi Goswami had become forever freed from his bonds to worldly existence (household life); yet his mind was distressed because of feeling separation from the Divine Young Lovers. He thus went straight to Siddha Manohar Dās Bābājī of Govindakuṇḍa at Govardhana. With torn clothes, soiled face, and eyes full of tears he rolled on the ground at Siddha Bābā's feet. Siddha Bābā laughed and said: "Gõsāi! What desire is in your heart?" Prabhupāda, drenching his chest with his tears, replied: "Mahārāja, please don't tell me to return home again. This time show me your grace and finding me a place at your feet, make me fulfilled." Siddha Bābā feeling amazed said: "What is this, Gõsāi? You are of the family of *ācāryas*.[86] Living beings bound to worldly existence are fulfilled by taking shelter at *your* feet. Such talk from your lips does not become you. Rise up. Calm down and rest now without worry." In this way Prabhupāda stayed with Siddha Bābā for some time and after receiving from him many instructions on the esoteric worship of Vraja, he felt himself gratified.[87] His initiation (*dīkṣā*) mantra he had received previously from his father Harimohan Goswami.

---

[86]The families of the *ācāryas* are the families that trace their ancestry back to close associates and companions of Śrī Caitanya. Prabhāpāda's ancestor, Śrī Guṇanidhi Goswami, was a direct disciple of Nityānanda Prabhu and Mā Jāhnavī, the wife of Nityānanda Prabhu.

[87]This is to say that Siddha Bābā became Prabhupāda's *śikṣā* or instruction *guru*.

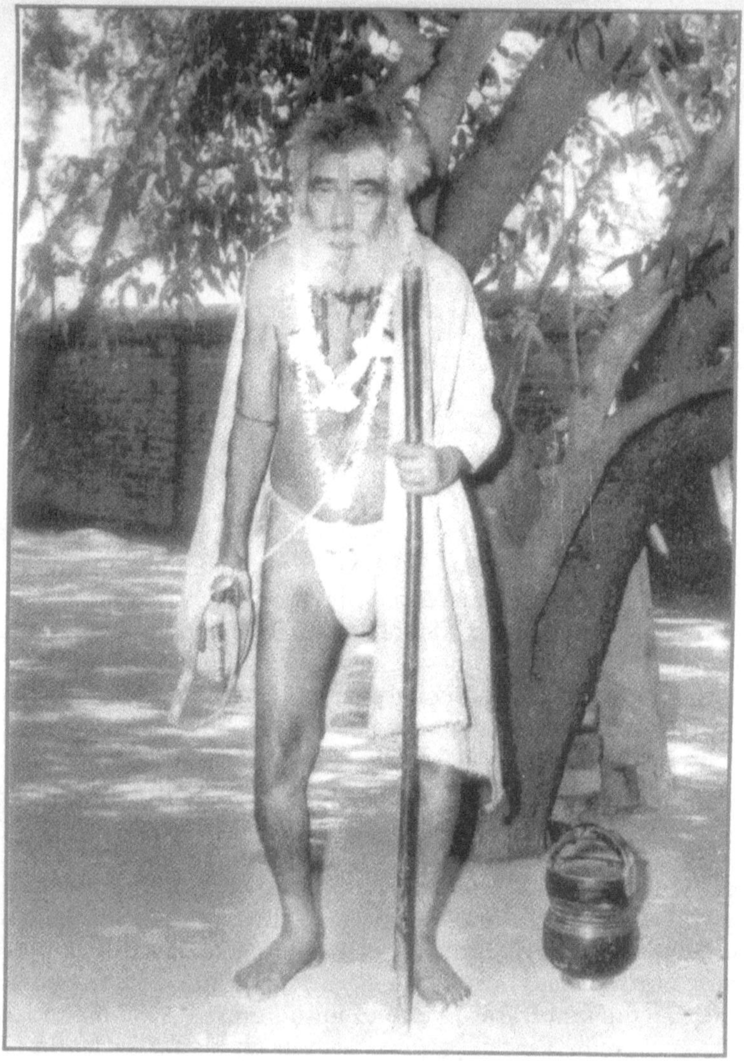

श्रीश्री नित्यानन्दवंशावतंस
प्रभुपाद श्री श्री 108 तीनकौड़ी गोस्वामी जी महाराज

Then, Prabhupāda's mind became anxious to do private worship (*bhajana*) in an exclusive way. He went to some deserted forest within the circle of Vraja and in body, mind and word became fully engaged in exclusive private worship. But time and again the thought came to him: "I have left behind worldly life, but I have not changed my worldly garb (*veśa*).[88] Therefore, before everything else I have to change this garb." Thinking in this way, Prabhupāda one day expressed this wish to change his garb to Siddha Bābā. Siddha Bābā became troubled at this request and replied: "Look, Gōsāi. You are of the family of *ācāryas*. How can I give you the [renunciant's] habit and become your *guru*? It will not happen through me. Besides that, what need is there for you to change your garb?" Prabhupāda was not satisfied with this statement of Siddha Bābā. After this, he went to many of the highest-level Mahātmas (saints) of Vraja and requested that they administer the rite to change his garb. But no one was willing to give him the change of garb rite and thereby become his *veśa-guru*. Then Prabhupāda decided to change his garb himself. One day he he took one of Siddha Bābā's rope loin-clothes *kaupinas* and making the Lord his witness changed his garb [into that of a Vaiṣṇava renunciant, i.e. a *bābājī*]. Along with that he took up a water pot and a staff. He made a vow that as long as he remained alive he would not touch money and not see the face of his wife again. It goes without saying that as long as he lived he kept his vow fully. After this, Prabhupāda, begging permission from Siddha Bābā, went forth to do private worship in some solitary place.

When Prabhupāda came to Vṛndāvana he brought a servant with him. His name was Śibu Adhikārī. Prabhupāda was living along with him on the bank of Rādhākuṇḍa. Suddenly, after a sickness of only a few days, Śibu Adhikārī left his mortal body and went to the next world. Receiving news of his death, his son Nitāi Adhikārī came from his home to Rādhākuṇḍa. After staying with Prabhupāda for a few days he decided that he, too, would not return to his home and instead he became engaged as Prabhupāda's servant. A few days after that Prabhupāda went to Keśīghāṭa with Nitāi Adhikārī. After staying there for some time, Nitāi Adhikārī also fell sick and departed for the next world. When Nitāi Adhikārī passed away Prabhupāda became rather worried. A few days after Nitāi Adhikārī's passing a youth by the name of Ayodhyā Dās be-

[88]Tinkaḍi Bābā is referring here to the formal rite of becoming a renunciant, or *bābājī*, in the Caitanya tradition. In addition to taking vows of poverty and abstinence, one simplifies one style of dressing, replacing one's household clothes with a simple white, cotton, cloth tied around the waist and another wrapped around the shoulders. One also dons an undergarment called a *kaupin* which represents and supports the practice of celibacy. All other possessions, except for a water pot are to be given away. One also generally shaves one's head.

came engaged in Prabhupāda's service. This Ayodhyā Dās' service was truly inspiring. Prabhupāda was very pleased by his whole-hearted service.

Prabhupāda now taking Ayodhyā Dās with him went to various deserted forests in the circle of Vraja and became deeply engaged in intense private worship. Sometimes under a tree and sometimes in a lonely and abandoned hut (*kuṭira*) Prabhupāda did his private worship. At that time Prabhupāda had no *āśrama* in Vraja. He used to observe rules of private worship in a most unbending way. At one o'clock in the morning he would sit for private worship and after that at around four o'clock in the morning he would go out to take his bath and so forth. After bathing he would again sit in his determined seat and practice private worship the rest of the day in a state of silence (*mauna*). Then at sunset he would get up. Ayodhyā Dās, after going to beg for alms in the nearby villages, would take care of Prabhupāda's service. Unpopulated forest settings were especially dear to Prabhupāda. As his habitual dress he only used to wear a burlap loin cloth and over his body a burlap shawl or wrap. In this way, sometimes at Prema-sarovara, sometimes at Barṣāṇā, sometimes at Pāvana-sarovara, sometimes at Kāmyavana, or Ādibadrī, or Rasaulī, or Cāmelīvana, or Tapovana, or Akrūra Ghāṭa, or Pāni Ghāṭa, or at Durvāsā-kuṇḍa, he passed his time in the bliss of private worship.[89] He did not stay at one place for a long time. When the arrival of people to visit him increased, then, without saying a word to anyone he would go somewhere else. Since of all the places in the circle of Vraja where Prabhupāda did private worship Rādhākuṇḍa was the place most dear to him, from time to time he would stay for a while on the bank of that blessed pond and then again head out to some solitary forest. Prabhupāda was fearless. Even while staying in many dangerous places he remained absorbed with a peaceful mind in the thought of the Divine Youthful Couple. Not ghosts, nor ghouls, nor tigers, nor snakes, nor any other living creatures were able to infuse fear into him.

Once at Prema-sarovara Prabhupāda was absorbed in private worship. When he was unable to complete the number of holy names he wanted to, he was deeply distressed. His longing for the Divine Couple began to increase more and more. He made then a solemn vow to perform even more intense private worship. Let there be practice of the *mantra* as long as the body does not fall away. His desire was that

[89]These are sites, generally off the beaten path, scattered all over the region known as Vraja, the land believed to have been Kṛṣṇa's home while he was growing up.

he would take his bath at two in the morning and then in one sitting perform his private worship. But since there is the regulation for taking one's bath during the *Brahma-muhūrta*, one has to wait until then to complete one's bath and other rites.[90] One day after being absorbed in private worship late into the night, Prabhupāda was overcome by drowsiness for a little while. Suddenly, he was startled by someone's shout. It sounded like someone was shouting: "Hey, get up! Take your bath and then sit for worship!" When Prabhupāda did not find anyone around even though he searched everywhere, he was astonished. The next day again there was that same shout: "Hey, get up! Take your bath and then sit for worship." Again Prabhupāda searched around a great deal, but he was not able to find anyone. He then thought to himself that it certainly must be Mahāprabhu's order. From that day on he took his bath at two in the morning and then sat for his private worship.

Since his mind even then had not reached a state of steadiness, Prabhupāda felt great sadness. Even with many great efforts he was not able to be fulfilled. In this condition, one night in the third hour, as he was seated on his seat, suddenly, Prabhupāda saw a tall Vaiṣṇava standing before him with a well-shaped body, a shining golden complexion, a shaven head, a top knot, and *tilaka*[91] on his forehead. Prabhupāda lowered himself to the ground and offering obeisance to him, asked who he was. He replied: "I am Vallabhācārya. I am pleased with your attachment to private worship. I will give you a *mantra*. If you repeat this *mantra* your mental fluctuations will quickly become peaceful and your mind will become steady." Saying this he gave Prabhupāda a *mantra* and disappeared. Prabhupāda repeated that *mantra* and in a short while attained an unprecedented result. His mental operations became peaceful and became identified with the thought of the Lord.

On another night in the third hour, while sitting on his private worship seat (*āsana*), Prabhupāda saw that a Vaiṣṇava like the one before with a shining golden complexion was standing before him. In his hands was a string of *tulsī* beads. Prabhupāda bowed like a stick before him and asked who he was. He said: "I am Viṭṭhalanātha. I wish to place

[90]The moment (*muhūrta*) of Brahman begins an hour and thirty-six minutes before sunrise.

[91]*Tilaka* are markings made on the body with sandalwood paste or a paste of sacred earth that represent the consecration of the body to the service of Viṣṇu or Kṛṣṇa. This is generally done before one sits for private worship. Each different community of Vaiṣṇavas marks the body in its own distinctive way. Thus, by seeing the *tilaka* of an unknown Vaiṣṇava one can tell which community or sub-community that Vaiṣṇava belongs to.

this garland of beads around your neck." Prabhupāda became worried. He anxiously saw that if he took the neck beads from Viṭṭhalanāthjī, the son of Vallabhācārya, he would be changing his Vaiṣṇava community [from the Caitanyite to the Vallabhite community]. Fearing this, Prabhupāda in a very humble manner said: "Master! I already have neck beads. Please give me your blessing instead that I may attain pure *bhakti* for the lotus feet of the Young Lovers." After this Viṭṭhalanāthjī, with a pleased expression, gave his blessing to Prabhupāda and disappeared.

After that Prabhupāda's private worship sharply increased in intensity. Through his absorption in private worship, consciousness of his own body gradually decreased. While performing this extremely intense private worship in this way, one day his heart and exterior became illumined with the light of consciousness. Prabhupāda opened his eyes and saw standing before him Śrīmatī Rādhārāṇī, the embodiment of the pleasure-giving power, radiating the light of a million moons, smiling in her form as the bestower of great fearlessness. At that very sight alone it was as if every one of the molecules and atoms of Prabhupāda's body was drenched in a shower of invisible love-nectar (*premāmṛta*). Even though he gazed upon her without blinking he was not satisfied. He thought that if he had unlimited eyes it would help him a little to relish the sweetness of her beauty. Priyājī, the beloved of Kṛṣṇa, said: "Your wish has been fulfilled. Still, even now there will be much for you to accomplish. In proper time you will meet me again." Saying this Priyājī disappeared. And Prabhupāda fell unconscious at her disappearance. When his consciousness returned he thought: "Have I seen a dream? No! Even now my molecules and atoms are being bathed in a shower of consciousness-nectar from seeing Priyājī. Alas! When will I again attain such a vision of Priyājī?" Saying this he began to cry with a troubled heart. In this way he began to pass his days in an extraordinary condition of deep absorption. Since Prabhupāda had a close friendship with the scholar of Govardhana's Cākleśvara, Priyācaraṇa Dās Bābājī Mahārāja, one day when the two of them were enjoying *iṣṭagoṣṭhī*[92] Prabhupāda gave an account of his vision of Priyājī to Bābājī Mahārāja.

One day Prabhupāda's devoted attendant Ayodhyā Dās suddenly became ill with cholera. He was seen by a few nearby doctors, but there was no good result. Gradually, his condition worsened. At that time there were a few other *bhaktas* staying with Prabhupāda. Prabhupāda

[92] *Iṣṭagoṣṭhī* means discussions held between *bhaktas* about the objects of their deepest, heart-felt desires (*iṣṭa*), Rādhā and Kṛṣṇa.

asked one of those *bhaktas* to bring a new cloth. In a short while the new cloth was brought. Prabhupāda himself put a loincloth on Ayodhyā Dās and changed his habit [gave him formal initiation into the renunciant order of *bābājī*]. In his ear he began to repeat the name of Kṛṣṇa. In this way while hearing the name of Kṛṣṇa that devoted servant of Prabhupāda, Ayodhyā Dās, left his perishable body and departed for the eternal sport. Prabhupāda was deeply pained by Ayodhyā Dās's passing and began to worry about the well-being of his inner self (*ātman*). He went to Govardhana and for the benefit of Ayodhyā Dās organized a seven-day reading of the *Bhāgavata Purāṇa*. But he was not satisfied even with that. Ayodhyā Dās had served him for so many days and in such a devoted way, what was his state? Prabhupāda worried about this. He was then staying at the place where Rūpa Gosvāmin performed his private worship, Ṭeri Kadama. One day while he was worrying about what the outcome had been for Ayodhyā Dās he became drowsy. Suddenly, he heard Priyājī saying: "Hey! Why are you ruining your private worship by worrying about him? He has been engaged in my service even before you." Prabhupāda then became free of worry.

Prabhupāda spontaneously used to praise this Ayodhyā Dās. He used to say: "His renunciation, detachment and devotion to service were beyond comprehension. Such service no longer exists. Ayodhyā had some sort of spiritual power. It was as if somehow he was able to read one's mind. I thought to myself, 'I will go get cleaned up,' and before saying a word I would find that Ayodhyā arrived with my waterpot filled with water. Sometimes perhaps my body was not well and I had a desire to eat another kind of food. I would see that before I said anything Ayodhyā would have brought the very thing I had been thinking about. How many times did I scold him, almost to the point of striking him, and yet I never saw his face become dejected." Whatever the case may be, after the death of Ayodhyā Dās, Prabhupāda's service was somewhat impaired. A little while later, a *bhakta* named Gopīdās took up his service. After that Prabhupāda, taking Gopīdās with him, wandered around the circle of Vraja in the bliss of divine love (*prema*), tasting in rapture flavors of the divine sports (*līlā-rasa*).

In the meanwhile, Prabhupāda found he had to return once more to Manoharpur for the marriage of his youngest daughter. It goes without saying that after Prabhupāda had put on the loincloth he never again saw the face of his wife. When Prabhupāda used to visit Manoharpur, his wife, Sarasvatī Devī, had to stay somewhere else. They used to follow this practice even before this occasion. At the auspicious return of

Prabhupāda to Manoharpur there was excitement in all the neighboring towns and villages. Manoharpur was again flooded with the *saṅkīrtana* of the holy names. After staying there a few days and planting the seed of contemplation on Kṛṣṇa in everyone, Prabhupāda returned to Navadvīpa.

At the news of Prabhupāda's auspicious return to Navadvīpa, waves of joy began to swell up among his disciples. Hundreds and hundreds of disciples came to visit him, gathering into crowds. When Prabhupāda expressed a desire to stay on the bank of the Ganges his *bhaktas* built a bamboo and wicker hut for him to stay in. In great bliss he began to reside on that golden bank of the Ganges. At the auspicious arrival of Prabhupāda, a unceasing great rite (*mahā-yajña*) of the holy names started there. Along with that the *Bhāgavata* was regularly recited, songs about the divine sports sung and so forth. At the time countless people chose him as their *guru* and were satisfied. In this way, Prabhupāda stayed for some time in Navadvīpa amidst a surge of love for the holy names, and then returned to Vṛndāvana.

After arriving in Vṛndāvana, Prabhupāda wandered around to various locations of the divine sports and then went to Rādhākuṇḍa. At that time, a *bhakta* from Prabhupāda's home region came to him. He decided that he would not return again to his home and engaged in Prabhupāda's service. Prabhupāda had Gopīdāsa administer the change of habit rite for him[making him a renunciant or *bābājī*]. He was named Sītānātha Dās. A little while after that, Gopīdāsa left his mortal body, passing on to the next world. After Gopīdāsa departed, Sītānātha Dāsa became Prabhupāda's primary servant. After that, gradually more and more servant-*bhaktas* began to stay with Prabhupāda.

Prabhupāda became increasingly engaged in the work of spreading the faith. With a group of *bhaktas* he spread the holy names from village to village in the circle of Vraja. In each village Prabhupāda used to put on a seven-day recitation of the *Bhāgavata* and *saṅkīrtana* of the holy names. Along with that, festive feasts used to be sponsored. Whatever village Prabhupāda visited, Vrajavāsīs would come each day desiring to see him. The ladies of Vraja, gathering together in groups, used to come to see him singing songs the whole while. Since, at that time, too, Prabhupāda practiced a vow of silence all day long, the Vrajavāsīs started to call him Maunī Bābā (Silent Father). When he visited a village he would not stay in the middle of the village. Instead he stayed in some isolated place nearby. Prabhupāda used to sit the whole day under some isolated tree and do his private worship. His servants stayed in a nearby hut. Prabhupāda's rule was that at three in the morning everyone, after removing their soiled clothes, taking their baths and doing other cleaning rites, had to take part in *kīrtana*. If anyone wanted to do other than this, he had to go somewhere else. Whatever rice, flour, and vegetables the villagers used to give, that was used to serve guests and Vrajavāsīs. His own servant-*bhaktas* would subsist by begging for alms (*madhukarī*) from local villages. Every evening everyone also had to participate in the performance of *kīrtana*.

Once Prabhupāda was staying at Keśīghāṭ. Suddenly he had a desire to do private worship in Bhāṇḍira Forest on the other side of the Yamunā. The rainy season had just ended, and everyone said that if one went to Bhāṇḍira Forest, it would not be good, because everything would still be waterlogged from the high waters. After a few days, they said, going there would be fine. Prabhupāda, not listening to anyone's advice, started out for Bhāṇḍira Forest. With him went one servant. After arriving he began to stay in an abandoned hut. Since the floor was soaked his servant gathered some dry straw and spread it out on the floor. The hut's walls were not dry either and there was a musty odor. Prabhupāda nevertheless stayed there in the bliss of divine love. One day at about two in the morning Prabhupāda sat down for private worship. His servant was singing songs about the sports of the Young Lovers at the end of the night. Suddenly, hearing Prabhupāda's voice the servant quickly went to him and saw that he was shaking. When it appeared that he was about to collapse the servant quickly caught hold of him. Before his servant's eyes, Prabhupāda went unconscious. The servant became extremely agitated and started to think of what to do.

Before sunrise the news was given at Keśīghāṭ to a Vrajavāsī who had received Prabhupāda's grace.[93] That Vrajavāsī without any delay went to Bhāṇḍir Forest and was ready to take Prabhupāda to his own house. In the meantime Prabhupāda had returned to consciousness, but he was unable to speak. Since he was also unable to stand, three or four people together lifted him into a *ṭāṅgā* (a two-wheeled, horse drawn carriage). It was discovered then that the left side of his body was paralyzed. Receiving the news that Prabhupāda was paralyzed, many *bhaktas* came to Vṛndāvana from Bengal to see him. He was examined by some very good doctors and his treatment was started. In that condition Prabhupāda stayed at Keśīghāṭ and though some recovery oc-

[93] That is, who was an initiated disciple of Prabhupāda.

curred he was not able to move well. After that, at Prabhupāda's wish he was taken from there to Rādhākuṇḍa. Even then he was not able to do anything with his left arm and he was not able to speak clearly. In the meantime, at Prabhupāda's wish two *āśramas* were acquired, one in Rādhākuṇḍa and one in Govardhana. Though Prabhupāda underwent treatment for a long time at the *āśrama* in Rādhākuṇḍa and became more or less better, he never again reached full recovery. After that time he always used a staff and moved on foot very slowly.

Many days had passed since Prabhupāda had left Navadvīpa for Vṛndāvana. At the request of the residents of Navadvīpa Prabhupāda expressed a desire to visit Navadvīpa again. He had attained the highest treasure of human life. Now he was anxious to distribute that priceless treasure and to drive away the sufferings of living beings scorched by the three fires.[94] On the appointed day Prabhupāda started out for Navadvīpa along with some of his disciple-servants.

Prabhupāda arrived in Navadvīpa on schedule. Countless residents of Navadvīpa came out to welcome him at the Navadvīpa station. When Prabhupāda got off the train he was garlanded with flower garlands and as *saṅkīrtana* of the holy names filled the air he was taken to the Śrī Śrī Rādhāvallabha Temple on Maṇipur Ghāṭ Road. This time, too, by Prabhupāda's wish a hut was constructed on the bank of the Ganges for him to stay in. In front of the hut in which he stayed, in an excellent place a huge canvas awning was put up. At the news of Prabhupāda's auspicious visit to Navadvīpa many of his disciples came from various parts of Bengal to see him. As a result of that, more and more people gradually began to arrive. Arrangements were made for hundreds of people to receive grace-food (*prasāda*) everyday. If someone sat down, that person received grace-food. There was no waiting for an invitation. Then, too, Prabhupāda used to practice his vow of silence during the day. In the evenings he would speak. In the afternoons readings of the *Bhāgavata* were arranged. Many readers were eager to present their readings before Prabhupāda. Therefore, specific times were assigned for everyone's readings. Many, not getting a chance to read, expressed their disappointment to Prabhupāda. At night there were *kīrtans* of the *padāvalī*.[95] Many of the famous *kīrtana* singers of Bengal came and sang

[94]The three fires or sufferings are: sufferings relating to the body and mind (*ādhyātmika*, physical sickness, mental illness, etc.), to other beings (*ādhibhautika*, wild animals, bugs, other human beings, etc.), and to nature (*ādhidaivika*, natural calamities, etc).

[95]These are Bengali and Brajabuli songs about Śrī Caitanya and the sports of Rādhā and Kṛṣṇa.

kīrtans for Prabhupāda. All day long, like the current of a river, people came and went. To make a few *paisā* at this opportune time, on both sides of the road Pan shops, snack shops, roasted cashew shops and such sprang up. In these surroundings on the bank of Gaura's Ganges, Prabhupāda in the bliss of divine love increased the joy of the *bhaktas*.

At this time, one of Prabhupāda's special recipients of grace, a *bhakta* named Subal Māiti, had a dream in which Prabhupāda told him: "Subal, I have come to Navadvīpa. Quickly come here." Subal Māiti, too, had been thinking of a way to sever his ties to the worldly life made of *māyā*. He did not waste any time starting out for Navadvīpa. As soon as he arrived in Navadvīpa Prabhupāda said: " Who? Subal? Good! I was thinking about you." Prabhupāda became pensive for a little while and then said with a little smile: "That face has not worked. Turn your face around!" Subal Dādā was startled by Prabhupāda's words. After this, he firmly made up his mind that he would not return again to worldly life. A few days after this at Prabhupāda's order he changed his garb and became engaged in Prabhupāda's service.

Many people used to come to ask all kinds of questions of Prabhupāda. But since he spent his whole day practicing a vow of silence no one could ask him anything during the daytime. When the daytime was over he used to break his silence and speak with everyone. Prabhupāda answered all kinds of questions using beautiful expressions. With many kinds of scriptural arguments he would teach that worldly existence is impermanent and that for living beings the worship of Hari was the most important thing to be performed.

One night, at around eleven o'clock, Prabhupāda was walking slowly on the bank of Gaura's Ganges. With him was one a disciple, Nārāyaṇa Viśvāsa, and a few other *bhaktas*. In the moonlight there was a softness everywhere. The Ganges, river of the gods, was flowing with a gurgling sound. A soft, slow breeze was blowing. Along with that there was an unprecedented sweetness in everyone's hearts because of Prabhupāda's sweet closeness. Everything became quiet. Suddenly, Prabhupāda said: "Well, Nārāyaṇa, what beautiful moonlight! Is it not?"

Nārāyaṇa Viśvāsa with an exultant heart said: "Yes, Bābā."

Then Prabhupāda said: "See, what a beautiful breeze is blowing. Is it not?"

Everyone replied: "Yes, Bābā."

"How do you like it?"

"We like it very well."

"Well, Nārāyaṇa. Have you bathed in the Ganges?"

"Yes, Bābā."

"How was it? Tell me."

"Bābā, taking into account all the places I bathe, the kind of peace I feel when I bathe in the Ganges, I don't feel anywhere else."

Prabhupāda seemed to become very pensive. A few moments later he broke the silence of the night and said: "Okay, Nārāyaṇa, do you have electricity at your house?"

"Yes, Bābā."

"A fan?"

"Yes, Bābā."

"Okay. For the lights that you burn and the fans that you run you don't have to pay some tax?"

"Bābā, one has to pay tax. Without tax how would we have such facilities."

Prabhupāda became very thoughtful and then said: "Now tell me, Nārāyaṇa. Bhagavān is providing this free air—without which, if it were stopped even for a short time, we human beings would lose our lives. He is giving the light of the sun and he is giving the lovely sweet light of the moon. If all these lights were stopped the whole earth would be in darkness. The beautiful water of the Ganges and the water beneath the soil; if this water were not there, no living being would be able to remain alive. Bhagavān provides all these things for us our whole lives and for that Bhagavān there is nothing that we should do? Look, Nārāyaṇa, aren't we grateful? Bhagavān is providing for us in such a beautiful way and we can't find even spend the little bit of time needed to think about him? There is no mention of having to give him anything. One doesn't have to give him anything; he doesn't want anything in exchange. He has only mentioned saying his name with our lips. I can do all the work of mundane life, but all I need to do for him is say his name with my mouth and just see how unfaithful we are, how ungrateful: without making any great effort we are to say his name with our mouths and that little bit we cannot do. Nevertheless, see how compassionate Bhagavān is. Even if you don't give him anything and even if you do not accept him he does not deprive you of his grace. Who else is so merciful? Those who I think love me in this worldly existence, they, too, love me for some self-interest. Those for whose happiness we are wasting through neglect this rare human birth, they all love out of self-interest. Notice how Bhagavān is exactly the opposite of that. I don't love him; nevertheless take note of how much effort he makes to support us. Even before we are born he places milk in the breasts of our mothers so that we may survive. But we can't even spare the little bit of time it takes to say his love-rich name. And those for whose happiness we would give up our very lives, they waste our present lives and in the afterlife set us on the path to becoming guests in hell. And the one who desires nothing at all, who only goes on giving, who even if we do not love him loves us, we will not even think about such a loving person as him for a little while. So ungrateful!" Prabhupāda's words made a deep impression on everyone's minds. With extremely beautiful turns of speech such as this, Prabhupāda lifted everyone's minds to contemplation on Śrī Kṛṣṇa.

During that period so many *bhaktas* used to come that everyday was like a festival in the temple. From two o'clock in the day until two o'clock at night *bhaktas* used to receive grace-food. Prabhupāda would request all those who came to see him to receive grace-food. By Prabhupāda's desire it was never heard that someone came and did not receive grace-food. Since it was not known when Prabhupāda would send someone to have some grace-food, a little extra was always kept aside. Many times it was seen that after everyone had had grace-food and enough for five or six more people was put aside, Prabhupāda would send fifteen or twenty *bhaktas* to partake of grace-food. Perhaps then too there would not be time enough to cook again. Nevertheless, it was noted that everyone was satisfied with that little bit of grace-food. One day at around four o'clock Ramā Devī came with about thirty to thirty-five people to see Prabhupāda. In order to honor Prabhupāda's request they all went to the temple. At the temple there was only enough grace-food kept aside for three or four people and there was not enough time then to cook again. With no other choice, that insufficient grace-food was distributed to everyone and what a wonder! Everyone was fully satisfied with that small amount of grace-food and returned happily to their homes. This kind of incident occurred many times.

There was another incident from the same time. Seeing so many people come to visit Prabhupāda at that time, many *bhaktas* and non-*bhaktas* were anxious to come to see him too. Some who were full of devotion to God and some who were just extremely curious used to come to him. One day a young atheistic man who was acquainted with a *bhakta* who was a recipient of Prabhupāda's grace made a vow that he would never go visit any holy man and that he would never eat any of that stuff they call grace-food. The person who had been graced by Prabhupāda tried many times to get that young man to visit Prabhupāda, but the youth would not agree to visit him through any urging. One day that young man said to Prabhupāda's (*bhakta*): "Look, I don't accept any of that holy man business. I have heard, however, that your *gurudeva* is a perfected great-soul (*siddha mahātmā*). Therefore, if your *gurudeva* is able to bring me to see him, I will know that he really is a perfected saint (*siddha mahāpuruṣa*)." With no other choice, that *bhakta* decided he would never again ask the youth to go see Prabhupāda and left. As soon as he had departed, that atheistic youth started to feel some kind of strong attraction towards Prabhupāda. He thought again and again: "If I go now, see him and then return, I will know what sort of holy man he is. So many people are going to see him. What could that be about?" He thought to himself in this way, but still, he could not muster the courage to go. He thought that if any of his friends or relatives saw him there they would make fun of him. They would say: "What's this? Aren't you the one who won't go see any holy man? Why have you come now?" For fear of such comments he was unable to gather up the courage. Nevertheless, he was also unable to control his intense desire to visit Prabhupāda. With no other choice, he decided privately that when no one else was around he would go see him. With this idea in mind, right at two o'clock, looking nervously this way and that, the young man went to Prabhupāda's hut. Prabhupāda was then observing his vow of silence. By signs he motioned the young man in. As if he were enchanted by some *mantra* the young man entered inside and began looking at Prabhupāda. Prabhupāda began to smile at him tenderly. Then Prabhupāda, motioning, requested that the young man go to have some grace-food. The young man also, like an extremely well-behaved boy, bowed down to him and went to the temple to have some grace-food.

Anyway, Prabhupāda stayed several months in Navadvīpa surrounded by many incidents like these. Before he left Navadvīpa arrangements were made for an extraordinary festival there. At that festival grace-food was distributed to thousands and thousands of people. Then, after planting in this way the seed of contemplation on Śrī Kṛṣṇa in countless people in Navadvīpa, Prabhupāda went to Nīlācala (Jagannātha

Purī). There, too, after infusing grace into many living beings who were scorched by the three fires, he returned to the holy land of Vṛndāvana.

When he returned to the holy land of Vṛndāvana, he stayed at Rādhākuṇḍa. Gradually, the number of *bhaktas* there increased. Many of the new arrivals among them changed their garb [became renunciants] and stayed with Prabhupāda. After this, whenever Prabhupāda went anywhere he always had ten or twelve renounced *bābājīs* living with him. Most of the time he remained at Rādhākuṇḍa, the slope of Girirāja, Prema-sarovara, and Tapovana. From time to time he would visit some of the other sites of divine sport. When the arrival of people would increase, Prabhupāda would start out for another place. Where and when he would go most of the time nobody was able to say. Many times Prabhupāda would just suddenly start out for somewhere. His servant would ask: "Bābā! Where are you going?" Prabhupāda would mention another place. The servant would perhaps beg for a little time to pack up the supplies and utensils and in response Prabhupāda would say: "You pack up. I'm going." Saying something like that, he would simply start off. With little other choice, the servant would quickly gather a few necessary supplies in a bag and hurry off after him.

Once Prabhupāda was residing by the side of Girirāja [Mount Govardhana]. One day a rascal came to Prabhupāda to get a lucky number for gambling. Prabhupāda was then observing silence. The fellow, calling out "Bābā, Bābā," entered into the hut. Prabhupāda raised his hand and showed him five fingers to indicate that he should come back in the afternoon after 5 o'clock. The fellow thought that Prabhupāda was telling him to use the number five. Happily he went off and indeed in the game he bet a good amount of money on the number five. He bet and he bet again on the number five. The fellow won a lot of money that way. After that, with a little token of a gift, he visited Bābā and told him the whole story. When Bābā heard about it, he was speechless. The very next day he picked up his sitting mat and said: "Let's go. Even here there is calamity. We will go somewhere else."

One time Prabhupāda was living at Rādhākuṇḍa. Meanwhile there was to be a feast for the sixty-four Mahāntas[96] at Nityānanda Dhāma, the *aśrama* that Prabhupāda had established in Govardhana. His disciples

[96]Mahānta means great saint. The sixty-four Mahāntas are the sixty-four great saints who were companions of Śrī Caitanya in his sports. On special days of commemoration or to honor the passing of a great Vaiṣṇava a feast is often held in which the food is first offered to the sixty-four Mahāntas.

came to Rādhākuṇḍa to take him to Govardhana. Prabhupāda didn't want to go to Govardhana. Everyone became thoroughly obstinate and fell down at his feet. With no way out, Prabhupāda, even though he really didn't want to go, went to Govardhana at their request. That night Prabhupāda came down with a serious fever, so serious that he nearly fell unconscious. In that condition he said: "Rādhārāṇī has again and again warned me: 'now don't you leave Rādhākuṇḍa and go anywhere else.' Not listening to her words I have come to Govardhana. Therefore, I am in this sorry state." Then everyone understood why Prabhupāda did not want to leave Rādhākuṇḍa and go to Govardhana. They all felt sorry for their mistake. Prabhupāda became better again after a few days.

At this time Prabhupāda visited the outlying forests as if for the last time. Niyama-sevā[97] was not very far off. Prabhupāda spent a few days at the side of Girirāja-Govardhana in the bliss of private worship and then for Niyama-sevā went to Rādhākuṇḍa. His *bhakta*-servants followed Prabhupāda there. Receiving word that Prabhupāda was staying at Rādhākuṇḍa, many *bhakta* Vaiṣṇavas from many places in Bengal came to Rādhākuṇḍa to observe Niyama-sevā. All four directions were alive with *saṅkīrtana* of the holy names. Circumambulations began and Prabhupāda's *āśrama* was buzzing with the arrival of *bhaktas*. In this way after having bathed in a shower of the nectar of *prema* on the banks of Rādhākuṇḍa for one month, the *bhaktas* at the end of their Niyama-sevā vows returned to their homes. Prabhupāda after staying a few days at Rādhākuṇḍa went to Govardhana. He stayed there for the whole winter season. When the fury of the cold became calm Prabhupāda started out for Prema-sarovara with his *bhaktas*. There, after increasing the joy of *bhaktas* and Vrajavāsīs alike for more than a month through *saṅkīrtana* of the holy names, seven-day readings of the *Bhāgavata*, and such, he went to Kokilāvana. After spending a few days there at the request of Vrajavāsīs he went to Durvāsākuṇḍa in Kāmavana. After a few days' stay at Durvāsākuṇḍa ,Prabhupāda began to feel a particular pain in his stomach and at the insistence of his *bhaktas* he went to Keśīghāṭa in Vṛndāvana for diagnosis. He stayed there more than a month under treatment and felt somewhat better as a result.

[97]*Niyama-sevā* is a regime of special practices and austerity undertaken by Caitanya Vaiṣṇava renunciants during the month of Kārtika (October-November) each year. Practitioners are to eat less, not shave, and increase their chanting and singing of the holy names and perform circumambulations of holy places.

After that, at the request of some Vrajavāsī *bhaktas* he went from Vṛndāvana to the Rāmajānakī temple at Akṣarabaṭa near Tapovana. After staying there a few days he went on to Tapovana. Then, after spending a few days in the bliss of divine love in Tapovana, in most charming surroundings on the bank of the Yamunā, he returned to Govardhana. After this, Prabhupāda's body gradually became more ill and he no longer went wandering from forest to forest. He only stayed at Govardhana, Rādhākuṇḍa, and Vṛndāvana after this.

Prabhupāda's Final Days

Prabhupāda at this time desired to go to Nīlācala [Purī]. He deputed one of his servants to write a letter to Navadvīpa. In a short while letters were written to Prabhupāda's disciples Dr. Śuśīl Bhaumik in Navadvīpa and Dilīp Kumār Mitra in Kolkata expressing his desire to go to Nīlācala. A few days later at the request of his *bhaktas* who were living in Vṛndāvana that he not go to Nīlācala, he changed his mind accordingly and asked his servant to send a telegram to Kolkata and Navadvīpa. His request was duly followed. Meanwhile, as fate would have it, the telegram was delayed in arriving and Dr. Bhaumik and Mitra Mahāśaya had started out for Vṛndāvana with the intention of taking Prabhupāda to Purī. Back in Vraja, Prabhupāda without the worry [of travel] had decided to sponsor a seven-day reading of the *Bhāgavata* to be performed at Śrī Śrī Rādhāmurārimohan Kuñja[98] in Vṛndāvana. To attend the seven-day reading of the *Bhāgavata*, at Prabhupāda's invitation, Śrī Priyācaraṇa Dās Bābāji[99] came from Govardhana to Śrī Rādhāmurārimohan Kuñja. Two days after the beginning of the reading, Dr. Bhaumik and Mitra Mahāśay arrived in Delhi by airplane and after reserving four tickets for travel from Delhi to Purī, they continued to Vṛndāvana to take Prabhupāda to Purī. They had reserved tickets for a plane from Delhi to Bhuvaneśvara for the day following the day they arrived in Delhi. Because Prabhupāda's telegram did not arrive in time this crisis arose. Hearing that Prabhupāda will not go to Purī they were extremely mortified. After this, because they

[98]This was the name of Prabhupāda's *āśrama* at Keśighāṭa.

[99]Priyācaraṇa Dās Bābājī was a great Vaiṣṇava who specialized in seven-day recitals of the *Bhāgavata* and who in his day maintained records of many of the initiation and guru lineages. He was a friend and confidant of Tinkaḍi Goswami and had his *āśrama* next to Prabhupāda's in Chakleshar at Govardhana.

specially begged Prabhupāda to go to Purī, Prabhupāda agreed to go to Purī. Meanwhile, the *bhaktas* who lived in Vṛndāvana did not want to let Prabhupāda go. On one side were the supplications of the *bhaktas* who had come from Bengal and on the other side the heart-felt petitions of the *bhaktas* who lived in Vṛndāvana. On top of it all there was the performance of the seven-day reading of the *Bhāgavata*. Prabhupāda became specially anxious. Moreover he was drawn powerfully by the misery of the countless human beings scorched by the three heats [miseries] in Nīlācala and Bengal. He knew it was not much longer until he entered eternal sport. Indeed, a few months before this incident while he was staying at Rādhākuṇḍa, he told a servant that the end of his sport was near. Therefore, perhaps his mind became specially anxious to quell the tears of externally focused livings beings who had been swallowed by the *māyā* of ignorance and point out for them the path of genuine light one last time. One imagines that thinking of the well-being of living beings, Prabhupāda decided to go to Purī. The next day at daybreak Prabhupāda started out for Purī. Priyācaraṇa Dās Bābā was mortified at the news that Prabhupāda was going to Purī. But he did not put forward any sort of objection. In the morning, with two servants with him and the *bhaktas* from Bengal Prabhupāda left Vṛndāvana for the last time. After that, he was never able to return to the holy abode of Vṛndāvana while he was alive.

The taxi taking Prabhupāda arrived at Palam Airport at around 10 o'clock. Meanwhile, four tickets had been bought, but there were five people. Mitra Mahāśaya tried specially hard to get one more ticket. Because the Asian Games were in progress then, getting an extra ticket was difficult. Around that time one of the high-office-holding employees at the airport came to see Prabhupāda. When he saw Prabhupāda he was enchanted. By then, Mitra Mahāśaya had returned, unable to acquire another ticket. Fortunately, however, an extra ticket was quickly acquired with the help of that employee. When the time for the plane's departure arrived, Prabhupāda was boarded and seated with the help of a few people. At the scheduled time the plane taxied for the sky.

The plane arrived at the Bhuvaneśvar airport at around two in the afternoon. After that, the *bhaktas* started towards Purī in a taxi with Prabhupāda. The news of Prabhupāda's coming arrived before he did. He arrived in Purī and went to the temple of Ṭotā Gopīnātha to stay. Since the news of his coming had spread, *bhaktas* living in Purī began to come to Ṭoṭā Gopīnātha with great enthusiasm. The room at the temple in which Prabhupāda stayed was not very healthy because little light and air were able to enter it. One day the abbot of the Haridāsa Maṭha, Nitāipada Dāsa Bābājī, came to see Prabhupāda. Seeing that Prabhupāda was staying in a room without light, he invited him to come with him to the Haridāsa Maṭha. Prabhupāda accepted with great joy. A fine room at the Maṭha of the tomb of Haridāsa, which had lots of exposure to the light and air and lots of room for him to walk about in, was reserved for him. The very next day Prabhupāda moved from Ṭoṭā Gopīnātha to the Haridāsa Maṭha. Nitāipada Dāsa Bābājī was determined with all his heart and soul that Prabhupāda should not feel any sort of difficulty or discomfort.

When they received news that Prabhupāda was in Purī, *bhaktas* from various places in Bengal came, so that Haridāsa Maṭha was floating in waves of bliss. Even before this, because of cataracts in Prabhupāda's eyes, he was not able to see very well. The *bhaktas* of Nīlācala brought an eye specialist to see him. Since the cataract in one eye was worse, the doctor recommended an operation. On the appointed day the operation was performed by an eye specialist from Bhuvaneśvara. Though two months after the operation Prabhupāda had more or less recovered, because of a small mistake in the operation, he did not get his full vision back.

Meanwhile, many *bhaktas* began to arrive from various places for Prabhupāda's birth day. On the day of the celebration, Vaiṣṇavas from all the four religious communities (*sampradāya*)[100] of Nīlācala were invited. As a result of that, many holy men and residents of Nīlācala were satisfied with grace-food and took their leave. In bliss such as this three months went by. Now it was time to change locations.

After receiving the news of Prabhupāda's presence in Nīlācala, a few *bhaktas* of Navadvīpa came to Nīlācala with the intention of bringing him to Navadvīpa. At first Prabhupāda did not show any special interest in going to Navadvīpa. But, at the despair-filled pleading of the *bhaktas* from Navadvīpa he finally agreed to go. The *bhaktas* reserved a seat for him in an air-conditioned car of the Purī Express. On the appointed day Prabhupāda took his leave of the *bhaktas* of Nīlācala and

---

[100]The four Vaiṣṇava communities are generally the Śrī Vaiṣṇava community of South India, the heirs of the ancient Tamil Alvars and the tradition of Rāmānuja (12th cent.). The Mādhva community of Karnatak founded by the saint Madhva (12th cent.). The Vallabha community which was founded or renewed by Vallabha (15th-16th cents.). Finally, the Caitanya Vaiṣṇava community founded by Caitanya (15th-16th cents.). There is also the Nimbārka tradition traceable to the teacher Nimbārka (12th cent.) also of South India (Andhra Pradesh). This latter community may not have much of a presence in Purī.

went to the Purī station. The primary ritual specialist (*pūjārī*) of the Jagannātha Temple came there and put the silk rope of Jagannātha on him. At the scheduled time, the train for Kolkata departed. With tears in their eyes the residents of Nīlācala bid farewell to Prabhupāda.

News of Prabhupāda's coming to Navadvīpa had been sent ahead. After receiving the news, the *bhaktas* of Navadvīpa were waiting for Prabhupāda at the Howrah station. The *bhaktas* of Kolkata also came to the Howrah station after hearing the news. When the train arrived at the platform, there was great excitement among them all. When the train stopped, Prabhupāda was escorted off and seated in a taxi decorated with flower garlands. The Kolkata *bhaktas* offered their prostrations to Prabhupāda and then waited on him. Then the car departed for Navadvīpa with Prabhupāda.

Countless people, having received news of Prabhupāda's auspicious coming, were waiting for him with impatient enthusiasm at the Rādhāvallabha Temple. When Prabhupāda arrived in Navadvīpa there was unprecedented excitement in every direction. After so long their own great saint had returned to Navadvīpa. Because his body was not well, no arrangements were made this time for Prabhupāda to stay on the bank of the Gaṅgā. Instead it was arranged for him to stay in a house close to the Rādhāvallabha Temple.

With Prabhupāda's auspicious arrival, in each neighborhood *saṅkīrtana* parties for the holy name were formed. Each *saṅkīrtana* party would parade in the morning, performing *saṅkīrtana,* and then go to the Rādhāvallabha Temple. As soon as morning began, one after another, *saṅkīrtana* parties, filling the air with the names of Hari, began to arrive at the Rādhāvallabha Temple to see Prabhupāda. In that way a hundred morning *saṅkīrtana* parties were created at that time. In each party the number of young boys and young men was greater [than all the other age groups]. Also at that time, there were regular readings of the *Bhāgavata Purāṇa* in the afternoons and at night there was singing of Vaiṣṇava songs.

Previously Prabhupāda did not give initiation to anyone very quickly. But this time, coming to Navadvīpa, he became different. If someone desired to receive initiation he gave initiation. As a result, there was a rush to receive initiation from Prabhupāda.

News of Prabhupāda's arrival in Navadvīpa even reached Manoharpur. Some *bhaktas* came to Navadvīpa with special enthusiasm to take him to Manoharpur. "If Prabhupāda goes to Manoharpur, he will never return to Navadvīpa"—with this worry the *bhaktas* of Navadvīpa did not want to let Prabhupāda go to Manoharpur. After receiving the promise that after visiting Manoharpur he would return to Navadvīpa, Prabhupāda decided to go to Manoharpur. On the appointed day Prabhupāda started out for Manoharpur with some servants and *bhaktas.*

Prabhupāda's son-in-law, Anil Kumar Bandyopadhyay, lived in Arambag in the district of Hugli. He made arrangements on behalf of the residents of Arambag for Prabhupāda to visit there for a little while on his way to Manoharpur. The weekly paper of Arambag had previously announced the news of Prabhupāda's coming. Many people gathered there for Prabhupāda's auspicious arrival. For Prabhupāda's visit a high platform was constructed so that everyone would be able to see him even from afar. In honor of his coming *saṅkīrtana* of the names of Hari was arranged in advance. Everyone was beside themselves with enthusiasm when the car carrying Prabhupāda with his *bhaktas* arrived. Prabhupāda remained there for two hours before continuing on to Manoharpur.

After receiving the news of Prabhupāda's auspicious coming to Manoharpur, a *saṅkīrtana* party from Manoharpur gathered to wait for him. In time, the car passed through Ghāṭāl and headed in the direction of Manoharpur. Seeing that Prabhupāda's car was coming, the *bhaktas* of Manoharpur loudly began to perform *saṅkīrtana* of the names of Hari. Countless villagers wishing to see him lined both sides of the road waiting. The car began to move forward slowly. In order to give everyone a chance to see him, the car would stop for a while and then again move slowly forward. In front was the *saṅkīrtana* party; behind it slowly moving was the car with Prabhupāda. Eventually, it arrived at the Gaura-Balarāma Temple in Manoharpur.

At Prabhupāda's request arrangements were made for his wife, Sarasvatī Devī, to stay at a *bhakta's* house in Ghāṭāl. After a long time Prabhupāda had returned to Manoharpur. In less than a hour this news was spread far and wide. Every day numerous villagers, beside themselves with excitement, came to Manoharpur from many distant places wanting to see him. So that everyone would receive grace-food, lavish arrangements were made. Since they came from afar by foot, many *bhaktas* spent the night in the *āśrama*. When morning came they returned to their own homes. In this way because of the arrival of people day and night, the *āśrama* was always full. At night many people stayed in the audience hall. Those who did not find a place in the audience hall laid themselves down under the open sky along with their sons and daughters. At night it was an extraordinary sight—hundreds of people—wives, children, and the old—laying down wherever they could find a place and going to sleep where they were. Near someone's foot was someone's head; beneath them the soil and above the open sky. They were pleased with just having a sight of Prabhupāda. In this way, hundreds of people, willing even to accept numerous discomforts, came to see Prabhupāda. As long as Prabhupāda was in Manoharpur the *āśrama* was always full because of the ceaseless arrival of people.

As long as Prabhupāda stayed at Manoharpur, it was as if a Rājasūya sacrifice[101] were being performed in the *āśrama*. Many poor villagers used to come just at the right time to receive grace-food and after honoring it, they went home feeling the joy of love. If someone merely sat down, that person would receive grace-food. There was no restriction or obstacle at all.

There was one incident during this time. One of Prabhupāda's childhood friends came to see him. It was then wintertime. Since there had been no rain the farmers' worries had no limits. Because of lack of water, it was not possible to plant the crops. The proper time for planting was slipping by. Prabhupāda's childhood friend said to him: "Look, Gõsāi! Haven't I heard that you are a great accomplished [perfected] soul? So give us a sample this once of your accomplishment. In the next two days, if rain comes, then I will know that you really are an accomplished being. And if rain does not come, Gõsāi, I will not believe anything people say about you. I will grab a hold of you and throw you into the pond." Prabhupāda, after hearing his words, began to laugh softly. It was then noted: the very next day it rained down mallets and clubs. The farmers' anxiety was ended. The earth, too, warmed by the rays of the sun and bathed by the rain showers, blossomed.

In Manoharpur, too, Prabhupāda gave initiation without discrimination. It was as if the door of his compassion had been flung open. The time arrived for him to say goodbye to Manoharpur. *Bhaktas* came from Navadvīpa to take Prabhupāda back. The *bhaktas* of Manoharpur, shedding tears again and again, bid him farewell. Prabhupāda, with his *bhaktas* and servants, started out for Navadvīpa again.

---

[101]This is the royal crowning ceremony of ancient Hindu culture. No one has ever seen one, but there are elaborate descriptions of them in the *Mahābhārata* and the *Purāṇas*.

Prabhupāda indeed returned to Navadvīpa, but he was not like he had been. He began to always remain absorbed inside himself. He almost completely gave up eating. This time Prabhupāda became very nearly like a child. With much coaxing perhaps he would eat a little food, and he always would close his eyes. He had no knowledge of what food he was eating. Closing his eyes, whatever came to his hand he would put in his mouth. Perhaps he did not like it. Then he would spit it out wherever he could. At that time only a little curds and apple, boiled, would be given to Prabhupāda. Sometimes at night in the second *prahara* he would say: "I'm hungry." His servant would light a lamp and give him something to eat like milk sweets. Just as much food as a six month old baby would eat, Prabhupāda would eat. If someone begged him to have more, he would show no desire.

Previously an operation on Prabhupāda's eye had taken place, but since he could not see well by means of that, at his wish an appointment was made for an operation on the cataract of the other eye. Before the coming of cold weather, on the appointed day, the operation was performed by the famous Indian eye specialist, Dr. I. S. Ray.

After the operation the condition of Prabhupāda's body gradually began to worsen. He also gradually became more withdrawn. Because of the cold weather he began to experience special difficulty with breathing. Some *bhaktas* started to encourage Prabhupāda to go to Purī. On the other hand, the *bhaktas* of Navadvīpa were not willing to allow him to go anywhere other than Navadvīpa. However, when Prabhupāda expressed a desire to go to Purī again, Dilip Kumar Mitra Mahāśaya came with a car from Kolkata to take Prabhupāda to Purī. On the designated day, Prabhupāda, with a group of his servants, started out for the holy abode of Purī once more.

The car sped along towards the Howrah station. A first class ticket had been reserved for Prabhupāda on the Purī Express. The Purī Express would depart around seven in the evening. Then, because of a traffic jam on Kolkata's Central Avenue, Prabhupāda's car sat for over an hour. The time for the departure of the Purī Express had nearly arrived. The *bhaktas* became extremely upset. "Everyone will be unable to catch the train"—this kind of worry arose in them. Then the greatest worry of all arose—if the train departs without them, where would Prabhupāda spend the night? Even if he stayed somewhere, Prabhupāda would be faced with great discomfort because of his unwell body. Everyone became extremely anxious. Mitra Mahāśaya then began to console everyone, saying that when Prabhupāda was with them no kind of danger could arise.

In the meantime, seeing no possibility of becoming free from the traffic jam, the driver of the car turned around and proceeded by some alternate route to the Howrah station. When the car was near the Howrah bridge it was an hour past the train's scheduled departure time. Everyone was sitting hopelessly, their faces pale, while in their minds they began to think of various ways of resolving the problem.

After receiving news of Prabhupāda's trip to Nīlācala, many *bhaktas* who lived in Kolkata came to the Howrah station. Seeing that his arrival was delayed the *bhaktas* were also upset and were waiting for him. As soon as the car carrying Prabhupāda entered Howrah station a *bhakta* raised his hand and stood in front of it. With great joy he gave the news that the train from Karsed had not arrived at the platform. The train would leave two hours later than the scheduled time. In spite of a great deal of inquiry, the reason that the train from Karsed was late could not be discovered. Everyone breathed a deep sigh of relief.

After this, Prabhupāda was taken and seated in a wheel chair. The *bhaktas* put flower garlands on his neck. In bliss many bowed to Prabhupāda and returned to their homes. After a little while the train arrived at the platform. Everyone took Prabhupāda and got on the train. After a short while the train blew its horn and slowly started out towards Purī.

This time arrangements had been made at Haridāsa Maṭha for Prabhupāda's stay. At the news of Prabhupāda's return, Haridāsa Maṭha was again, like before, resonant with the sounds of the arrival of *bhaktas*. Although this time Prabhupāda experienced good health for a few days after his arrival in Nīlācala, after that he became even more ill than before. He was examined by the specialists of that place, but his illness gradually began to increase. One day Prabhupāda's condition suddenly became extremely serious; he lost consciousness. In three days forty-two injections were given. After three days, Prabhupāda slowly became conscious again. Meanwhile, news of his illness was sent to Navadvīpa by telegram. Though indeed Prabhupāda became gradually somewhat better, he remained so withdrawn that he was not even aware of his body.

There was no string of beads for the holy name in his hand, but Prabhupāda was moving his fingers as if there were and doing *japa*.[102] He was thinking in his mind that there was a string of beads in his hand. A servant would perhaps come to him with grace-food; Prabhupāda would extend his empty hand and say "Take my *mālā* (garland or string of beads)." That servant would take hold of his hand and say "Bābā, I have taken your beads. Now have some grace-food." Since he was so withdrawn Prabhupāda was not able to eat grace-food properly. With no other recourse, his servants fed him with their own hands. At that point one could say that he was not really eating. It is doubtful whether in a whole day he ate even fifty grams of curd. From that time on, Prabhupāda never again held a *mālā* for the holy names. One day grace-food was brought for Prabhupāda. He was moving his empty hand doing *japa*. His servant said: "Bābā, I brought grace-food." Prabhupāda with his eyes closed said: "Wait! Let me finish my round." Even though there was no *mālā* in his hand, he thought "I am chanting on a *mālā*." When a round on a *mālā* was complete, the Sumeru or the central bead came; then one knows that the round is complete and can put the *mālā* aside. With this kind of expectation, Prabhupāda was waiting for the Sumeru bead. But without a *mālā* where will the Sumeru bead come from? Then a *bhakta* said: "Bābā! You have no *mālā* in your hand." Prabhupāda raised his empty hand and said: "Then this that I am doing *japa* on, what is it?" Everyone laughed. Another servant said: "Bābā! That is your mental *mālā*." Prabhupāda then became externally aware for a moment. What Prabhupāda was doing during that period was the result of his previous practice. His awareness of the external world was practically non-existent.

At night sometimes he would need to pass urine. After a servant washed his feet, Prabhupāda would think that dawn had come. He then would go to bathe. After that, it would be time to meditate on his *mantras*. Sitting on his bed, he would instruct his servant to bring his *pañcapātra*.[103] When the servant brought the *pañcapātra*, Prabhupāda would rinse his mouth (*ācamana*) and sit to meditate on his *mantras*. The servant would then say: "Bābā! It is now twelve at night. Is this the time to meditate on mantras?" Prabhupāda would then briefly become externally aware. He would say: "Oh! It is, isn't it. Therefore, shall I lie down now?"

One day at around one in the morning, Prabhupāda urinated and

---

[102]Japa refers to whispered or silent repetition of the holy names of Kṛṣṇa.

[103]This is a small metal cup with a spoon of the same metal. It is used to do *ācamana*, the ritual rinsing of one's mouth before the recitation of mantras.

when his servant had washed his feet and dried them, he sat on the bed and asked for his *pañcapātra*. His servant said: "Bābā! It is now one in the morning. Is now the time to meditate on your mantras?" Prabhupāda was then so much more withdrawn into himself that the words of his servant did not even enter his ears. He asked for his *pañcapātra* again and again. When his servant brought his *pañcapātra*, he rinsed his mouth and sat to call to mind his mantras. Catching hold of his sacrificial thread[104] over his shoulder, he thought it was his string of beads for reciting the holy names. He began to do recitation (*japa*) with it. When the sacrificial thread became tangled Prabhupāda thought that his beads had gotten twisted. When that happened, he became irritated. Then the servant would loosen and move the sacrificial thread over his shoulder. In this way the sacrificial thread became tangled and the servant had to loosen again and again. Nearly an hour passed in this fashion. After that the servant again said: "Bābā! It is one in the morning. Is this the time for remembering mantras?" This time his external awareness returned and he said with amazement: "What's that? It's now one in the morning? Then, should I go to bed?" The servant said reassuringly: "Yes, Bābā! Go to bed now."

At that time Prabhupāda kept his eyes closed all the time. Sometimes, while his eyes were closed he would say: "I am not able to see anything. Everything is dark." His servant would say: "Bābā! Your eyes are closed. How will you see anything? Open your eyes." Prabhupāda then, trying to open his eyes, would say: "Yes, I can see a little bit." Such was the nature of the internal absorption in which he used to stay.

Meanwhile, after receiving news of Prabhupāda's illness, *bhaktas* from Navadvīpa came to Nīlācala. Seeing that Prabhupāda's medical treatment was especially problematic they begged to take him back to Navadvīpa. Prabhupāda knew that the time of the end of his sport was drawing near; therefore, wishing to leave his destructible body in the holy abode of Śrīman Mahāprabhu, he accepted the proposal without any argument. The *bhaktas*, too, with great enthusiasm purchased a ticket on the Purī Express with the intention of taking Prabhupāda to Navadvīpa.

There are two things worthy of mention that occurred before the day Prabhupāda departed for Navadvīpa. One night at about one in the morning, Prabhupāda began to talk with one of his servants about his childhood and place of birth. He talked about his childhood days in

[104]The sacrificial thread is the thread given to members of the upper castes at the time of their Vedic initiation and worn by them the rest of their lives.

Manoharpur. The servant listening to those incidents from his childhood life from Prabhupāda's own lips considered it grace. On top of that, a few days earlier that same servant's left eye began to dance about in a violent way. He then began to suspect that Prabhupāda, his foremost shelter, was about to end his earthly sport.

On the appointed day, Prabhupāda started out for the holy abode of Navadvīpa with his *bhaktas*. The residents of Nīlācala bid him farewell, their hearts tormented by pain.

After arriving in Navadvīpa from Nīlācala, Prabhupāda was more or less well for a few days. But, compared to before, he was much more withdrawn into his own inner world. If one were to say that he practically did not speak much at all, it would be accurate. At that time, since he was unable to move his legs, he had to be lifted into the standing position and then seated. He was also not aware of whether it was day or night. One day at around twelve midnight some *bhaktas* said: "Bābā, it is time to go to bed." In reply Prabhupāda said: "Do I ever sleep in the middle of the day?"

In the meantime, because Prabhupāda experienced greater difficulty in breathing, arrangements were made to give him oxygen. Because of that he felt some relief, nevertheless his condition worsened. One day a letter arrived from Vṛndāvana. It was written by Kiśorīdāsa Bābā of Keśīghāṭa Ṭhor. He wrote: "Bābā, I had a dream one night in which a dark-skinned young boy to me said: 'Hey! You sent Gosvāmī home in the middle of a seven-day reading of the *Bhāgavata* and you did not bring him back. Go, quickly arrange to bring him back to Vṛndāvana.' I asked him: 'Who are you?' That boy replied: 'I am Murārimohana.' After saying that the boy disappeared. Bābā, come immediately to Vṛndāvana as soon as you read this letter."[105] After hearing the contents of that letter Prabhupāda did not speak with anyone again, did not even open his eyes again.

Two days went by in that way. In the afternoon of the third day, Prabhupāda developed a fever and with that his body began to shiver. He pulse, too, went from weak to weaker. His blood pressure decreased from around one hundred and forty to stay around eighty. Dr. Bhaumik Mahāśaya informed one of his servants of the seriousness of the condition Prabhupāda was in. Arrangements were made to give him more

[105]Murārimohana is the name of the sacred image of Kṛṣṇa in Prabhupāda's temple-*āśrama* at Keśīghāṭa. That was where the seven-day reading of the *Bhāgavata* was being performed when he was whisked away to Navadvīpa. See the previous narrative.

oxygen at night. After hearing the news, one of Prabhupāda's disciples, Dr. Balarām Datta of the Kāṭoyā Hospital, also came. Dr. Bhaumik spent the night near Prabhupāda and there was no limit to the worry of the *bhaktas*.

Daybreak was not far off and Prabhupāda's servants were one by one completing their morning ablutions. The thought of remembering their mantras was not on anyone's mind. That day one *bhakta* had made arrangements for *sādhu-bhāṇḍārā*[106] in the temple, but no one was paying much attention to that. Gradually, Prabhupāda's heartbeat began to weaken. Receiving the news that Prabhupāda's condition was critical, Prabhupāda Śrī Jīva Gosvāmī from Śrīvās Aṅgan came to see him. It was then about seven in the morning. One servant began to repeat the holy names loudly at Prabhupāda's feet. Śrī Jīva Gosvāmī embraced Prabhupāda and saying "Jaya Nitāi! Jaya Nitāi," began to weep. Some other *bhaktas* started to perform *saṅkīrtana* of the holy names in the audience hall of the temple. The hour reached 8:30 am. Prabhupāda's lips suddenly began to quiver. Uttering "Jaya Nityānanda Rām! Jaya Nityānanda Rām" in a barely audible voice, he gave up his destructible body and becoming situated in a body of consciousness he started out for the divine, blissful, non-material, eternal sport. In all directions the sounds of wailing arose.

Receiving the news of Prabhupāda's disappearance, countless people came running from all directions. In a short while the news of his disappearance spread everywhere. Innumerable people came weeping from all directions to have a glimpse of him for the last time. In this way viewings and obeisances continued until three in the afternoon. Many *bhaktas* came to Navadvīpa even from Kolkata after they received the news.

After that it was decided that a palanquin should be brought for a procession through the streets of Navadvīpa with Prabhupāda's body and after it was decorated in a very beautiful way with flower garlands, the procession began. Behind it innumerable people followed singing the holy names. When the procession reached the main road, because of the gathering of so many people, the movement of lorries, buses, rikshaws, and such was stopped. On both sides of the road numerous people watched that beautiful procession from their verandas and roofs. If one looked upon it from a high place, no matter how far one could see,

---

[106]This is feast in which food is generously distributed to *sādhus*, the saintly or those who have devoted their lives to spiritual practice.

the road itself could no longer be seen; only the heads of innumerable people were seen. In this way after proceeding for three or four hours, the beautiful parade arrived back at the Rādhāvallabh temple at around seven in the evening.

Prabhupāda's son, Vṛndāvana Gosvāmī had at that time gone to the house of one of his disciples. Someone was sent to bring him back. The night before the day on which Prabhupāda left his body, Vṛndāvana Gosvāmī had had a dream in which Prabhupāda said to him: "Hey! Come home right away." Seeing this kind of dream, Vṛndāvana Gosvāmī became specially disturbed. The very next day the messenger came to him with the news that Prabhupāda had disappeared. In a short while he set out and arrived back in Navadīpa at around twelve midnight.

Meanwhile, the guru-brothers were debating how the final rites for Prabhupāda's corpse were to be performed. One party argued that the rites should be performed on the bank of the Ganges. Another party said no, they should be performed near the temple. After this, in agreement with the opinion of Prabhupāda Śrī Jīva Gosvāmī of Śrīvās Aṅgan, it was decided that his final rites should be performed on the bank of the Ganges where Prabhupāda previously used to love to do private worship.

By then it was one o'clock in the morning. The *bhaktas* carried Prabhupāda's corpse to the bank of the Ganges. A pile of wood was prepared. The body of Prabhupāda's human sport was washed with Ganges water and new clothes were put on it. Sacred markings (*tilaka*) were put on the twelve places on his upper limbs and his body was laid out on the arrangement of wood. The sounds of *mṛdaṅga*, cymbals, and the holy names broke the silence of the late night on the bank of the Ganges and spread far into the distance. The bank of the Ganges was a dense forest of people. Slowly Prabhupāda's form in his human sport was transformed into ashes. One very bright star in India's auspicious spiritual firmament had gone out. Overwhelmed with sorrow the *bhaktas* brought water from the Ganges in hundreds and hundreds of pots and silently cooling the cremation embers, returned to their homes.

Meanwhile the news of Prabhupāda's wrapping up his earthly sport reached the holy land of Śrī Vṛndāvana. A dense darkness descended among the *bhaktas* residing in Vṛndāvana. Among them one of Prabhupāda's Vraja disciples at Premasarovara had a dream at night in which Prabhupāda told him: "My time for departure has arrived. I'm going. Don't be sad." That resident of Vraja, becoming troubled by the sight of that kind of dream, went to Nityānanda Dhām in Cākleśvar and heard that it was true. Prabhupāda had gone to the eternal abode.

Even now one can hear from the lips of Vrajavāsīs: "Bābā! We have never seen a *sādhu* like him. A *bābā* indeed was that Tinkaḍi Bābā." Even today as they talk about Bābā their throats get choked up and their eyes fill with tears. They have lost one of their own great ones, Tinkaḍi Bābā.

Part II

Prabhupāda's Sweet Nature

Various Supernatural Incidents and Traits

A Miraculous Event

At one time Prabhupāda was staying at some place near Kokilāvana. Suddenly, he wanted to move to another place. The *bhaktas* wondered how he would be able to make such a move. Then at Prabhupāda's instruction a *bhakta* went to a Vrajavāsī by the name of Jīvanlāl Netājī of Baḍa Baiṭhān. He had a tractor. The *bhakta* revealed Prabhupāda's desire to move to another place and requested him to take Prabhupāda there by tractor. At that time all the wheat was ripe and he was threshing the wheat with his tractor. That Vrajavāsī thought about it and realized that if he stopped the threshing and took Prabhupāda where he wanted to go he would lose about two hundred rupees per day. Thinking in this way he did not agree to the request. With no other choice the *bhakta* went back to Prabhupāda. A little while after the *bhakta* arrived back, one piece of cloud came and right where that Vrajavāsī was threshing his wheat it began raining down like a shower of clubs and everything became soaking wet. That wheat would not be able to be threshed for at least two days. That Vrajavāsī searched around and saw that the rain did not fall any where else. Then, thinking that this was the result of his not agreeing to move Prabhupāda, with great dispatch he brought his tractor and moved Prabhupāda. That was not all. He offered himself at Prabhupāda's feet and became his disciple.

Protecting With His Subtle Body

That same Jīvanlāl of Baḍa Baiṭhān was traveling along a road one day. Behind him came a tractor. When the tractor got very close to him, as he went to stand off to the side he tripped and fell. Right along with that, the front wheel of the tractor rolled over Jīvanlāl's waist. Jīvanlāl screamed: "Jaya Gurudev!" and lost consciousness. Before the big back wheel of the tractor could crush him, however, the tractor tipped over for no apparent reason. The incident was over in an instant. After that, Jīvanlāl was taken unconscious to the hospital. His condition was extremely serious. Jīvanlāl was unconscious in the hospital for three days. The bones of his midsection were broken and he had been placed in a cast. When after three days Jīvanlāl returned to consciousness, he saw that Prabhupāda was slowly circling around him with his holy name beads in his hands. Prabhupāda said to him: "Don't you worry. You will be fine." Jīvanlāl beckoned to Prabhupāda asking him to sit and then fell unconscious again. When he again became conscious, he, just as before, saw Prabhupāda circling him. This time he touched him on the head with the string of beads in his hands. Like this, for three days Jīvanlāl saw Prabhupāda in the hospital. With words of reassurance like "Don't worry; you will recover," Jīvanlāl became free from his fears. After he stayed for forty-five days in the hospital, the bandage around his waist was removed. Then the nurses tried to get Jīvanlāl to stand up, but without any success. He was completely unable to stand up on his own. After that the doctors were led to the firm conclusion that he would never be able to walk again. At everyone's crying Jīvanlāl realized that he would not be able to move his legs again. Then Jīvanlāl, too, began to weep with a troubled heart. Again and again he asked at Prabhupāda's feet why he had survived. Now for the rest of his life he would be a burden on others. Everyone would only think of him as dead weight. Thinking is this way he cried out loudly, "Bābā! Why have I survived?" Suddenly, he saw that Prabhupāda was standing behind him. Prabhupāda said: "Don't you worry about anything. You will certainly be fine." Saying this Prabhupāda disappeared, and at his words of reassurance Jīvanlāl became peaceful.

Three days after that incident Jīvanlāl actually became able to stand with the help of crutches and slowly, placing his weight on the crutches, he was able to move his legs. After some more days had passed, Jīvanlāl became able to move about on his own [without the crutches]. The doctors were speechless. They could not imagine that this was possible.

Then, after Jīvanlāl returned to his home, he wanted to know where Prabhupāda was staying. After asking around he learned that Prabhupāda had gone to Navadvīpa a few months previously.

When fluid began to build up in the spinal column of one of Prabhupāda's very special disciples named Caitanyacaraṇ Pāl of Barackpore near Kolkata, he had to be taken to the hospital in very serious condition. The doctors examined him and began a treatment but had little hope of his survival. The spinal column was pierced and the fluid was released. When he received the news, one *bābājī* of Vṛndāvana (a relative of Caitanyacaraṇ Pāl) went to Bengal to see him. Caitanya Pāl was then in the hospital in a state of unconsciousness. His relatives went to the hospital to visit him. That *bābājī,* too, arrived at the hospital. Caitanya Pāl's condition was then extremely serious. Just at the most dangerous time, that *bābājī* saw that Prabhupāda was standing at Caitanya Pāl's head. Prabhupāda touched Caitanya Pāl's head with the string of *japa* beads in his hands and disappeared. Witnessing that sight, the *bābājī* became extremely amazed.

After that incident, by Prabhupāda's supernatural influence Caitanya Pāl began to get gradually better. The doctors had determined that that patient was not in any way going to survive, but seeing his return to health they were thoroughly dumbfounded.

In the midst of this incident another incredible thing happened. That Caitanya Pāl, before he became unconscious, asked that his *japa* beads be put in his hands. That was done. The extraordinary thing was that when Caitanya Pāl was unconscious and was wrestling with death, even then the beads in his hands kept on moving. The doctors seeing this amazing phenomenon were astounded. After he returned home Caitanya Pāl wrote a letter to Prabhupāda saying, "Bābā! It was as if there were some unseen power chanting three *lakhs*[107] of the holy names through me every day while I was unconscious."

Once another one of Prabhupāda's disciples, a teacher from Burdwan, suddenly saw, as he was walking down a path, Prabhupāda beckoning to him. After a moment he disappeared. The *bhakta* was astonished and after some inquiry learned that Prabhupāda was then staying in Navadvīpa. Without any further delay he went to Navadvīpa and when he was with Prabhupāda told of the incident. In response Prabhupāda said: "Yes. I was thinking about you."

---

[107] A *lakh* is a hundred thousand, or sixty-four rounds on a set of Vaiṣṇava chanting beads. Caitanya Pāl did three *lakhs*, three hundred thousands names or 192 rounds on the beads.

In this way there are many incidents of Prabhupāda's moving about in his subtle body. For fear of making the book too large I have not written about all of them. One of his servants asked Prabhupāda one day about this ability to move around in his subtle body and in response he said, "That's nothing. That's such an ordinary thing." The servant was speechless with amazement. Thinking, "Would such an uncommon thing be *that*?" he became bewildered.

Acquiring By Wish Alone

Here is another incident. Prabhupāda then resided at Rasaulī. One day some *sannyāsīs* arrived there. Prabhupāda invited them to have grace-food and in response they said that they ate only fruit. And among fruits they listed all the names of fruit that at that time under no circumstances could possibly be gathered. Prabhupāda was worried. He asked them to come back after bathing. At just that moment a Śeṭha (merchant) arrived by car to visit Prabhupāda. He gave Prabhupāda all the various fruits that the *sannyāsīs* had previously listed and, bowing before him, returned to his home. The *sannyāsīs* completed their baths and rituals and returned. When grace-food of the very types of fruit they had requested was distributed to them they were extremely amazed and, praising Prabhupāda enormously, they returned to their homes with gladness on their faces.

A Novel Incident

Once Prabhupāda was residing with his *bhaktas* at a lonely place called Pāṇḍavagaṅgā not far from Kokilāvana. At Pāṇḍavagaṅgā there is a pond and in that pond there were many lotus plants. When Prabhupāda was residing there there were no blossoming lotuses in the pond. One afternoon there was a reading of the *Śrīmad Bhāgavata* on the bank of that pond. Prabhupāda was sitting nearby. At that time someone noticed that two blossoming lotus flowers slowly moved from two opposite edges of the pond and met one another in the middle. As long as the reading went on the two lotuses were joined together. When the reading was over the two lotus flowers slowly moved apart in opposite directions. Everyone saw this and was extremely amazed.

Curing Disease by Compassionate Glance

By Prabhupāda's simple glance of compassion many were freed from difficult situations.

At one time one of his servants had been suffering from a fever for some days. Suddenly one morning his hands and legs became uncontrollable. Raising his hands he was unable to take hold of anything. Seeing no other recourse he went to Prabhupāda and told him of his condition. Prabhupāda told him that it was a symptom of palsy and reassured him saying, "Don't worry about it at all. Everything will be fine." Indeed, in a few days that servant's health gradually returned.

Another time another servant had a fever. Because of the severity of the fever the servant was practically unconscious for a few days. After three days the fever increased even more. The servant then with great difficulty went to Prabhupāda and told him of his suffering. Prabhupāda said, "Don't worry even a little bit. Put water on your head and you will be fine." The servant did that. Even without any treatment in a few hours that servant began to feel well again.

Grace Through Dreams

Prabhupāda was then staying in Navadvīpa. At that time every day many used to recite books on *bhakti* for him. Among those reciters was one named Suresh Mukherjee. He had a stomach disease. At that time because his stomach ache [his diarrhea] increased, he was not able to recite for Prabhupāda for three days. Because of that he felt great torment in his mind. On the fourth day at night he had a dream in which Prabhupāda came to him and said, "Suresh, where is your pain. Show me." Suresh showed him his stomach. Prabhupāda then rubbed his hand on his stomach and said: "No, no. You have nothing there. Now you are well." Indeed, after he woke from sleep he no longer felt any pain in his stomach. Not only that. He was free of disease for a long time.

Ability to Know of Things From Afar

About thirty years earlier a *bhakta* came from Kolkata to Vṛndāvana to visit Prabhupāda. At that time he did not have initiation. Prabhupāda was then staying at Rādhākuṇḍa. As soon as that *bhakta* came into Prabhupāda's presence, Prabhupāda told him, "You remain here even now? You should return to your home immediately. One of your sons has died." That *bhakta* quickly returned to his home and saw that indeed one of his sons had passed away.

Knowing Mental States by Supernatural Power

I noticed in Prabhupāda some supernatural power by which he was somehow able to know a person's mental state.

One day a servant of Prabhupāda went to circumambulate Girirāja. When he reached Pucharī he met with an older guru-brother, Gopāladāsa Bābājī. Gopāladāsa Bābājī gave some grace-food from Jayapur's Govindajī to that younger bābājī to give to Prabhupāda. When he was returning with that grace-food a boy of Vraja he met on the path said, "Bābā, give me some grace-food." That servant thought to himself, "how many ways does Bhagavān test the practitioner? Perhaps this is Bhagavān in the form of a boy." Thinking in this way, he gave that boy one sweet and then started on again. After going a little further another boy approached him and asked for grace-food. He also gave him a sweet from the grace-food. After that he arrived at Rādhākuṇḍa and just as he was giving Prabhupāda the grace-food from Gopāladāsajī Prabhupāda said: "Look, if someone gives something to you for your *gurudeva,* you should not give any part of that to someone else before giving it to him."

Another time when a guru-brother had an altercation with that same servant he thought to himself after moving a good ways away from Prabhupāda, "No! There is no further need for me to serve my *guru.* I will go somewhere else." Then again he thought, "No, whatever mental anguish there may be, giving up one's service to one's *guru* and going somewhere else would just be foolish." As he was thus arguing with himself suddenly Prabhupāda roared at him, "You are fiercely debating with yourself in your mind. That is very bad. By that you will be greatly harmed. I am able to know all about it." The servant was stunned.

One other time that same servant, after placing some distance between himself and Prabhupāda, was thinking that if one's mind is not pure, service to one's *guru* does not really take place. He had no idea how many offenses had occurred while serving his *guru.* In the end, the burden of offenses would be very heavy. Suddenly, Prabhupāda began to laugh and then he said, "How many times does a child in a mother's womb kick the mother. Is it a sin for the child?"

On another day this incident occurred. That same servant used to massage Prabhupāda's body every night. One night just as he touched him in order to give him a massage, Prabhupāda said with anger, "Go away! Go do some *kīrtan*! You don't have to serve me now." At this statement from Prabhupāda the servant was struck to the core. He thought to himself that when he touched Prabhupāda while his heart was blemished, Prabhupāda did not experience any pleasure. Instead, who knows how much pain he must have experienced in his body of clarity (*sāttvika śarīra*) as a result? In addition, if one cannot perform even the most ordinary service for him while living near one's *gurudeva*, what is the use of leaving home in the first place? That kind of anxiety was poisoning his mind. He no longer performed *kīrtana*.

At that time that servant used to sleep by the side of Prabhupāda's bed, and at night sleep no longer came to his eyes. Again and again only that subject came to his mind and streams of tears began to flow. Then, one night about one o'clock, Prabhupāda suddenly began to call that servant's name, "Binode, Binode!" The servant was awake and went to Prabhupāda. Prabhupāda said: "My body is aching something terrible. Give me a little massage." Now the servant fell into a deeper difficulty. He thought that at his touch Prabhupāda would certainly experience pain in his purified body. Therefore, how could he give him pain once more by touching him? Prabhupāda again said: "My body is aching fiercely. Give me a massage."

One has to honor the orders of one's *gurudeva*. With no other recourse the servant while keeping his feet as far away as possible began to massage him. Prabhupāda said, "It is not working. Get on top of me and massage me more forcefully." The servant now began to get extremely anxious. How is that possible? Yet, there is no other way. He then got on top of Prabhupāda's chest while keeping his head and feet as far away as possible and began to press on him harder than before. In addition, the servant began to worry that if his breath touched Prabhupāda's blessed body, there was no telling how much trouble it might cause him. Prabhupāda again said, "It's not working. Put your complete body on top of me and press." After that the servant gave up all of his reservations and hesitation and pressed on Prabhupāda with his whole body. Prabhupāda said, "Now that's right." In this way after five or ten minutes

Prabhupāda said, "Go now. Go back to bed." The next day Prabhupāda again called that servant and said, "Give my body a massage. It's aching a great deal."

Kṛṣṇa's Qualities in His Bhakta

Now I will endeavor to give some indication of the exemplary behavior and moral standards held by Prabhupāda. Prabhupāda's morality and exemplary practices are vast like an ocean. I, an ant trying to describe the ocean, am a source of hilarity even for children. Still, by the urging of my Śrī Gurudeva I will try to touch a drop of that ocean. Generous readers will cleanse away the audacity of this lowest of human beings.

In the eighth and ninth verses of the sixth chapter of the *Bhagavad-gītā* it is said that: "One whose mind is satisfied by knowledge born of the instructions of scripture and the direct perception of the truth, who is unmoved in the presence of sense objects and in control of his senses, who sees a lump of mud, a stone, and a piece of gold as equal, and who looks upon a chum, a friend, an indifferent person, an enemy, someone despicable, a family member, a holy man and a sinner with equanimity, such a person is a *yogī* and the best of all."[108] Prabhupāda's behavior was a match for this statement of the *Gītā*. Those who associated with Prabhupāda will certainly agree with this statement. In the *Caitanya-caritāmṛta* it is said in connection with the definition of a Vaiṣṇava:

> All these qualities define a Vaiṣṇava.
> I cannot mention them all; I can just give a hint.
> Compassionate, unoffensive, truthful, equal,
> faultless, generous, gentle, pure, without possession,
> helpful to all, peaceful, sheltered only by Kṛṣṇa,
> desireless, unattached, steady, conqueror of the six qualities,
> moderate in eating, unexcitable, respectful, not arrogant,
> deep, sympathetic, friendly, poetic, clever, and silent.[109]

[108]I translated from Binode Bihari Das Bābājī's Bengali translation, not directly from the *Gītā*.

[109]Kṛṣṇadāsa Kavirāja, *Caitanya-caritāmṛta*, 2.22.44-7.

All of these Vaiṣṇava qualities described by the *Caitanya-caritāmṛtra* existed in Prabhupāda. I will try to demonstrate these qualities by means of particular incidents.

Compassionate

Prabhupāda was the very image of compassion. He was always saddened at the misery of the living beings scorched as they were by the three flames and deluded by *māyā*. How much did he himself not suffer by taking on all the sins and sufferings of his disciples? Still, without hesitation he gave initiation to raise up thousands and thousands of living beings who were befuddled by *māyā* and in return he did not want anything. He was not affected in the least by his fame and high standing. Many times I heard Prabhupāda say with deep sadness, "When there is a celebration in the house of an important person relatives and friends are invited and they gather and eat the leftovers from the plate of that person. That is how those who are dear to Rādhārāṇī got their *prema-bhakti*, and to me she gave respect, worship, and high standing." Towards the wealth of his disciples he did not have the least interest. He himself also did not touch wealth. How many people were there who after bowing before him gave him wealth and yet he never used to even glance in that direction. Prabhupāda only gave. He did not ask for anything in return.

Once a young man from Kolkata took a vacation from his work and came to Vṛndāvana. When he came to see Prabhupāda, Prabhupāda with effort kept him near him for a few days. After that when he revealed to that young man his desire to give him initiation, the young man, as if enchanted by mantra, agreed. On the appointed day he gave the fellow the initiation mantra. Prabhupāda's whole-hearted desire was that that young man not return any more to the mundane world of illusion. When his vacation was over the young man made known to Prabhupāda his desire to return to his home. Prabhupāda did not give any reply. The very day that the young man was to start for home, his mental attitude completely changed. He began to think:

> Why should I return to mundane life? After gaining this rare human birth and then finding a true *guru*, if worship of Kṛṣṇa does not occur then what is the point of gaining such

> a birth? If enjoyment and pleasure are the main goals of living beings then there is plenty of such enjoyment in births as animals. Is enjoyment the purpose of human life? And if in youth one does not worship Kṛṣṇa, then how can it be done in old age? "In youth one worships Kṛṣṇa out of a desire to have him. In middle age one worships Kṛṣṇa, out of desire or not out of desire. In old age one worships Kṛṣṇa out of fear of death." Therefore, now is the best time. Let there be no more foolishness for wasting this human birth neglectfully out of a desire for the pleasures of false enjoyment.

This kind of thinking powerfully invaded his thoughts. On the other side there was his government job, his friends and relatives, to attract him. After a while he decided to give notice at his job and in the morning went to see Prabhupāda. At that time Prabhupāda was doing private worship in a solitary cottage by the slope of Govardhan and it was then about seven in the morning. Prabhupāda, after meditating on his *mantras*, would communicate as needed around nine in the morning. When that young man arrived at the slope of Govardhan, he saw that Prabhupāda had come outside and was standing. It was as if he were there waiting for someone. The young man went running up to Prabhupāda and rolling on the ground at his feet said that he would not return again to his home. Hearing this Prabhupāda raised his hands and, shouting "ho ho" loudly like a madman, began to laugh. It seems that when Prabhupāda's wishes were fulfilled he showed that kind of delight. After that, that young man never again returned home. Resigning his job at Prabhupāda's request and changing his garb he attained Prabhupāda's service and became blessed.

By this incident it is very clear that if Prabhupāda had even the least bit of greed he would not have told the young man to leave his job. Instead, he would have advised that with wealth gathered in an honest way he should serve his *guru*. In this way only for the upliftment of the living beings he extended his grace and bestowed initiation.

At this time there was one *bhakta* who, having lost for some reason the ability to see in his two eyes, came to Prabhupāda in Vṛndāvana. Prabhupāda gave him initiation and instructed him to stay in Vṛndāvana and do private worship. At that instruction, the *bhakta* begged in extreme despair: "Bābā! I am blind. If I stay in Vṛndāvana who will look after me? I won't be able to beg for alms."

In response Prabhupāda said, "Enough with, 'there is nobody.' I am here. I will look after you." At this statement the *bhakta* began to weep. A little while after this, at Prabhupāda's instruction he changed his garb. Even until the present he is doing private worship in Prabhupāda's temple at Govardhan.

By this incident it is demonstrated that Prabhupāda, without any self-interest, being troubled by the sufferings of others, gave them initiation.

Compassionate Salvation from the Wombs of Ghosts

With extraordinary compassion Prabhupāda, through arranging for seven-day recitals of the *Śrīmad Bhāgavata*, saved many living beings who had been born as ghosts.

Once Prabhupāda was staying at Rādhākuṇḍa. One night he was lying down and one of his *bhaktas* was massaging his feet. It was about ten at night. The servant finished his service and went to have some grace-food. Prabhupāda had almost gone to sleep when suddenly he felt as if someone were massaging his feet in the dark. Prabhupāda was not able to see anything in the dark. Then he said: "Hey, who is it? Who are you?" and there was no answer. Prabhupāda again said: "Hey! Who are you who are massaging my feet?" When there was no answer Prabhupāda began to call loudly for his servant: "Gauragovinda, Gauragovinda!" His servant, hearing his call, put aside his grace-food, quickly entered his room, and asked why he was calling. Prabhupāda said: "Who is massaging my feet now?"

The servant was extremely surprised. He had put the chain on the door from the outside when he had gone and at that time there was no one in his room. He said: "Who, Bābā? There was no one in the room." Then Prabhupāda understood that this was not work of any human being. It was learned that before it was sold someone had committed suicide in that house. At the beginnings of dark nights there used to be the sounds of someone walking on the roof. Even after much searching no one was ever found. After that Prabhupāda arranged for a seven-day recital of the *Śrīmad Bhāgavata* in that place for the redemption of that deceased soul. After that no other incident was ever heard of.

A *bābājī* who was one of Prabhupāda's disciples used to have a ghost always following after him because of some mistake he committed. At that time, that *bābājī* did his private worship in a cottage near Uddhava-kuṇḍa. After evening started the mischief began to occur. Sometimes that ghost would take the form of a horse and come and stand there and then as one watched it would change to the form of a cow. Sometimes it would take the form of a woman and stand there and then before one's eyes it would disappear. Sometimes in the dead of night it would forcefully shake the thatched hut of the *bābājī*. In various ways like this it would cause frights in the *bābājī*. The *bābājī* brought many exorcists and fakirs but to no avail. Gradually, he began to become sick from the anxiety. One day the *bābājī* got a charm from an exorcist and wore it around his waist. One night after the sun went down, the *bābājī* was sitting. At that time the ghost pushed down his shoulder and took that charm from his waist. With no other recourse, he went to Prabhupāda and told him in distress all about the situation. Prabhupāda knew about it even before he was told. He instructed the *bābājī* to arrange for a seven-day recital of the *Śrīmad Bhāgavata*. The *bābājī*, asking for alms from many places, gathered three hundred rupees and gave it to Prabhupāda. Prabhupāda said: "Good. If there is any left over I will return it to you. Still, you have to fast the whole day and in a pure condition listen to the *Bhāgavata* seven-day recital." The *bābājī* agreed to that.

Prabhupāda at that time was staying near the slope of Girirāja (Govardhan). In order to perform the *Bhāgavata Saptāha* he arranged for Kṛṣṇadāsa Bābājī to come from Barsāṇā. On the second day of the *Saptāha*, in the morning, the *bābājī* in question was listening and a little further away another *bābājī* was sitting. The second *bābājī* noticed that the first *bābājī* seemed to be talking with someone with his hands folded and yet there was no third person present there. The second *bābājī* was overcome with curiosity to know who the first *bābājī* was talking with and thus he asked him. The first *bābājī* told him the story half in Hindi and half in Bengali. Weeping profusely he said: "Look. You folks don't see it, but I see it all. Look there. That ghost is just standing here up till now. Till now it does not leave." Hearing his words the second *bābājī* could not decide whether he would laugh or cry. Anyway, on the evening of the third day after the beginning of the *Bhāgavata's* recital, right at eight o'clock, that ghost broke the boundary wall of Prabhupāda's Govardhan *āśrama* from one end to the other and took its leave.

Once Prabhupāda was staying at a place called Hoḍel in the circle of Vraja. One day in the middle of the night someone began to call from outside in the voice of a woman: "Bābā, Bābā!" His servant went outside quickly but was unable to find anyone. It should have been mentioned before that Prabhupāda did not sleep much at night. The servant asked Prabhupāda whether he had heard the woman's voice calling or not. In reply, he said that he too heard it. The next day in the third watch of the night Prabhupāda had gone for his bath and with him sent a servant. At that time in the middle of the darkness they heard the call of that woman's voice, "Bābā, Bābā!" The servant after much searching was again unable to find anyone and became extremely astonished. The next day when a Vrajavāsī of Hoḍel came to see Prabhupāda they told him about the woman's voice at night. In response the Vrajavāsī said that a few days previously a woman had committed suicide there. Then Prabhupāda realized that that women had come back as a ghost. After that, Prabhupāda arranged for a seven-day recital of the *Śrīmad Bhāgavata* there and gave that ghostly spirit liberation.

Inoffensive to Others

I have never heard that Prabhupāda in his life ever caused injury to anyone. Instead, if he came to know that anyone had caused him harm, he would regard himself as the great offender and feel sadness. Thus, Prabhupāda used to think that it was because of his own faults that others caused him harm. It was seen that if anyone gave Prabhupāda even the slightest glance askance and if he came to know of it, he would treat that person with so much more respect that, without seeing it for themselves, it would be hard to make anyone understand with words. There was one *bābājī* in Vṛndāvana who used to engage in unseemly criticism of Prabhupāda. After Prabhupāda heard of it, when that *bābājī* came for a visit, Prabhupāda would try to give him great attention and affection. He would invite him to eat and, having him seated nearby, would feed him himself. Seeing that *bābājī*'s cordial reception everyone was astonished. Another *bābājī* of Govardhan used to look askance at Prabhupāda. I have seen that Prabhupāda used to show him, too, respect with an inordinate amount of affection.

Once Prabhupāda was staying at a place named Akṣayavaṭa near Tapovana. The abbot of the Sītārāma Temple of that place was a Rāmānandī *bābā*. He did not look upon Prabhupāda with eyes of affection. Moreover, I have seen that Prabhupāda used to show that *mahātmā* uncommon respect. A holy man coming from Akṣayavaṭa to Tapovana arranged for a feast. Prabhupāda invited that Rāmānandī *bābā* of Akṣayavaṭa, but he did not come. Then Prabhupāda instructed one of his servants to deliver a portion of that food to the Rāmānandī *bābā* and return. Not only that—he began to inquire again and again whether a portion had been sent or not. In this way I was aware many times of his absence of harmfulness. Prabhupāda was the very image of the idea of absence of harm.

Truthful to the Core

He made the only true object, the lotus feet of the Divine Couple, Śrī Śrī Rādhā and Kṛṣṇa the essence of his life. Saying that is more than enough.

Equable

Equable means seeing all living beings as equal. Put in another way, the one Lord resides in all living beings. One who perceives this attains a genuine condition of equal mindedness. This state of equal-mindedness is characteristic of a great Bhāgavata or devotee of the Lord (Bhagavān). In the *Gītā* the Lord says: "Hey Arjuna, let there be joy or let there be sorrow. A person who looks with an equal eye upon all, seeing them as similar to himself, is the best of *yogīs*. This is my opinion."[110] In Prabhupāda's life this equal-mindedness existed in full measure. No matter who approached him and no matter what level they were on, he would respect and honor all in the same way.

Once Prabhupāda's son Vṛndāvana Gosvāmī came to Vṛndāvana along with his dependents. I noticed that Prabhupāda did not show even the most ordinary joy at the coming of his son. When the young sons of Vṛndāvana Gosvāmī came near to Prabhupāda, he did not once turn and look at them. I saw that the way he behaved with ordinary people was the same way he behaved towards his own son and grandsons. The way he behaved towards those who were always engaged in his service was the same way he behaved towards ordinary people.

At one time Prabhupāda used to do private worship by the slope of Girirāja. Near his cottage a sickly dog used to live. From time to time that dog would come into Prabhupāda's cottage and eat the sweets given to him by his *bhaktas*. Prabhupāda seeing that never said a word.

[110] *Bhagavad-gītā*, 6.32.

One day in Prabhupāda's temple in Govardhan there was a special offering of food. At Prabhupāda's instruction a portion of that food was sent to offer to Girirāja. After offering the food to Girirāja for two periods Prabhupāda instructed his servant, "Take some *luci* and sweets and give them to that dog. All day the dog has not eaten anything. It's very hungry." The servant was amazed at Prabhupāda's equal-mindedness.

Even among holy men he did not distinguish who was higher and who was middling. Who took pleasure in private worship and who did not do private worship; this did not fall into his view. He thought of all without distinction as Vaiṣṇavas. Holy men of all communities and of all levels were to him objects of the same respect.

If true equal vision arises in someone, that is, if the direct perception that one God is present in all living beings occurs, not even an iota of malice remains in that person's mind. As a result no living being behaves violently towards that person either.

The Nonviolence of Living Beings Towards Prahbupāda

Prabhupāda performed his private worship even while living in the midst of many dangerous forest animals. But, no animal ever attacked him.

One time Prabhupāda was living with a few *bhaktas* in a grove called Ratan Kuṇḍa not very far from a village called Candorī which was a few miles from the town of Chata. It was then winter. One day in the morning Prabhupāda was absorbed in private worship in an open space. It would have been around nine o'clock in the morning. A servant went to bring Prabhupāda a glass of *sarbat* and saw that a long poisonous snake had entered into Prabhupāda's body-wrapping and was moving about. The tail of the snake was sticking out. Prabhupāda was immersed in relishing the *rasa* of the sports of the Divine Couple in his meditation-intent mind. The servant seeing this from a distance returned to the cottage. After a little while the servant again returned and saw that the snake was taking his leave of Mahārāja. The servant breathed a deep sigh of relief.

In Tapovana Prabhupāda used to do his private worship under a Pilu tree. That place was the habitat of many poisonous snakes. Even in the face of many entreaties, he selected that place as the best place for private worship. One day a servant saw that above Prabhupāda's head a cobra had spread its hood and was swinging back and forth. Prabhupāda with a placid expression on his face just remained in the bliss of private worship.

Even the crooks, thieves, and thugs did not trouble Prabhupāda. Once Prabhupāda was staying in Tapovana. On the news of his presence there, many wealthy people would come and go. As a result, suspecting that there was a lot of wealth with Prabhupāda, a gang of thieves appeared before him at twelve o'clock one night, armed with guns and pistols. Prabhupāda in a very calm way offered them places to sit and asked them to sit down. Then he asked whether they had eaten or not. In response they admitted that they were indeed hungry. Prabhupāda called a servant and asked him to arrange food for them. In a little while the food was ready and he fed the gang of thieves until they were satisfied. Seeing this kind of heart-felt, affectionate behavior the gang of thieves forgot their purpose in coming. Thinking about returning home, they bid him farewell. Prabhupāda, looking on them with affection like he would his own people, forbid their going so late at night and requested that they stay there with him. How would the thieves be able to depart? They then offered a gift of one hundred rupees at Prabhupāda's feet and bowing to him said, "Bābā! We are not good men. Don't worry, though. You remain here with love. As long as we are around, nothing bad will happen to you." After saying this, the gang, bowing again to Prabhupāda, took their leave.

Prabhupāda at one time used to do private worship in a place called Goālapukur near Kusumasarovara. It was dense forest. In the middle of one night Prabhupāda was resting. With him was one servant. At that time two thugs arrived there and asked how much money they had. That day a *bhakta* had come to show respect to Prabhupāda and had given him some money. The servant brought out that money and offered it into the hands of the thieves. After that they asked for something to eat. At that time, because Prabhupāda was ill, a kind of sweet ball had been made for him out of ghee and cow's milk. Out of that the servant gave them four. They devoured those four and asked for more. Then, Prabhupāda asked his servant to give them all of the sweets and the servant did as asked. The thugs took two more sweets and after going off a ways, they came back to Prabhupāda, returned the money they had taken, and departed.

Faultless

There are many kinds of faults. Among them there are eighteen major ones. Those are: bewilderment, weariness, error, astringent flavor, useless labor, unreality, anger, acquisitiveness, apprehension, universal folly, inequality, strong urges, agitation, arrogance, envy, harm, distress, dependence on others. Prabhupāda was free of all those faults. I will try briefly to throw some light on this topic.[111]

Bewilderment (Moha)

Prabhupāda was not in the least bewildered by worldly things. Since this is known to everyone, I have not given any specific examples.

Weariness (Tandrā)

In his life as a practitioner (*sādhaka*) or in his life as accomplished being (*siddha*) no one found Prabhupāda overcome with weariness. Only at night an ordinary state of weariness used to remain and that too only for a half an hour.

Useless Labor (Pariśrama)

Useless labor is labor performed to attain worldly things without any focus on Śrī Kṛṣṇa. On this subject, too, much already has been said.

Rough or Dry Flavor (Rūkṣa-rasa)

This is feeling or love without any connection with divine love (*prema*). For one who has achieved an object that consists of inconceivable divine love, where is his interest in any rough or dry flavors?

---

[111] The source of these eighteen faults is not known. They are given in Dr. Radhagovinda Nath's commentary on the *Caitanya-caritāmṛta*, 2.22.45. There are another eighteen faults enumerated in the *Mahābhārata*, Book Five, Chapter 43. They are associated with pride (*mada*), but that seems to be a different list than the one used here.

Unreality (Asatya)

What previously was not, is now, and later will not remain—that is the unreal. The only real thing is Śrī Kṛṣṇa. One who with his body, mind, and speech has sought shelter with that reality, for him what place is there for the unreal?

Anger (Krodha)

Prabhupāda was without anger. Nevertheless, in order to correct his disciples he from time to time showed imitation anger. Clever people will notice this.

Acquisitiveness (Ākāṅkṣā)

This is the desire to obtain the things of this world. In the matter of obtaining worldly things Prabhupāda had no interest. Whatever of Prabhupāda's temples and *āśramas* there were, he had no interest in them. They arose because of his *bhaktas'* desires.

One *bhakta* revealed a desire to spend lots of money to renovate Prabhupāda's temple at Rādhākuṇḍa. If one said that Prabhupāda showed only a small amount of enthusiasm for it, that would be correct. Nevertheless, the *bhakta* many times submitted his desire to Prabhupāda. In response, Prabhupāda said: "Do as you desire." Prabhupāda did not clearly display any kind of enthusiasm for the project.

Once when Prabhupāda was staying at Nīlācala, a *bhakta* asked of him, "Bābā! Please go to Vṛndāvana. If you don't go to Vṛndāvana, Brajen Dhar will not build a temple at Rādhākuṇḍa." Hearing this, Prabhupāda showing the thumb of his right hand[112] said, "If he doesn't do it, I don't care at all." Take it from that how free from desire he was.

Apprehension (Āśaṅkā)

For one who had no desire to obtain worldly things, there was certainly no apprehension about the loss of those worldly things.

---

[112]This hand gesture is sometimes called green or unripe bananas. It indicates that the person making the gesture does not care about whatever is being discussed.

Universal Folly (Viśvavibhrama)

This consists of the desire to protect the universe of *bhaktas* like Brahmā and others. For one who wants only to attain the menial service of Śrī Rādhikā, where is there a chance for universal folly?

Inequality (Vaiṣamya)

This topic has been thoroughly discussed previously.

Strong Urges (Ulvakāma)

This is worldly desire which only results in sorrow. On this topic I will not repeat examples already given.

Agitation (Lolatā)

This is a kind of restlessness. One who has attained a direct vision of the Young Couple (*Yugala-kiśora*, Śrī Rādhā and Kṛṣṇa) has become truly peaceful. Prabhupāda was free of real agitation.

Arrogance (Mada)

Prabhupāda was completely free of conceit. This anyone who has had association with him even for the smallest while would accept unanimously. Not only was he free of arrogance himself, if even the slightest amount of arrogance were seen among any of his *bhaktas* he would not tolerate it.

One time a servant said to Prabhupāda, "Bābā! In practices of ritual purity we are not any less demanding than any other community (*sampradāya*). Rather, the Gauḍīyas practice greater ritual purity than many other communities. Why then do many other communities not accept food cooked by the hands of Gauḍīyas?" Prabhupāda in an extremely serious manner fiercely protested, "This is just your arrogance. You should think to yourself that they have much greater practices of purity than you. This kind of arrogance is not good." The servant became ashamed of himself at this statement from Prabhupāda.

A servant was telling Prabhupāda about his misdeeds in his previous stage of life (*āśrama*). After that, the servant said to Prabhupāda, "You know, Bābā. I was previously very bad." Prabhupāda became very pensive and then said, "You mean you want to say—now you have become good?" The servant was completely unprepared for this question from Prabhupāda. He realized that in that statement of his—"now I have become good"—there was an arrogance lurking. That arrogance was unable to hide from Prabhupāda's faultless sight. Then the servant said, "No, Bābā! I have not even now become good. Still, before I made no effort to be good. Now I am trying. That is the only difference."

Envy (Mātsarya)

This is being pained when one sees another's good fortune. It is a most reprehensible mental state. There is no need to mention this in connection with Prabhupāda.

Harm (Hiṃsā)

Harm is not appropriate even in ordinary human beings. Not just humans, Prabhupāda did not harm any living being.

One time there were a lot of bugs in the bed that Prabhupāda was sleeping on. His servants said that if they cleaned the bed in the best manner with hot water, the bugs would all die. Prabhupāda did not accept that suggestion. He said: "If one puts the bed in the sun, then the bugs will all run off."

Because Prabhupāda did not harm any living being, no living being harmed him. Sparrows used to come in bliss, land on his head for a while and then fly off again.

In Prabhupāda's temple at Rādhākuṇḍa there were many mice. Prabhupāda did not scare off even one of them. Many times I saw that mice being chased would run into Prabhupāda's outer garments and take shelter there. It was as if they had a long friendship with him.

Distress (Kheda)

Prabhupāda did not have even the least attachment to worldly things. Therefore, when worldly things were destroyed he felt no distress.

Dependence on Others (Parāpekṣā)

In the first stage of his practice Prabhupāda used to perform all activities even cooking with his own hand. He was not dependent on anyone at any time. At a later time, after he was overcome with paralysis, even though it is the root of obligations he used to accept service. But, in his mind and in his heart he did not depend on anyone.

The eighteen faults have been considered here, more or less.[113]

I noticed that if anyone talked about anyone else's faults in Prabhupāda's presence, he would become extremely irritated with the person talking. That was so whether he spoke justly or unjustly. Prabhupāda usually used to say that of all the kinds of character faults there were, the worst was that of finding faults in others. No one ever heard any discussion of the faults of anyone from Prabhupāda's lips. Because he was himself without fault he saw no faults in others.[114]

Generosity

Prabhupāda was extraordinarily charitable. What can one say about his charity? No matter who it was, *brāhmaṇa*, Vrajavāsī, *bābājī*, or whoever it may be, if they came to Prabhupāda in some need, he would without agitation give to them. *Bhaktas* used to give clothes and other materials for his service and he without hesitation would distribute them among the *brāhmaṇas*, Vrajavāsīs and holy men.

One descendent of a Gosvāmī used to come to see him from time to time. As soon as he arrived he used to talk about the troubles of his household life. Then whatever was in Prabhupāda's possession, money, clothes, and so forth he would give to him without hesitation. I have seen this kind of generosity in him in many ways.

Softheartedness

He was by nature tender and soft. What other example will I give about Prabhupāda's tender nature? Those who have come into contact

[113] Actually, Binode Bābā has forgotten one of them, error (*bhrama*). That is a hard one to demonstrate the absence of for anyone.

[114] This ends the subsection on Tinkaḍi Bābā's absence of faults. We now return to his virtues.

with Prabhupāda know it in the best way.

One time Prabhupāda was staying at Kokilāvana. He had come from Premasarovara to Kokilāvana. A few days after that a severe hail storm destroyed the crops of nearly all the places of the region of Vraja. Prabhupāda began to say again and again with extreme sadness, "See what kind of holy man I am! They have served us with so much effort and look at the result of serving a holy man like me. All their crops have been destroyed." Saying this again and again he showed sadness.

It is particularly noteworthy that at that time the only place that did not have any sort of hail storm or damage was around where Prabhupāda was staying.

Purity

Purity is of two kinds: inner and outer purity. Prabhupāda with great firmness protected this state of purity. Outer purity he used to observe indeed and with that inner purity. For example, if such things as calumniating anyone, harming anyone, being pained at another's good fortune, lust, anger, greed and so forth appear, then one's inner purity is destroyed. Prabhupāda with extreme effort and enthusiasm protected his inner purity.

Being Without Possessions

One is possessionless who has rejected all forms of enjoyment and pleasure for Śrī Kṛṣṇa. Prabhupāda left behind wife, son, family, all the earthly joys for the sake of Śrī Kṛṣṇa.

Offering Help To All

Prabhupāda by seeing all as the same used to help everyone without distinction. To him, when it came to helping there was no such thing as self and other.

Once Prabhupāda was living at Tapovana. Needless to say, wherever Prabhupāda stayed, there charity cases also appeared. Even Tapovana was no exception. There was a Vrajavāsī *brāhmaṇa* who had received

Prabhupāda's grace. Whenever there was a charity feast (*bhāṇḍāra*), he used to come with his whole family and have grace-food. Not only that—his daughter's marriage was coming, please give cloth. His *dhoti* had become torn—please give a *dhoti*. In the winter I feel such difficulty—please give me a blanket. In this way, whenever there was any need, he would ask for it from Prabhupāda. Prabhupāda, without argument, used to give to him whenever and whatever he asked for. One day one of Prabhupāda's servants said: "Bābā! If you invite him, he will come along with ten or twelve people. Apart from that when he wants some cloth or something you give it to him. He is your disciple. Therefore, he should serve you. But you are serving him." Hearing this statement from his servant, Prabhupāda said in a very gentle way, "Look. For one who is hungry, food is necessary. For one who has no clothes, clothes are necessary. His needs are greater. He is a *brāhmaṇa* and on top of that a Vrajavāsī. If one has to give, giving to him is proper. They are not able to eat well. If it doesn't happen here the game will be over for him and his family in a few days." Seeing this magnanimous outlook of Prabhupāda's, that servant began to condemn his own miserly attitudes.

Peaceful

A *bhakta* of Kṛṣṇa is desireless and therefore peaceful. All those who desire sense enjoyment, liberation, and yogic power are without peace. In Prabhupāda's case what more exemplification shall I give?

Without Lust

This means being without the deep-seated inclinations or urges (*vāsanā*) to satisfy one's own senses. Prabhupāda always remained immersed in the flavor (*rasa*) of divine sport. Therefore, it goes without saying that in him there was not the slightest degree of inclination to satisfy his own senses.

Indifferent

This means being without effort for any other matter except for serving Śrī Kṛṣṇa. This, too, took concrete shape in the life of Prabhupāda.

Calm

One never saw any agitation in Prabhupāda on any matter. Once one of Prabhupāda's disciples was shoved by the monkey and fell off a roof. Having fallen down that servant was badly injured and lost consciousness. The news was given to Prabhupāda. Hearing this news he was not in the least upset. He only said, "For this reason my left eye has been twitching since morning. I knew that there would be some loss." After saying this, he began to talk normally with another *bhakta* on another subject.

One of Prabhupāda's disciples, a *bābājī* by the name of Śaṅkarāraṇya Dāsa, without telling anyone entered Nidhuvana at night desiring to see the divine sport. The next day in the morning the guard opened the main entrance to the forest and found the *bābājī* unconscious on the path entering the forest. When they received the news the guru-brothers came running. A doctor was brought. Foam was coming out of the *bābājī*'s mouth. After much examination and consultation the doctors could not find any cause for this. After remaining a day in this state the *bābājī* was taken unconscious to Prabhupāda's *āśrama* in Govardhan. Prabhupāda was then engaged in private worship at the slope of Girirāja. News was sent to Prabhupāda and the amazing thing was that he did not show the slightest degree of disturbance. After that some of Prabhupāda's foot wash was brought and placed in the mouth of Śaṅkarāraṇya Dāsa Bābājī and a few moments after that he left his mortal body and went to the next world. News of Śaṅkarāraṇya's passing was sent to Prabhupāda, but the result was another astounding matter. At this too Prabhupāda did not show even a little agitation. He only said, "If he had gone in a little more mature state of worship, it would have been better."

Conquered the Six Vices

The six vices are: lust, anger, greed, illusion, intoxication, and envy. By another accounting they are: hunger, thirst, old age, disease, grief, and delusion.[115] Prabhupāda was one who conquered those six vices

---

[115]The first set of vices are listed in Dr. Radhagovinda Nath's commentary on the *Caitanya-caritāmṛtra*, 2.22.46. The second list which are not really vices but weaknesses is also given there. They are also mentioned in Śrīdhara Svāmin's commentary on *Bhāgavata*

as well. Since the first set of bad vices are among the previous eighteen faults, the following six vices are discussed here.

Hunger and Thirst

In Prabhupāda's behavior, I have never seen him to be troubled by thirst or hunger. On Ekādaśī[116] and on other waterless fasts especially on summer days, we used to become extremely troubled, but we never found Prabhupāda to be troubled.

Old Age and Disease

Prabhupāda's old age and disease that were seen were only to give others a good opportunity to perform service and thus to bring about their ultimate well-being. The old age and disease that were seen in him were not produced by his past actions starting to fructify. Below I have tried to clarify the matter.

One day Prabhupāda said to one of his close servants: "Look, for saints (*mahāpuruṣa*) nothing remains that can be called fructifying (*prārabdha*) *karma*. But, in order to give others an opportunity to perform service and to bring about their ultimate good fortune, they ask the Lord for him to create new fructifying *karma* for them." After saying this Prabhupāda went to do his ablutions. When he returned from his bath, the same servant began to dry off his feet. At that time Prabhupāda said with a smile: "O Lord! Please create some *karma* and again cause more service. This is your sport." By Prabhupāda's statement, it is proven that for him there was no more fructifying *karma*. Nevertheless, to fulfill others by giving them an opportunity to serve, he had created fructifying *karma*.

I have noticed that if anyone came to visit him, Prabhupāda would talk about the sufferings of his body. But, when no guest was there, I have noticed that he did not think that he had any kind of suffering. With an affectionate, peaceful, and satisfied face he would relish the flavors of divine sport. In order to hide himself from the view of the people

---

Purāṇa, 11.11.31. In fact, that section of the *Purāṇa* (11.11.29-32) appears to be the source of the list traits of the *bhakta* found in the *Caitanya-caritāmṛta* on which this part of Binode's biography is based.

[116] This is the eleventh day and night of the monthly full and new moon fortnights. These two days in the month are observed by fasting, even from water, among the renunciant communities of Caitanya Vaiṣṇavism.

he would show this external illness. The truth of the matter was proved many times and in many ways. How many times was his blood tested, his stool, his urine and so forth and how many times were xrays taken, but in all of that not the slightest problem was ever found.

His sport of illness did not remain the same either. After a few days his illness would change. Sometimes it was, "My stomach is aching. Bring a doctor." The doctor was brought and the medicine begun. Then it was, "My teeth are aching. Bring the doctor." The doctor was brought. After the teeth were done, it was difficulty breathing, "Bring the doctor." Soon the difficulty of breathing was forgotten. Then a cough started. When one illness started, the prior was forgotten. In this way he revealed his illness-sport and kept his servant-*bhaktas* busy.

Grief and Delusion

These topics have been discussed before.

Moderation in Eating

Prabhupāda was always a moderate eater. In the early stages of his practice he used to eat only fruit during the day and then just a little. Later he would eat a little milk and tapioca in the morning and in the afternoon water-chestnut flat-breads and vegetables without oil or spice. In his final days he only ate curds and some boiled apple once a day.

Without Frenzy

I never saw Prabhupāda become frantic or maddened by any matter. Let any delightful or disturbing incident occur, he was in all circumstances free of madness or frenzy.

Humility

One who thinks of himself as lower than anyone else and does not desire the respect or honor of anyone else is humble.

This feeling of humility existed in full measure in Prabhupāda. If any Vaiṣṇava came to see him, he would bow down and in a very modest way say: "I am unfit. I cannot go anywhere. Therefore, you have gracefully come to give me a sight of you and make me fulfilled." Whoever the holy man on whatever stage they were on, when he came, Prabhupāda would show him respect through this sort of humble statement. It was not only that he was free of arrogance, if he noticed even the slightest arrogance in any of his disciple-servants he would severely condemn it.

One day one of Prabhupāda's servants had an argument with one of his older guru-brothers. At that Prabhupāda called that younger servant and said, "Look, you should not regard the judgment of an older guru-brother as unjust. You should think that the fault is yours. If you ever see someone's faults, you should think that it is because of your ignorance and arrogance that you see others faults. Even if your elder brother strikes you you should think that the fault is yours. Keep in mind that if one is able to tolerate, one is chaste; and if one is not able to tolerate, one is a whore. If you are able to be tolerant, you can be a holy person (*sādhu*). And if you are not able to be tolerant you will fall. If you cannot be free of pride, you will not be able to obtain *bhakti* at any time. As long as you are proud, you will not receive Bhaktidevī's grace. Another name for Bhaktidevī is the Mother of Humility. If a small child is at home then one should know that the mother is nearby. She doesn't go very far away. In that same way, one should know that where there is humility, Bhaktidevī is nearby. The tree that bears fruit bows down. In the same way, the head of one who has received even a little of the grace of Bhaktidevī is bowed. In other words, he continues to think of himself as lower than others. 'The Lord shows greater grace to the lowly. The high-born, the scholar, the wealthy have great arrogance.'[117] If one is able to think of oneself as lower than all others, that person has no more fear. You should not go out to defeat anyone. This is the Vaiṣṇava world. Here the one who defeats loses. We, after losing everything, have come here. We constantly remain losing. You, too, should lose. You will see then that you have actually won." Prabhupāda always gave special emphasis to the "lower than a blade of grass" verse.[118]

---

[117]Kṛṣṇadāsa Kavirāja, *Caitanya-caritāmṛta*, 3.4.64.

[118]Third verse of the *Śikṣāṣṭaka* attributed to Śrī Caitanya: तृणादपि सुनीचेन तरोरिव सहिष्णुना। अमानिना मानदेन कीर्तनीयः सदा हरिः॥, "More humble than a blade of grass, as tolerant as a tree, without conceit giving respect, one should always praise Hari."

Taciturn

In Prabhupāda inscrutability was particularly noteworthy. Knowing his inner moods was difficult.

Compassionate

One who is not able to tolerate the sufferings of others is compassionate. This subject has been discussed before.

Friendly

I leave aside this topic to avoid repetition.

Poetic

One who is good at creating sentences that are sweet to the ear, possess beautiful meanings, and arrangements of deep feelings is poetic. This subject has been discussed in the treatment of the life of Prabhupāda.

Expert

One who is capable of getting things done is expert. Expert also is one who is not lazy and who is able to complete difficult tasks quickly. Before he was affected by paralysis, he was expert in all his undertakings.

Silent

One who does not talk about anything other than the names, forms, qualities and sports of the Lord is called silent. In the first stage of his practice Prabhupāda used to maintain complete silence (*mauna*). At later times during the day he remained silent and in the evening he would speak as needed.

An Actual True Guru

Prabhupāda was an actual authentic guru. I am not making this kind of statement just because he was my guru. Through the few incidents given below, I will try to make this matter more clear.

One time a lawyer from Kolkata took initiation from Prabhupāda. His line of thinking was that if he took initiation from an accomplished saint, by the grace of his guru all obstacles and calamities would be removed and his special earnings in business and trade would be improved. But, not seeing that kind of result after taking initiation he became disappointed. Gradually he began to lose his faith in his guru also. Then one of his so-called friends instructed him, "Brother, all that worship of the Divine Couple is worthless. Nothing will come of that. You should take to the *mantra* of the Goddess. The Mother is very much alive. Therefore, because of that your good fortune and earnings in business will increase." The lawyer believed his friend's words to be true and was initiated again into the goddess *mantra* by a worshiper of the Goddess. Immediately after receiving that initiation every kind of obstacle, calamity, disrespect, disease and sadness arose such that the lawyer became completely lost and began to search for some solution. One after another the troubles came. Then finding no other recourse he took shelter of a *brāhmaṇa* priest at Kālīghāṭa. He told him, "Brother, please implore the Mother on my behalf. I am worshiping the Mother; yet in spite of that why are there so many difficulties? And how can I become free of those troubles? Inform the Mother about my troubles. I will cover all of your expenses." The priest did that. A few days after imploring the Mother, the Mother one night took an extremely frightening form in the priest's dream and said, "Why are you beseeching me on behalf of that one? I am going to finish him off. He hasn't seen anything yet. I have only just begun with him. Didn't he reject an accomplished Vaiṣṇava guru and take shelter with me?" Saying this much the image of the Mother disappeared. The priest became extremely frightened. He went to that lawyer and told him what had happened. Hearing all that, the lawyer went all the way to Vṛndāvana and fell at Prabhupāda's feet crying like a baby.

There was a wealthy resident of West Bengal who, out of a desire to receive *mantra* initiation, was searching for an authentic guru. Many people from many different communities began to exert their influence to try to bring him into their fold. That person having no other recourse went to Tārakeśvara and supplicated Bābā Tārakanātha to obtain a genuine guru. A few days after the supplication Bābā Tārakanātha told him in a dream, "You should receive initiation from the Mitras' family guru." There was one Mitra with whom the gentleman was well acquainted and who was a disciple of Prabhupāda. After that he went to Prabhupāda and told the story of the dream and then, receiving the grace of Prabhupāda, he became fortunate.

Guileless Behavior like a Child

Prabhupāda from time to time behaved like a child. When he saw small children he used to become very joyful. Seating them close to him he would tell stories.

One of Prabhupāda's *bābājī* disciples used to tell him stories based on incidents from the *Rāmāyaṇa* and sometimes incidents from the *Mahābhārata*. Sometimes, in the course of describing various incidents, he would tell stories about Gopāla Bhāḍa as well. When he was describing some particular incident Prabhupāda would become amazed just like a child and say, "Bāhvā! How terrifying! What happened after that, Gauragovinda?" After this kind of listening he used to say, "You know a whole lot. I don't know anything at all!"

One day a big black ant bit into Prabhupāda's foot and held on. After many efforts to remove the ant, it became torn in half at the belly. Then that same *bābājī*, thinking of a riddle, recited it, "Black in color, munches on toe, though stomach's torn, it does not go."[119] Prabhupāda hearing the riddle became excited just like a child to know what the subject was. When the *bābājī* told him the meaning of the riddle, Prabhupāda began to laugh just like a child.

A *bhakta* often used to come from Vṛndāvana to see Prabhupāda. He used to wear on his head a Gāndhī hat. Prabhupāda suddenly had a desire to wear one of those hats. He requested that *bhakta* to have such a hat made for him. In a short while a hat arrived for Prabhupāda. Receiving that hat Prabhupāda's joy could not be restrained. He used to sit nearly all the time with that hat on his head. When he took the hat off his head he would ask again and again if the hat was carefully put

[119] *kālo varaṇ, chakhāna caraṇ, peṭ chiṛleo nāika maraṇ.*

away. One would think that that hat was his everything. After wearing it for a few days he forgot about that hat.

Unaware of Contemporary Affairs

One day a servant was talking about his occupation in his former life. After that he said to Prabhupāda, "Do you know, Bābā, in my work life I also used to take bribes (*ghuṣa*)." Prabhupāda said, "What sort of thing is a *ghuṣa* (bribe)?" Though the servant tried in many ways he was not able to make Prabhupāda understand what a bribe was.

One day a servant was talking with Prabhupāda about the modern or present age and mentioned as examples the cruel massacres at the villages of Pipaḍā in Bihar and Māndā Bazar in Tripurā. Prabhupāda said with great astonishment, "What's that? Do such things really happen in the present day?"

Vigilant Observation Even Though Unmanifest

At Premasarovara a Vrajavāsī was a disciple of Prabhupāda. He was advanced in age, too. A few days after Prabhupāda's disappearance, after being bedridden with illness he said one day, "Look! Guru Bābā has come to take me. Give him a place to sit." After saying that his body became motionless. Prabhupāda himself came to take him to the far shore of the mortal world.

When one of the other guru-brothers developed ill feelings towards a servant at the Govardhan temple, he decided that he would go elsewhere. That night Prabhupāda said to that servant in a dream, "Sudāmā, where have you decided to go?" That servant, Sudāmā Dāsajī, never went anywhere else again.

In Vṛndāvana at Śrī Śrī Rādhā Murārīmohana Kuñja when there was some disagreement on some matter, the servant decided that he was going to go somewhere else. At night in a dream he saw Bābā who said with an extremely sad face,"No one will serve me. No one will serve me." That servant never went anywhere else.

One day Prabhupāda's wife Mātā Gosvāminī came to Prabhupāda's *āśrama* in Govardhan. When she came she revealed her wish to stay in Prabhupāda's private worship hut at the temple. At night Prabhupāda said to Sudāmā Dāsa in a dream, "Put her out of my room immediately! Otherwise, I will not be able to go into it."

On Kauśīka Mountain in the Himālayas a Daśanāmī Sannyāsī holy man used to perform private worship. At the order of his guru there he went to Śrī Dhāma Vṛndāvana wishing to worship the Divine Couple. After arriving in Vṛndāvana he was specially enthusiastic to associate with Vaiṣṇavas of the Caitanyite tradition. But as he went for their company, in some places he encountered special attacks. Since he was a *māyāvādin sannyāsin*, many nourished a disgust toward him and used to give him fierce glances. In many places they disrespected him as well. At this he felt great pain in his heart. Coming to Vṛndāvana he saw a picture of Prabhupāda and became specially faithful towards him. One night he had a dream. Prabhupāda was sitting at the base of a tree on the shore of Premasarovara. The renunciant prostrated himself before him. Prabhupāda with great enthusiasm offered him a seat. After that the renunciant expressed his mental anguish before Prabhupāda, "Master! Why is there so much constriction in *dharma*? Being a *sannyāsin* one is not qualified to attain the lotus feet of the Divine Couple? Members of other communities are not able to attain the lotus feet of Bhagavān, or become *bhaktas* of Śrīman Mahāprabhu? Or, is this a monopoly of Gauḍīyas? I came to Śrī Dhāma Vṛndāvana with so many hopes, but now I see that here nearly everyone is happy to remain bound within the limits of restrictions. Going to associate with Vaiṣṇavas, I have gained only mental anguish and my mind has become saddened."

In response to that Prabhupāda said with a smiling, peaceful face, "Look! If one ignites wood that is wet one gets smoke and a sputtering, crackling noise. When that wood has been burned by the fire and turned into ashes then there is no more smoke and no more noise. In the same way as long as the mental operations are covered with ignorance there are many kinds of disagreements and clashes. When those mental operations are burned away by the fire of knowledge then there are no more disagreements. Where there is no perception of the world of consciousness (*cinmaya-jagat*), there are many communal disagreements. Where there is investigation of the realm of consciousness illumined by the light of *bhakti*, there is peace." The renunciant being pleased by this answer of Prabhupāda accepted him in his heart as his guru.

Although Prabhupāda has become unmanifest, he is still present among us through his vigilant observation. Fortunate practitioners know the truth of this.

Jaya Śrī Gaurasundara, Jaya Nityānanda Rāma!

Part III

Prabhupāda's Sūcaka Kīrtanas

Kīrtana One

শ্রীশ্রীতিনকড়ি বাবার সূচক কীর্তন

A Song Introducing Śrī Śrī Tinkaḍi Bābā

A *sūcaka kīrtana* is a special kind of song of praise that introduces or indicates the greatness of the traits or qualities of a saint. It usually is composed by one of the disciples of that saint and sung on special occasions when the saint is remembered, occasions such as his or her appearance or disappearance celebrations. This song is one of two written for Śrī Tinkaḍi Bābā. The authorship of this one is given at the end as poor Caitanya Dāsa, or a poor servant of Caitanya, which may be the name of an actual disciple of Tinkaḍi Bābā or it may refer to a disciple who wishes only to be known as a poor servant of Caitanya. It may also be the work of Binode Bihari Das Bābājī. It is printed in the back of his Bengali book on the life of Śrī Tinkaḍi Bābā. Another *sūcaka kīrtana* was written for Bābā by Śrī Hṛdayānanda Dāsa Bābā who, though not a disciple of Tinkaḍi Bābā, was a special object of his affection. It is printed for the first time along with a translation in the next chapter.

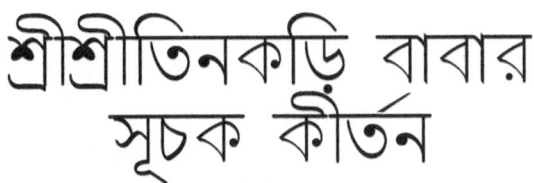

জয় নিত্যানন্দ রাম

পরমারাধ্যতম শ্রীগুরুদেবের
গুণলেশ সূচক কীর্তন

জয় রে জয় রে জয়, শ্রীগুরু করুণাময়,
প্রভু মোর তিনকড়ি গোস্বামী মহাশয়।
ভক্তি ধর্ম আচরিয়া, জগভরি প্রচারিয়া,
পতিত উদ্ধারিল যিঁহো অমায়ায়।।

মেদিনীপুর ঘাটাল মাঝে, এক পুণ্যভূমি আছে,
নাম যার মনোহরপুর।
প্রভু গুণনিধি মোর, শাখা হয়ে নিত্যানন্দের,
বসতি করেন সেই পুর।।

পিতা হরিমোহন গোস্বামী, সর্বগুণে গুণমণি,
যাঁকো পুরে 'ঠাকুর' বলে গায়।
মাতা দেবী সুরধনী, যেন পতিত পাবনী,
যাঁর গর্ভে আইলা মহাশয়।।

তের শত তের সনে, শুভ মাঘী পূর্ণিমা দিনে,
অবতীর্ণ হৈলা অবনীতে।
সর্ব সুলক্ষণ দেখি, সবার জুড়ায় আঁখি,
উঠিল মঙ্গল ধ্বনি আচম্বিতে।।

Victory to Nityānanda Rāma!

A song of praise introducing
a few of the good qualities
of the most worshipable *śrī gurudeva.*

Victory! O Victory! O Victory!
To the compassionate *guru,*
My magnanimous master,
Tinkaḍi Gosvāmī.

Practicing the religion of *bhakti*
And spreading it till it filled the world,
He uplifted the fallen so guilelessly.

In the district of Medinīpura,
There is an auspicious land
called Manoharapura.

My master, a treasure chest of virtues,
In the branch of Nityānanda
Resides in that town.

His father was Gosvāmī Harimohan,
A virtuous gem among all virtues;
As "Ṭhākura" in the village he was sung.

His mother was Suradhanī,
A purifier of the fallen;
To her womb the great one came.

In the year thirteen hundred and thirteen,
On Māgha's fortunate fullmoon day,[120]
He descended to the earth.

Seeing all his good features,
Everyone's eyes were pleased.
There arose suddenly a joyful sound.

---

[120]The month of Māgha corresponds to January-February in the English calendar. The Bengali year 1313 corresponds to 1907 in the Common Era (C.E.)

বাড়ে প্রভু মাতৃকোরে,　　পরম আনন্দ ভরে,
　　নাম হৈল কিশোরী কিশোরানন্দ।
পঞ্চ বর্ষ বয়ঃকালে,　　জননী বিদায় নিলে,
　　পিতার হইল বড় দ্বন্দ্ব।।

পিতা অতি সদাশয়,　　ইষ্টে গাঢ় নিষ্ঠা হয়,
　　সমর্পয়ে কিশোরি চরণে।
হেনকালে এক আত্মীয়া,　　সাগ্রহে আসিয়া,
　　ভার নিল সেবার কারণে।।

তিনটি কড়ি বিনিময়ে,　　আইসেন প্রভু ক্রীত হয়ে,
　　নাম হইল প্রভু তিনকড়ি।
ধাইমার নয়নমণি,　　মোর প্রভু গুণমণি,
　　পালিলেন অতি যত্ন করি।।

বাল্য চাপল্য মতি,　　পাঠাভ্যাসে নাহি রতি,
　　বিদ্যালয়ে প্রবেশয়ে যেই।
কপট ক্রন্দন করে,　　ধাইমার থাকি কোরে,
　　পাঠশালার নাম শুনিলেই।।

নবম বর্ষ যবে,　　উপনয়ন হইল তবে,
　　ভাবান্তর হইল প্রভুর।
গাঢ় অনুরাগ ভরে,　　গীতা গ্রন্থ বুকে ধরে,
　　ঘুরয়ে ফিরয়ে নিরন্তর।।

The master grew on the lap of his mother,
In the fullness of the highest joy,
His name became Kiśorīkiśorānanda.

When his age was only five
And his mother bid him farewell.[121]
His father then faced a major dilemma.

His father was very noble-hearted.
He had deep faith in his beloved deity.
He offered prayers at the feet of Kiśorī.[122]

At that time a lady relative
Came forth with enthusiasm
And took responsibility for the sake of service.

In exchange for three cowries,
The Master had been purchased.
Thus, his name became Tinkaḍi [Three Cowries].

He was the jewel of his nurse's eye,
My Master, gem of virtues.
She raised him with great care.

His childhood mind was fickle.
He had no love for studies,
When he entered the local school.

He cried false tears
And clung to his nurse's lap
Whenever he even heard the word "school."

When he was nine years old
His *brāhmaṇa* initiation took place.
And Master's feelings changed completely.

Filled with deep attachment,
He took the *Gītā* to his heart.
And wandered out, around, and back ceaselessly.

---

[121]She passed away.
[122]Śrī Rādhikā.

পিতা ঠাঁই দীক্ষাতে, বাড়ে অনুরাগ চিতে।
থাকি মাতি কীর্তন বিলাসে।
পিতার সহিত শেষে, ফিরেন পহুঁ দেশে দেশে,
পরানন্দে সততই ভাসে।।

শান্ত সৌম্য ক্ষমাবান, সাক্ষাৎ যেন মূর্তিমান,
দৈন্যাদি গুণের হয় খনি।
স্বজাতীয় আশয় সঙ্গে, লীলা রস পর সঙ্গে,
উল্লাসে ভরিত মুখখানি।।

অতি শিশুকাল হৈতে, কৃষ্ণ অনুরাগ চিতে,
পরম বৈরাগ্য সদা মন।
পঞ্চদশ বর্ষ পরে, একদিব্য বালিকা হেরে,
পিতৃদেব কৈলেন চিন্তন।।

মনোহরপুর নিকট গ্রাম, খাঞ্জাপুর সুখ ধাম,
গোপীনাথ গোঁসাঞির বসতি তথায়।
সপ্তম বর্ষীয়া কন্যা, রূপে গুণে অসামান্যা,
তোমার করেতে সমর্পয়।।

শীতলা সুন্দরী সতী, সহধর্মিণী ভক্তিমতি,
আনুকূল্যে করয়ে সেবন।
সদাচার পরায়ণা, নিষ্ঠারুচি নাই তুলনা,
পরানন্দে হইলা মগন।।

When he received initiation from his father,
Deep attachment increased in his heart.
His mind remained in the joy of *kīrtana*.

Finally, in the company of his father
Master toured from place to place,
Always floating in the highest bliss.

"Peaceful, calm, and tolerant,
As though he were their embodiment,
A mine of the virtues, humility and such,

In the company of those with similar desires,
In the company of those who relish divine sport,
His face was filled with joy."

From a very early age
Feeling for Kṛṣṇa was in his heart
And the highest apathy[123] always in his mind.

When he was fifteen,
His father began to worry,
searching for a saintly girl.

Near Manoharapura was a village
Named Khāñjāpura, a happy place.
There lived Gopīnātha Gosāñi.

"My daughter whose age is seven,
In beauty and virtue most uncommon,
Into your hands I wish to deliver."

The chaste Śītalā Sundarī
His sharer in *dharma*, heart filled with *bhakti*,
Performed his service very favorably.

Intent was she on pure behavior,
Her faith and beauty beyond compare.
In the highest joy she was immersed.

---

[123]towards the world

বিষয়ে বিপত্তি জান, সংসার স্বপন মান,
নরতনু ভজনের মূল।
ঠাকুর নরোত্তমের বাক্য হৃদে করি মহাশক্য
সদা হইয়া ব্যাকুল।।

এই মতে কত দিনে পিতৃদেবের অদর্শনে
ভজন বৈরাগ্য বাড়য়।
পতিত পাষণ্ড যত, প্রেমে হয় উন্মত্ত,
স্মরণ লইল রাঙ্গাপায়।।

আপনি ভজন করি, আদর্শ স্থাপন করি,
সর্বত্র করেন পরচার।
সঙ্কীর্তন প্রেম রসে, প্রভু নিরন্তর ভাসে,
পতিতেরে করয়ে উদ্ধার।।

এইভাবে কাটে প্রভুর সংসার জীবন।
বৃন্দাবন নামে পুত্র জন্মিল তখন।।
শিশু পুত্র ফেলি মাতা পরলোকে গেলা।
প্রভুর ধাইমা স্নেহে পালন করিলা।।
বৈরাগ্য উৎকণ্ঠা যবে চরম বড়িলা।
সর্ব তীর্থ পর্য়্যটনে বাহির হৈলা।।
ভ্রমিতে ভ্রমিতে প্রভু আইসেন গোবর্ধনে।
সিদ্ধ মনোহর বাবার পাই দর্শনে।।

"Know that in sense objects there's trouble;
Accept worldly life as a dream.
The human body is the root of worship."

These words of Narottama Ṭhākura
He made most powerful in his heart,
Always remaining impatient.

In this way after some time
When his father passed away,
His worship and renunciation increased.

All the fallen and godless
Became intoxicated by divine love
And took shelter at those reddened feet.

Performing worship himself
And establishing the model
He spread it everywhere.

In the juice of love and *saṅkīrtana*
The Master floated ceaselessly.
The fallen he lifted up.

In this way the Master passed his household life.
Then a son named Vṛndāvana was born.

Leaving behind her infant son,
the mother went to the next world.
The Master's former nurse affectionately raised him.

When his thirst for renunciation reached its limit,
The Master went wandering to all the holy sites.

Wandering around the Master came to Govardhana.
There he met Siddha Manohara Dāsa Bābā.

হেরিয়া সে সৌম্যমূর্তি ব্যাকুলিত হিয়া।
আত্ম নিবেদন করি আপনা উঘাড়িয়া।।

আজ্ঞা দিলেন যাও বাবা গৃহেতে পুনঃ।
কৃষ্ণ ইচ্ছায় হবে তব অভীষ্ট পূরণ।।

মহৎ আজ্ঞা শিরে ধরি আইলেন ঘরে।
রামচন্দ্র কবিরাজে যেমতি আজ্ঞা করে।।

পুনঃ দারপরিগ্রহ তবেত করিয়া।
সংসারে রহেন প্রভু অনাসক্ত হৈয়া।।

নবদ্বীপ-নীলাচল কভু বৃন্দাবন।
সঙ্কীর্তন প্রচারিতে সর্বত্র ভ্রমণ।।

পতিব্রতা পত্নি তাঁর দেবী সরস্বতী।
পতি আনুকূল্যে রহি সেবেন তেমতি।।

তাঁর গর্ভে দুই কন্যার হৈলে জনম।
সত্যকরি মানে গৃহ অনল সমান।।

স্থাপিয়া অখণ্ড নাম শ্রীমনোহরপুরে।
পরম ধাম জানি আইলা ন'দে পুরে।।

সুরধুনী তটে হেরি নিভৃত স্থান খানি।
ভজনস্থলী করিতে বাঞ্ছেন আপনি।।

নদীয়া বিহারী হরির ইচ্ছার কারণ।
ফলাহারি বাবার মন্দির করে সমর্পণ।।

পতিতপাবন হরি পতিত উদ্ধারিতে।
পাতিলেন ফাঁদ ইহা স্বকার্য্য সাধিতে।।

হেন কালে অপূর্ব এক যুগল বিগ্রহ।
ভঙ্গীকরি আসিলেন করিতে অনুগ্রহ।।

Seeing that image of serenity his heart became perturbed.
Offering himself [to Bābā] he opened himself up.

He [Bābā] gave him the order, "Go back, Bābā, to your house.
When Kṛṣṇa wishes it, your desires will be fulfilled."

Taking the order of the saint on his head, he returned home,
He followed the order like Rāmacandra Kavirāja of old.

Then once more he took a wife
And, though detached, remained in household life.

To Navadvīpa and Nīlācala and sometimes Vṛndāvana
He wandered everywhere to spread *saṅkīrtana*.

His devoted wife was Devī Sarasvatī.
Favorably disposed towards her husband, she served him in that way.

In her womb two daughters were born.
He truly considered his home to be the same as fire.

He established the unbroken holy names in Śrī Manohara-pura,
And moved to the town of Nadīyā, knowing it to be supreme.

Noticing secluded places on the bank of the Suradhunī,
He desired to create a place for his private worship.

Because of the wish of Hari, the Frolic of Nadīyā,
The temple of Frugivorous Bābā was given to him.

Hari, the purifier of the fallen, to uplift the fallen
Spread a trap there to achieve his own goals.

A matchless image of the Divine Couple arrived there
Striking an attractive pose, to bestow their grace.

বিগ্রহ পাইয়া প্রভুর হরষিত মন।
শ্রীশ্রীরাধাবল্লভ বলি করেন স্থাপন।।

নবদ্বীপে তেলিপাড়ায় এক গোসাঞি পরিবারে।
সেবিত হৈত যিঁহ বহুকাল ধরে।।

দৈবে গোসাঞি যবে পরলোকে গেলা।
এক শেঠ ঠাঁই বিকাইতে মনন করিলা।।

হেনকালে শ্রীবিগ্রহের স্বপ্নাদেশ হয়।
প্রাতে আসি প্রভু ঠাঁই কাঁদি সমর্পয়।।

যে বারেক দেখে তাঁরে সে ধৃতি ধরিতে নারে,
কিবা সে মূরতি মনোহর।
অদ্যাপিও বিরাজ করে, সেই মণিমন্দিরে,
মোর প্রভুপাদের চিত্তচোর।।

সদা প্রাণ উচাটন, কভু স্থির নহে মন,
সিদ্ধ বাবার করিতে স্মরণে।
ছিন্নমূল-বৃক্ষ প্রায়, কাঁদি তিঁহ উভরায়
(ত্বরা আসি) পড়িলেন অভয় চরণে।।

তব ক্রীতদাস জেনে, ইঙ্গিতে এনেছ টেনে,
অঙ্গীকার করহ মোরে।
আসিয়াছি এবার পালিয়া তোমার
আজ্ঞা ধরিয়া শিরে।।

হেরি বাবা প্রেমভরে তোমা পাই বক্ষ ধরে
অশ্রুনীরে সিক্ত কলেবর।
কহিলা মধুর বাণী কৃষ্ণ মোর কৃপাখানি
ছুটাইল বন্ধন তোমার।।

Receiving the sacred image the Master's mind was thrilled.
As Śrī Śrī Rādhāvallabha the image was installed.

In the family of a Goswami of Navadvīpa's Telipāṛā,
The image had been served for a very long time.

When by fate the Goswami went to the next world,
She[124] considered selling the image to a merchant.

At that time the image's dream instruction came.
The next morning, she went crying to Master and offered it to him.

One who even once sees him[125]
Is not able to remain composed.
How mind-capturing is that image!
Even now he resides
In that jeweled temple there,
Thief of my Prabhupāda's heart.

Always restless was his heart.
His mind was never tranquil
As he remembered the accomplished *bābā*.[126]
He was practically an uprooted tree;
At the top of his voice he wailed.
Coming quickly, he fell at those fearless feet.

"Knowing me to be your purchased slave
By signs you have drawn me here.
Please accept me now.
I have come now fleeing,
Holding your order on my head."

Seeing this, Bābā, filled with love,
(said) "I have found you" and embraced him,
Drenching his body with tears.
He spoke theses sweet words,
"My Kṛṣṇa is a mine of mercy;
He has broken all your bindings."

---

[124]The Goswami's wife
[125]The image.
[126]Siddha Manohara Dāsa Bābājī.

তোমা অতি সযতনে রাখি নিজ সন্নিধানে
যুগল ভজন শিক্ষা দিলা।
গৌরগণ-সুসম্মত ভক্তি সিদ্ধান্ত যত
কৃপাকরি সব জানাইলা।।

সিদ্ধবাবা আজ্ঞা লৈয়া গভীর বনেতে গিয়া
বাস করি নিয়ম করিলা।
গোস্বামিগণের যত আচরি অভিমত
আদর্শ ভজন জাগাইলা।।

চৌরাশীক্রোশ পরিক্রমা করি, ভাগবতসপ্তাহ পরচারি
রহিয়া এক এক ঠাঁই।
সপ্তাহ অন্তে ভাণ্ডারা করি মহাপ্রসাদ বিতরি
সেবাধর্ম সবারে শিখাই।।

ব্রজ হৈতে ন'দে পুরী কভু নীলাচল পুরী,
নামের তরীটি বাইয়া।
কে যাবি কে যাবি বলি প্রভু ডাকে বাহু তুলি
(আয় আয়) বিনামূলে যাব সবা লইয়া।।

শ্রীক্ষেত্র হৈতে পদব্রজে ধাইলেন শ্রীধাম ব্রজে
ঝাড়িখণ্ড পথ প্রান্ত ধরি।
ভাসাইয়া সবাকারে আবাল বৃদ্ধ বণিতারে
নাম প্রেম বরিষণ করি।।

With the utmost care, he keep you close to him.
He taught you worship of the Divine Couple.
All the conclusions of *bhakti*
Approved by the followers of Gaura —
Showing you his grace, he taught them all.

Honoring Siddhabābā's order,
Into the forests deep he went,
And living there he followed the rules.
Performing all the practices
That are approved by the Gosvāmins,
He awakened the very model of worship.

Circumambulating the eighty-four *krośas*[127]
And spreading the seven-day reading of the *Bhāgavata*,
he stayed in one place after another.
After a seven-day reading,
He would hold a feast, distributing holy offerings.
He thus taught the process of service to all.

From Vraja he went
Sometimes to Navadvīpa,
Sometimes to Nīlācala.[128]
Steering the boat of the holy names.
"Who will go? Who will go?"
Master called out, raising up his arms.
"Come! Come! Fare-less we will go,
Taking aboard one and all!"

From Śrī Kṣetra by foot
He went to the holy land of Vraja,
Taking the path through Jhārikhaṇḍa
And setting all adrift, young and old alike, in a flood,
By raining down divine love in the holy names.

---

[127] A *krośa* equals about two and a quarter miles or four thousand yards. Here eighty-four *krośas* refers to the circumference of the holy land of Vraja.

[128] Jagannātha Purī in Orissa.

চট কৌপীন পরিধান ফল মূল গব্য খান
অন্নাদি না করি আহার।
ত্রিসন্ধ্যা স্নান করি স্মরণ কীর্তন করি
রাধাপদ ভজন যাঁহার।।

অষ্টপ্রহার রাত্রিদিনে রাধাকৃষ্ণ গুণগানে
স্মরণেতে সদাই গোঁয়ায়।
একপ্রহার শুতি থাকে স্বপ্নে রাধাকৃষ্ণ দেখে
এক তিল ব্যর্থ নাহি যায়।।

তপোবনে

যমুনার তীরে আসি নিভৃত তপোবনে বসি
অশ্রুনীরে ভাসিয়া গোঁয়াও।
হা বৃষভানু রাজনন্দিনী ওহে রাজচক্রবর্তিনী
করুণা নয়নে বারেক চাও।।

কভু হুঙ্কার করি ক্ষণে কত আর্তিভরি
আবেশে পড়িয়া রও।
ভাবাবেশে কও কথা বিবিধ প্রলাপ গাঁথা
চাটুবাক্যে কাহাকে ফিরাও।।

শুনিয়া সে মধুর বাণী জুড়ায় সবার পরাণী
(অনুমানে) বুঝি কারো দর্শন পাও।
হারাইয়া সেই ধনে হাহাকার ক্রন্দনে
(পরক্ষণে) ধরণীতে পড়িয়া লুটাও।।

He wore a loincloth of jute
And ate only roots, milk and fruit,
Avoiding all grains and such.
He bathed at the three joints[129]
And performed recollection and *kīrtana*,
Whose worship was the feet of Śrī Rādhā.

In the eight periods of night and day,
He sang the virtues of Rādhā and Kṛṣṇa.
And in recollection he always spent his time.
Only one period did he sleep
And seeing Rādhā and Kṛṣṇa even in dream,
Not one second was spent in vain.

Tapovana

Coming to the bank of the Yamunā,
Residing in lonely Tapovana
You pass your time floating in tears.
(Saying) "O Daughter of King Vṛṣabhānu!
O Empress of the King, gaze on me once
With your compassionate eyes."

Sometimes shouting out loud,
Momentarily filled with so much pain,
Down you fall in a trance.
Absorbed in feeling you speak
tirades of various kinds of raving.
To what do you respond with such clever words?

Hearing those sweet words,
Everyone's heart is soothed.
(We infer that) perhaps you see someone.
Then, loosing that great treasure,
With weeping and piteous cries,
(the next moment) you fall to the ground and wallow.

---

[129] These are the three joints (*sandhyā*) of the day: sunrise, noon, and evening.

একদিন মধ্যাহ্নকালে নৈবেদ্য নষ্ট হৈলে
সহসা করিলা হাহাকার।
আহা বাছা কি করিলি, গাত্র ঘর্ম ফেলে দিলি
কি বিঘ্ন ঘটালি সেবার।।

ভাব নেত্রে দেখি ইহা জানিলেন সত্য তাহা
(ন'দে হতে) পত্র এক আইলা যখন।
সাবধান হৈয়া চিতে আজ্ঞা দেই বিধিমতে
শ্রীরাধাবল্লভের করিতে সেবন।।

প্রেম সরোবরে

প্রেম সরোবরে আসি এক তরুতলে বসি
নাম প্রেমে সদা পড়িভাস।
ধৈরয ধরিতে নার অদর্শনে পুড়িমর
হৃদয়ে বাড়য়ে উচ্ছ্বাস।।

কাঁদি প্রভু রাত্রিদিনে পুড়ি যায় তনু মনে
বিরহে হৈয়া কাতর।
যুগলরূপ মাধুরী বিহ্বল হৈয়া হেরি
গদ্গদ বাক্য সদা স্ফুর।।

দিবানিশি অবিশ্রাম জপে রাধাকৃষ্ণ নাম।
ভাব ভরে করয়ে হুঙ্কার।
ক্ষণে করে ভক্তি পুনঃ অন্তর্মনা অনুক্ষণ
কি কহব ভজন রীতি তাঁর।।

One time in the middle of the day
When the food offering was ruined,
Suddenly he shouted out in distress:
"O child! What have you done?
You've flicked the sweat off of your body!
What an obstacle to service you've created now."

With eyes of love he saw here
What he learned to be true there
When a letter came from Nadīyā.
"In your mind take special care,"
he ordered, "to serve properly
Śrī Rādhāvallabha."

At Premasarovara

Coming to Premasarovara and sitting beneath a tree,
You always glowed in love of the holy name.
Unable to maintain self-control,
You burned when your visions were lost.
In your heart your emotions swelled.

Master wept night and day; mind and body burned,
Scorched by love-in-separation.
Seeing in great agitation the sweetness
Of the beauty of the Divine Couple,
Your words were always choked.

Day and night without cessation,
repeating the names of Rādhā and Kṛṣṇa,
Filled with love he shouted out loud.
One minute he performed *bhakti*
The next he was lost inside.
How can I describe the way of his worship?

উজ্জ্বল প্রেমের তনু   রসে নিরমিলা জনু
    ভাব অলঙ্কৃত সব অঙ্গ।
শুনিতে শ্রীভাগবত   ধৈরয না ধরে চিত
    সাত্ত্বিকে ব্যাপিত সব অঙ্গ।।

আহা কি কণ্ঠের ধ্বনি   কোকিল লজ্জিত শুনি
    ঢালে কিবা সুধাতরঙ্গিণী।
আহা সে মধুর হাসি   উগারে অমিয়া রাশি
    কথা শুনি বিকায় পরাণী।।

প্রেমরস ঘনাবর্ত্ত   বিধাতা করি একত্র
    গড়ি কি পাঠাল ধরাতলে।
একবার যেই হেরে   তার মন প্রাণ হরে
    সদাভাসে সে প্রেমের হিল্লোলে।।

গিরিরাজ তটে ও রাধাকুণ্ডে

গিরিরাজ তটে বসি   কত ভাব পরকাশি
    দেখাইলা ভজনের কালে।
শ্রীকুণ্ডে বাস করি   নিয়ম সেবা ব্রত করি
    আকর্ষিয়া পতিত উদ্ধারিলে।।

His body was of shining love, as if made of *rasa,*
Each limb adorned with ecstatic feeling.
While listening to the *Śrī Bhāgavata,*
Unable to maintain his composure,
Each limb was covered with physical reactions.[130]

Alas! what a voice he had!
Hearing it, the *kokila*[131] was shamed.
Or was it really waves of nectar flowing?
Alas! That sweet laugh!
A mass of ambrosia bursts forth.
Hearing his speech, living beings were sold.

A dense vortex of the *rasa* of love
The creator collected together
And shaping it sent it to earth.
Whoever saw him even once
Had his mind and heart stolen
And forever floated on a wave of love.

At Girirāja Taṭa and Rādhākuṇḍa

Staying at the slope of Girirāja,
How many ecstatic feelings
Did you reveal during your worship?
Residing at Rādhākuṇḍa
Performing the vow of Niyama-sevā,[132]
You drew the fallen to you and lifted them up.

---

[130]These are the eight *sāttvika-bhāvas,* physical manifestations of powerful inner emotions. They are: being stunned, perspiring, horripilation, breaking of the voice, trembling, change of color, tears, and fainting.

[131]The *kokila* is the Indian cuckoo, the beauty of whose singing is praised in Indian love poetry.

[132]This is a vow of austerity that is practiced during the month of Kārtika (October-November.) See the glossary for a discussion of this month-long vow.

চারি সম্প্রদায় যত মহান্তের মিলন হৈত
নিয়মসেবা উদ্যাপনে।
ব্রজবাসী দীন দুখী সবে হৈত মহাসুখী
মহাপ্রসাদ করিয়া সেবনে।।

নবদ্বীপ মণিপুর ঘাটে

আসি সুরধুনী তটে বসিয়া মণিপুর ঘাটে
পাতিলেন নিত্যানন্দের মেলা।
যত দীন-হীন ছিল সবে প্রভু কোল দিল
নির্বিচারে নাম বিতারিলা।।

শ্রীমদ্ভাগবত শ্রীচৈতন্যচরিতামৃত
আর যত যত ভক্তিগ্রন্থ।
সকল ভকত সঙ্গে আলাপ করিয়া রঙ্গে
লীলাকথা ভকতি সিদ্ধান্ত।।

শ্রী নাম বিজ্ঞানাচার্য্যবরে কভু যান ভেটিবারে
কি সে মধুর মিলন রঙ্গ।
দুই প্রভু ভূমে পড়ি দৈন্যে শ্লোক উচ্চারি
ভাবে ভূষিত দোঁহার অঙ্গ।।

এইমত ন'দে পুরে কভু বা নীলাচলপুরে
সঙ্কীর্তন-রঙ্গে সদা ফিরে।
করি হরি-সঙ্কীর্তন মাতাইলা জগজন
ডুবাইলা প্রেমের সাগরে।।

All the leaders of the four Vaiṣṇava communities
used to meet together to observe Niyama-sevā.
The residents of Vraja, the wretched, and the sad,
all became happy at your serving them Mahāprasāda.

In Navadvīpa at Maṇipura Ghāṭa

After coming to the bank of the Ganges
and settling down at Maṇipura Ghāṭa,
he put on a fair for Nityānanda.
All the wretched and those without,
all of them the Master embraced
and without discrimination spread the holy name.

The *Śrīmad Bhāgavata* and Śrī *Caitanya-caritāmṛta,*
along with many other *bhakti*-books
he enjoyed discussing with all the *bhaktas,*
stories of the holy sports and *bhakti* teachings.

Sometimes he went to visit
the *ācārya* of the science of the holy name.[133]
The two masters would fall to the ground
reciting verses in humility,
both their bodies covered with symptoms.[134]

In this manner in Navadvīpa town
Or sometimes in Nīlācala's holy ground,
He always wandered in the joys of *saṅkīrtana.*
Performing *saṅkīrtana* of Hari,
he made like madmen the people of the world
and submerged them in a ocean of love.

[133]Śrī Kānupriya Gosvāmī. He was known through his writings, especially those on the theology of the holy name, as the exemplary teacher of the science of the holy name.
[134]The eight external symptoms of sacred rapture (*bhakti-rasa*).

শ্রীটোটা গোপীনাথে   সমর্পয়ে যবে হাতে
    কৈলা প্রভু সেবার বিধান।
জগতের হিতকারী   জগজন তাপহারী
    প্রভু মোর জগতের প্রাণ।।

হিতব্রতী দানবীর   কৃপালু বিনয়ী ধীর
    গুণ যত কি বলিতে পারি।
বিষয় সৎকুল ছিল   জীব লাগি তেয়াগিল
    ভ্রমে পথে হইয়া ভিখারী।।

অসাধনে গুণনিধি   আনি মিলাওল বিধি
    জীব লাগি কাঁদয়ে সদাই।
মহাপাপী তাপী দেখি   সদা সকরুণ আঁখি
    কোল দিয়ে বলে ভয় নাই।।

প্রভু মোর নিজগুণে   পতিত-পাষণ্ডীজনে
    অবিচারে প্রেম দান কালে।
কি বলিব অদ্ভূত   পশু-পাখি-শিশু কত
    নাচাইলা প্রেমের হিল্লোলে।।

বৈষ্ণব কি অবৈষ্ণব   কি নিন্দুক কি বান্ধব
    কিবা যোগী জ্ঞানী কর্মী ভক্ত।
কি ভিকারী কিবা ধনী   মূরখ বিদ্বান মানি
    গৃহী কিম্বা বিষয়-বিরক্ত।।

কি হিন্দু-ম্লেচ্ছ যবন   কি ভক্ত অভক্তাধম
    সবা-প্রতি সম ব্যবহার।
সুমধুর-সম্ভাষণে   তোষে সদা প্রতিজনে
    প্রভু মোর দয়ার আধার।।

When Ṭoṭā Gopīnāth[135] was given into his hands,
Master arranged for his service.
Wishing the whole world well,
Removing the sufferings of the world's people,
My Master is the life-breath of the world.

Determined to do good, heroically generous,
Compassionate, humble, and steadfast,
(he had) All virtues; what more can one say?
He had dominion and good family
But gave up everything for the living beings
And wandered the world as a beggar.

Without cultivating them, he was a treasury of virtues;
With those was joined destiny.
For the living beings he always wept.
Seeing the great sinners and sufferers
His eyes were full of pity.
Embracing them he bade them have no fear.

My Master through his own virtue
On those fallen and lacking belief
Bestowed divine love without discrimination.
What can I say? It was amazing.
How many animals, birds, and children
Did he make dance in the waves of sacred love?

Whether Vaiṣṇava or non-Vaiṣṇava;
Whether yogī, gnostic, ritualist, or *bhakta*;
Whether beggar or prince; fool, learned, or arrogant;
Whether householder or renouncer of sense objects;

Whether Hindu or *mleccha*;
Whether *bhakta* or worst of the *non-bhaktas* —
He treated them all the same.
With most sweet conversation
he pleased each and every one.
My Master was a reservoir of compassion.

---

[135] Ṭoṭā Gopīnātha is an important image of Kṛṣṇa in Purī. The image was worshiped and cared for by Śrī Gadādhara Paṇḍita who was very dear to Śrī Caitanya. Some accounts have Śrī Caitanya disappearing into the image of Ṭoṭā Gopīnātha.

অসুস্থ্য লীলাছল করি ব্রজ ন’দে হৈতে পুরী
শ্রীহরিদাস সমাধিতে রয়।
পুনঃ নবদ্বীপে আসি শ্রীগুরু কুঞ্জে বসি
অন্তর্মনা হৈয়া দিন যায়।।

শ্রীশ্রীরাধাবল্লভ অঙ্গনে আসি সব ভক্তগণে
নিরন্তর কীর্তন শোনায়।
সেদিন কৃষ্ণনবমী তিথি হৈয়া মঙ্গলারতি
মহাসঙ্কীর্তন শুরু হয়।।

তেরশত নবই সালে গোষ্ঠ সময়কালে
বারই ফাল্গুন শনিবার।
বিনা মেঘে বজ্রাঘাত অকস্মাৎ হৈল পাত
ত্রিভুবন করিয়া আঁধার।।

মামের সহিত প্রাণ কৈলা প্রভু উৎক্রামণ
জয় নিত্যানন্দ রাম শব্দ বলি।
চৌদিকে হাহাকার হরিধ্বনি অনিবার
কোথা গেলা আমা সবা ফেলি।।

দীন চৈতন্যদাস পড়ি কাঁদে হিয়া ধৈর্য নাহি বাঁধে
কাঁহা গেলা করিয়া অনাথ।
কোথা গেলে তোমা পাব হেরি প্রাণ জুড়াইব
ও চরণে বাঁধি লেহ চিত।।

সূচক সমাপ্ত

His illness I take to be a trick of his sport,
From Vraja to Navadvīpa to Purī.
Again he returned to Navadvīpa
And stayed in Śrī Guru Kuñja.
Absorbed inside himself the days passed.

To the courtyard of Śrī Rādhāvallabha
All of the *bhaktas* had come,
Making *kīrtana* heard without stop.
That day, the ninth of the month's dark half,
After the Maṅgala Ārati[136]
The great *saṅkīrtana* started.

In the year of thirteen hundred and ninety[137]
At the time of the daily gathering,[138]
The twelfth day of Phālguna,[139] Saturday,
Without a cloud in the sky
A lightning bolt suddenly fell
Making the three worlds dark.

His life-breath with his heart,
The Master made them cross beyond,
saying, "Jaya Nityānanda Rāma."[140]
In the four directions there were cries
and the sound of "Hari" without pause.
Where has he gone casting all of us aside?

Poor Caitanya Das falls down and weeps;
Self-control cannot bind his heart.
Where have you gone leaving me without protection?
Where can I go to find you again?
Seeing you my life will be healed.
Tie my mind to your feet and take me too.

---

[136]This is the first ritual greeting of the sacred Images of the day. It usually takes place an hour and a half before sunrise.

[137]1984.

[138]According to Binode's previous account Prabhupāda's passing happened at around 8:30 in the morning.

[139]February-March

[140]Glory to Nityānanda Rāma!

Kīrtana Two

প্রভুপাদ ১০৮ শ্রীল তিনকড়ি গোস্বামী মহারাজের সূচক

Prabhupāda 108 Śrīla Tinkaḍi Gosvāmī Mahārāja's Sūcaka

by

Śrī Hṛdayānanda Dāsa Bābājī Mahārāja

শ্রী শ্রী গুরুগৌরাঙ্গবিধুর্জয়তি

(ভজ) শ্রীকৃষ্ণচৈতন্য প্রভু নিত্যানন্দ।
হরে কৃষ্ণ হরে রাম শ্রীরাধে গোবিন্দ।।

জয় রে জয় রে জয় কিশোরীকিশোরানন্দ জয়
প্রাণভরে জয় দাও ভাই
শ্রীকিশোরীকিশোরানন্দ প্রভুর প্রাণভরে জয় দাও ভাই
কিশোরীকিশোরানন্দ সেইট
প্রভু তিনকড়ি নামে খ্যাত, কিশোরীকিশোরানন্দ সেইট
সেই তিনকড়ি প্রভুর জয় দাও
আমার আমার আমার গুণের, সেই তিনকড়ি প্রভুর জয় দাও
নিতাই গৌর প্রেমময়, সেই তিনকড়ি প্রভুর জয় দাও
যেন মূরতি ধরে এসেছিলেন
নিতাই গৌর যুগলভজন জানাইতে, যেন মূরতি ধরে এসেছিলেন
নিতাই গৌর কৃপার মূর্তি মানি
আমার প্রভু তিনকড়ি গোস্বামী, নিতাই গৌর কৃপার মূর্তি মানি

জয় রে জয় রে জয় তিনকড়ি গোস্বামী জয়
নিতাই গৌর কৃপার মূরতি।
নিতাই গৌরাঙ্গ ভজন যুগললীলা স্মরণ
আচরিয়া দেখায় জীব প্রতি।।

Glory to the Guru-Gaurāṅga Moon!

(Worship) Śrī Kṛṣṇacaitanya
Prabhu Nityānanda,
Hare Kṛṣṇa, Hare Rāma,
Śrī Rādhe Govinda!

Glory, glory, glory,
Kiśorīkiśorānanda, glory!

Give a wholehearted "glory," brother,
to Kiśorīkiśorānanda Master.
Give a wholehearted "glory," brother.

Kiśorīkiśorānanda is the one
famed by the name of Master Tinkaḍi.
Kiśorīkiśorānanda is the one.

Give glory to that Master Tinkaḍi!
My, my, my most meritorious,
give glory to that Master Tinkaḍi!
Filled with love for Nitāi and Gaura,
give glory to that Master Tinkaḍi!

It's as though he took a form
to teach the worship of Nitāi and Gaura,
and of the Loving Divine Couple.
It's as though he took a form.

I think he was an embodiment
of the grace of Nitāi and Gaura,
my Master Tinkaḍi Gosvāmī,
I think he was an embodiment
of the grace of Nitāi and Gaura.

Glory, glory, glory
Tinkaḍi Gosvāmī, glory!
Image of Nitāi and Gaura's grace.
Worship of Nitāi and Gaurāṅga and
remembering of the Loving Couple's sports,
he practiced these and showed them to living beings.

নিজে আচরণ করে দেখাইলেন
আমার তিনকড়ি প্রভু　　নিজে আচরণ করে দেখাইলেন
নিতাই গৌরাঙ্গ ভজন　　নিজে আচরণ করে দেখাইলেন
অষ্টকালীনলীলা স্মরণ　　নিজে আচরণ করে দেখাইলেন
গোপীগণের আনুগত্যে　　নিজে আচরণ করে দেখাইলেন

কি বলিব গুণ তার　　শুণে লাগে চমৎকার
যেন ভক্তিদৈন্যের মূরতি।
মৃদুভাষী আনন্দময়　　ভেদাভেদ নাহি রয়
সব প্রতি সমান পিরীতি।।

যাকে দেখে আপন কাছে
মৃদু হেসে বসায় কাছে　　যাকে দেখে আপন কাছে
নিতাই গৌর ভজ উপদেশে　　যাকে দেখে আপন কাছে

জেলা মেদিনীপুর নাম　　মনোহরপুর ধন্যগ্রাম
প্রভু মোর যাঁহা জনমিলা।
শ্রীহরিমোহন গোস্বামী পিতা　　সুরধনী দেবী মাতা
অষ্টম গর্ভে প্রবিষ্ট হইলা।।

অষ্টম গর্ভের অদ্ভুত শক্তি
অনুভব কর ভাই রে　　অষ্টম গর্ভের অদ্ভুত শক্তি
দ্বাপরে এসেছিলেন শ্রীকৃষ্ণ
এই অষ্টম গর্ভেতে　　দ্বাপরে এসেছিলেন শ্রীকৃষ্ণ
পঞ্চম পুরুষার্থ লীলা করতে　　দ্বাপরে এসেছিলেন শ্রীকৃষ্ণ

Practicing himself, he demonstrated it,
my Master Tinkaḍi,
practicing himself, he demonstrated it.
The worship of Nitāi and Gaurāṅga,
practicing himself, he demonstrated it.
The remembering of the eight-period sports
practicing himself, he demonstrated it.
In the train of the cowherd girls,
practicing himself, he demonstrated it.

What can I say about his merits?
When one hears of them one is amazed.
He was like an image of the humility of *bhakti.*
Soft-spoken and filled with bliss.
He made no distinctions;
he showed the same affection to all.

Whomever he sees nearby him
smiling gently he seats beside him,
whomever he sees nearby him.
He teaches the worship of Nitāi and Gaura
to whomever he sees nearby him.

The district named Medinīpura,
the fortune village, Manoharpur,
is where my Master was born.
His father was Śrī Harimohan Gosvāmī;
his mother was Suradhuni Devī.
He entered as their eighth child.

The eighth child has astonishing power.
Realize this, brother
The eighth child has astonishing power.

In the Dvāpara came Śrī Kṛṣṇa.
As this eighth child in the Dvāpara came Śrī Kṛṣṇa.
To perform the sport of the fifth goal of humankind
in the Dvāpara came Śrī Kṛṣṇa.

(আবার) পঞ্চম পুরুষার্থ প্রেম দান করতে
এলেন আবার গৌর স্বরূপে
রাধাভাব কান্তি ধরে শ্রীগোবিন্দ, এলেন আবার গৌর স্বরূপে

এইত হল দুই ঈশ্বরের তত্ত্ব
অষ্টম গর্ভে আসা তাৎপর্য এইত হল দুই ঈশ্বরের তত্ত্ব

আবার এলেন দুই ভক্ত স্বরূপে
এই অষ্টম গভে জনম হয়ে -
আবার এলেন দুই ভক্ত স্বরূপে
শ্রীল রামদাস আর তিনকড়ি গোস্বামী -
আবার এলেন দুই ভক্ত স্বরূপে
সেই পঞ্চম পুরুষার্থ প্রেম জানাবার তরে -
আবার এলেন দুই ভক্ত স্বরূপে
একজন নামকীর্তন দ্বারে, একজন ভজন দ্বারে -
আবার এলেন দুই ভক্ত স্বরূপে

বড় অপরূপ কথা ভাই রে
ভগবান শ্রীমুখে বলেছেন:

আমা হৈতে আমার ভক্তের পূজা বড়।
বেদে ভাগবতে এই কথা কৈল দৃঢ়।। (চৈচ, ?)

নইলে কে বা জানাবে
আমার ভজন কৌশল নইলে কে বা জানাবে
আমার প্রাপ্তির উপায় নইলে কে বা জানাবে

(Again) to give the fifth goal of humankind, divine love.

He came in the form of Gaura;
Śrī Govinda, assuming the feelings and coloring of Rādhā,
in the form of Gaura he came again.

This was the truth about the two lords,
the purpose for coming as the eighth child.
This is the truth about the two lords.

Again he came in the form of two *bhaktas*
taking birth as the eighth child.
Again he came in the form of two *bhaktas*,
Śrīla Rāmadāsa and Tinkaḍi Gosvāmī.
Again he came in the form of two *bhaktas*.
To make known that fifth goal of humankind, divine love,
Again he came in the form of two *bhaktas*.
One by means of *kīrtana* of the holy names,
One by means of private worhsip,
again he came in the form of two *bhaktas*.

A most amazing thing, o brother.
The Lord himself has said:

Worship of my *bhakta*
is greater than worship of me.
This topic is firmly stated
in the Vedas and *Bhāgavata*.[141]

Otherwise, who would have taught me?
My expertise in private worship,
otherwise, who would have taught me?
My means to attainment,
otherwise, who would have taught me?

---

[141] Śrī Kṛṣṇadāsa Kavirāja, *Caitanya-caritāmṛta*, ?

আমি ত আমার কথা বলিতে পারি না
আমায় ব্যক্ত করে ভক্তজনা -
আমি ত আমার কথা বলিতে পারি না

তাই এলেন তিনকড়ি নাম ধরে
কলিজীবে ভজননিষ্ঠা জানাবার তরে -
তাই এলেন তিনকড়ি নাম ধরে
একমাত্র সাধ্য নিতাই গৌর জানাইতে -
তাই এলেন তিনকড়ি নাম ধরে

সর্ব অবতার সার গৌরহরি
কলিজীবের একমাত্র সাধ্যনিধি সর্ব অবতার সার গৌরহরি
রাইকানু মিলিত তনু সর্ব অবতার সার গৌরহরি

একমাত্র সাধ্য গৌরচরণ
জানাইলা তিনকড়ি প্রভু রতন একমাত্র সাধ্য গৌরচরণ
(মাতন)

অষ্টমগর্ভে প্রকট হইলা
তেরশত তের সনে মাঘী পূর্ণিমা শুভক্ষণে
জীবে পূর্ণ কৃপা করিবারে।
পূর্ণিমা চাঁদের মত হইলেন আবির্ভূত
(মাতা) সুরধনী কোল আলোকয়ে।।

(প্রভু) নিত্যানন্দ শাখা বংশধর মা জাহ্নবা পরিবার
নাম শ্রীগুণনিধি গোস্বামী।
তাঁর বংশের ধারা (যেন) নিত্যানন্দ প্রেমে গড়া
(সেই) বংশে জন্ম তিনকড়ি গোস্বামী।।

বাল্য হইতে প্রেমময় সদাই আনন্দময়
অনাসক্ত সংসারে উদাসীন।
করে বিদ্যা অধ্যয়ন সদা যেন অন্যমন
কারে অন্তরে করে অন্বেষণ।।

But I am not able to talk about me
The bhaktas have revealed things to me.
But I am not able to talk about me.

Therefore, he came taking the name Tinkaḍi
to teach firmness in private worhsip to Kali's living beings.
Therefore, he came taking the name Tinkaḍi
to teach the only objects of worship, Nitāi and Gaura.
Therefore, he came taking the name Tinkaḍi.

The essence of all descents is Gaurahari,
the treasure of goals for Kali's living beings;
the essence of all descents is Gaurhari.
Whose body is Rādhā and Kṛṣṇa joined,
the essence of all descents is Gaurhari.

The only goal is the feet of Gaura
Tinkaḍi taught, that jewel of Masters;
the only goal is the feet of Gaura.

He appeared as the eighth child
in *sana* thirteen hundred and thirteen (1907 C.E.),
at an auspicious moment on the fullmoon day of Māgha,
to bestow his full grace upon livings beings.
Like the full moon he appeared
lighting up the lap of (his mother) Suradhuni.

A lineage holder of (Master) Nityānanda's branch
and a close companion of Mā Jāhnavā
was Śrī Guṇanidhi Gosvāmī by name.
The current of his descendents was shaped by love of Nityānanda.
In that family Tinkaḍi Gosvāmī was born.

From childhood he was full of love and always joyful
and detached, indifferent to mundane life.
He cultivated knowledge as if always absent-minded.
Who was he seaching for within?

পিতা শ্রীহরিমোহন আনন্দের নিমগন
পুত্র তিনকড়িকে মন্ত্র দিল।
গৌর কৃষ্ণ মন্ত্র পেয়ে আনন্দে ভরিল হৃদয়
নামপ্রেমে বিভোর হইল।।

কিছুই ভাল লাগে না রে
সংসার সুখবিলাস কিছুই ভাল লাগে না রে
সদা রহে অন্তর্মনা কিছুই ভাল লাগে না রে

পুত্রের এই ভাব দেখি পিতা হলেন মনে দুঃখী
ভাবে পুত্র সন্ন্যাসী হয়ে যাবে।
কেমনে রাখিবে তারে তাই মনে বিচার করে
স্থির কৈলেন বিবাহ দিতে।।

বাল্য হইতে মাতৃহারা পিতার নয়ন তারা
তাই মনে মনে ভয় করি।
গৃহী করে রাখিবারে বিবাহ দিলেন তারে
(পিতা) হরিমোহন আনন্দ করি।।

প্রথম যৌবনকালে বিবাহবন্ধন ছলে
পিতা তারে সংসারী করিল।
গৌরপ্রেমের পাগল যে বল তারে বাঁধিবে কে
লোকাচারে বিবাহ করিল।।

কেবল পিতার সুখের তরে দার পরিগ্রহ করে
কিন্তু ভজনে নিমগ্ন সদাই।
নির্জনে সদা বসিয়া কাঁদে যে ব্যাকুল হইয়া
দয়া কর হা গৌর নিতাই।।

His father Śrī Harimohana was submerged in joy
when he gave his son Tinkaḍi the mantras
Receiving the Gaura and Kṛṣṇa mantras,
his heart was filled with bliss.
He became lost in the love of the holy names.

O. he did not like them at all,
the pleasured sports of worldly life.
O, he did not like them at all.
He always remained directed within.
O. he did not like them at all.

Seeing that condition in his son,
his father became sad in his heart.
"By his feelings my son will become a renunciant.
How can I keep him from that?"
That he considered inside his heart.
He decided then to give him in marriage.

From his childhood he was without his mother,
that star of his father's eyes.
Therefore, in his heart of hearts he feared.
Making him a householder, to keep him
he gave him away in marriage;
so did his father Harimohana happily.

In the first blush of his youth
by the contrivance of the bonds of marriage
his father made him a householder.
But one who is mad in love for Gaura
who will be able to tie him down?
By the ways of the world he was married.

Only for the pleasure of his father did he take wife.
But he was always absorbed in worhsip.
Always sitting apart he wept in distress,
saying, "Oh Gaura and Nitāi! Show me your grace!

(হায়) কুলের দেব প্রভু নিতাই এ অধমে দেখ চাই
এ সংসার-কূপ তুলিয়া।
শকতি সঞ্চারিয়া তোমার গৌর ভজাইয়া
রাখ যুগলচরণে বাঁধিয়া।।

আমার কুলের দেব নিতাই
বসুধাজাহ্নবার প্রাণ আমার কুলের দেব নিতাই
অধমতারণ পতিতপাবন আমার কুলের দেব নিতাই
এবার আমায় দয়া কর

কেউ নেই প্রভু তোমা বিনে
এ পতিতে উদারিতে কেউ নেই প্রভু তোমা বিনে

হা প্রভু নিতাই দয়া কর
মায়াবন্ধন ঘুচাও আমার হা প্রভু নিতাই দযা কর (মাতন)

এইমতে লোকাচারে (শ্রী) পিতা সুখের তরে
কিছুদিন সংসারে রহিল।
শ্রীবৃন্দাবন গোস্বামী নামে এক পুত্র হইল শুভক্ষণে
(তার) কিছুদিনে পত্নী বিয়োগ হইল।।

পত্নী বিয়োগের পরে এই সুযোগ মনে করে
তীর্থভ্রমণে বাহির হইল।
সারা ভারত করে ভ্রমণ কত মহাত্মা করি দরশন
চার ধাম দর্শন করিল।।

সর্বতীর্থ করি ভ্রমণ তিরপিত নহে মন
শেষে উপনীত বৃন্দাবনে।
বৃন্দাবন দরশনে নিত্যলীলা স্মরণে
প্রেমধারা বহে দু নয়নে।।

"Alas! my family's deity, Prabhu Nitāi!
I beg you glance on this low person.
Raise me from this well of mundane life
and filling me with your power
make me worship your Gaura.
Binding me, keep me at the Divine Couple's feet.

"O My family's deity, Nitāi,
the life breath of Vasudhā and Jāhnavā,
O my family's deity, Nitāi.
Deliverer of the lowly, purifier of the fallen,
give me your grace just once.

"There is no one else beside you Master
to save this fallen soul.
There is no one else beside you Master.

"O Master Nitāi show me your grace.
Undo these bonds of *māyā*.
O Master Nitāi show me your grace."

In this way, in accordance with the ways of the world
and for the satisfaction of his father
he remained in family life for a while.
By the name of Śrī Vṛndāvana Candra
a son was born at an auspcious time
and a little while later his wife passed away.

After the passing of his wife, he,
considering it a good opportunity,
went out wandering to the holy places.
While wandering all over Bhārata,
he met so many great souls
and saw the four holy abodes.

After visiting all the holy places,
his mind was still not satisfied.
Finally, he came to Vṛndāvana.
When he saw Vṛndāvana
and remembered the eternal sports,
streams of love flowed from his eyes.

শ্রীগোবিন্দ গোপীনাথ মদনমোহন সাথ
সাত দেবালয় দরশন করি।
রাধাকুণ্ড শ্যামকুণ্ড হেরি দু নয়নে বহে বারি
পরিক্রমা কৈল গোবর্দ্ধন গিরি।।

নন্দগ্রাম বরষাণে যাবট দ্বাদশ বনে
ব্রজবন ভ্রমণ করিল।
ব্রজভ্রমণ করিতে করিতে গোবর্দ্ধন গোবিন্দ কুণ্ডে
সিদ্ধ মনোহর দাস দর্শন পাইল।।

ব্রজের মহাত্মা হেরি প্রভু মোর তিনকড়ি
স্থির কৈলেন মনে মনে।
গুরুরূপে করি বরণ ধরিয়া যুগল চরণ
কাঁদিয়া বলয়ে শ্রীচরণে।।

এ অধমে কৃপা করি ভেক্ষাশ্রয় দান করি
সংসারবন্ধন ছিন্ন করেন (?)।।
শ্রীচরণে সেবা দিয়া নিতাই গৌর ভজাইয়া
দাস করে রাখ চিরতরে।

তিনকড়ি কথা শুনে সিদ্ধ বাবা বলিলেন।
শুন মোর কথা স্থির চিত্তে।
নিত্যানন্দ বংশে জন্ম এ দেহ করহ যত্ন
(বহু) জীব উদ্ধার হবে তোমা হইতে।

আমার আদেশ ধরে দার পরিগ্রহ করে
ভগবৎ ভজন সংসার গড়িবে।
যারা গৃহী সংসারী তোমার আদর্শ হেরি
নিতাই গৌর ভজন করিবে।।

Śrī Govinda, Gopīnātha
along with Madanamohana,
he visited the seven temples.
Seeing Rādhākuṇḍa and Śyāmakuṇḍa,
tears flowed from his eyes.
And he cicumambulated Giri Govardhana.

Nandagrāma, Barṣāṇa, Yābaṭa,
and the twelve sacred groves —
he wandered about all of Vraja's forests.
Wandering around the land of Vraja,
at Govindakuṇḍa near Govardhana,
he had a holy sight of Manohara Dāsa Siddha.

"Show your grace to this lowly one
and give me shelter as a renunciant.
Cut to pieces my bonds to material life.
Give me service at your lotus feet
and make me worship Nitāi and Gaura.
Keep me forever as your servant."

Hearing these words of Tinkaḍi,
Siddha Bābā said in reply:
"Listen to my words, steadying your mind.
You are born in Nityānanda's family;
take good care of this body.
From you many living beings will be lifted up.

"Follow my orders and take another wife.
You should mold your mundane life to the worship of Bhagavān.
Those who are householders, engaged in material life
seeing your example, will worship Nitāi and Gaura.

কাদা হতে তুলতে গেলে
নিজেকে কাদায় নামিতে হবে কাদা হতে তুলতে গেলে

সব তো দেখাইয়া গেছেন
প্রভু নিতাই প্রাণ গৌর সব তো দেখাইয়া গেছেন
সংসারী জীবনেতে যেমন ভজন সব তো দেখাইয়া গেছেন

তুমি ভগবৎ সংসার গড়ে তোল
ভয় নাই লিপ্ত হবে না তাতে সব তো দেখাইয়া গেছেন

সব আসা পূর্ণ হবে
সংসারে থেকে ভজন কর সব আসা পূর্ণ হবে
কলিজীব উদ্ধার হবে সব আসা পূর্ণ হবে

সিদ্ধবাবার আদেশ পেয়ে পুনঃ ফিরে এসে গৃহে
দ্বিতীয় দার গ্রহণ করিলেন।
শ্রীসরস্বতী দেবী নাম পত্নী রূপে করি গ্রহণ
ভগবৎ সংসার কৈলেন গঠন।।

নামমাত্র সংসারাশ্রম সদা ভাবে নিমগন
তিন লক্ষ নাম জপ করে।
দীন হীন জন দেখি সদা সকরুণ আঁখি
কৃষ্ণমন্ত্র জপ উপদেশ করে।
পেয়েছ দুর্লভ জন্ম কেন কাটাও অকারণ
আর কি মনুষ্য জন্ম হবে।।

চৌরাশী লক্ষ যোনি ভ্রমণের পরে জানি
এ জন্ম বৃথা না কাটাবে।
অনিত্য নশ্বর দেহ শৃগাল কুক্কুর খাদ্য এহ
মলমূত্র পূঁজ পূর্ণ দেহে।।

"If one wants to pick someone up from the mud
one will have to get down in the mud,
if one wants to pick someone up from the mud.

"You are demonstrating everything,
Prabhu Nitāi and our life-breath, Gaura,
you are demonstrating everything.
The way one should worship in household life
you are showing everything.

Establish a model for *bhagavān*-centered household life
Fear not, you will not be affected by that,
you are demonstrating everything.

All your hopes will be fulfilled;
worship from within household life,
all your hope will be fulfilled.
Living beings of Kali will be lifted up,
all your hopes will be fulfilled."

Receiving the instructions of Siddha Bābā,
he again returned to his home
and married his second wife.
Śrī Sarasvatī Devī by name,
he accepted her as his wife
and created a *bhagavān*-centered household life.

It was a householder stage only in name:
he was always absorbed in divine emotion.
He chanted three *lakhs* of holy names a day.
Seeing wretched and miserable people
his eyes were always full of compassion.
He taught chanting of the *kṛṣṇa-mantra.*
"You have attained this rare human birth;
why do you pass it without purpose?
Will a human birth occur again?

"After wandering though eight million,
four hundred thousand wombs,
you should not waste this birth.
This body is temporary and destructible,
food for jackals and hounds.
In this body is a mass of urine and feces.

এ অনিত্য দেহদ্বারে নিত্যবস্তু পাবার তরে
নিতাই গৌর ভজ শ্রীগুরু আশ্রয়ে।
এই কলিযুগের ধর্ম হরিনাম সংকীর্তন
যুগাবতার শ্রীগৌরাঙ্গহরি।।

শ্রীগুরু আশ্রয় করে নাম কর প্রাণ ভরি
নিশ্বাসেতে বিশ্বাস না করি।
স্ত্রীপুত্র পরিবার বল আমার আমার
শেষ দিনে বাঁধিয়া পোড়াবে।
এ সংসারের অনিত্যতা দেখে যেন বুঝ না তো
দিন রাতে ভজ ভাই সবে।।

এই মত উপদেশ দানে কত দীনহীন জনে
শ্রীচরণে আশ্রয় দান দিল।
গৌরকৃষ্ণ মন্ত্র দানে মাতাইল নাম প্রেমে
শত শত আশ্রয় লইল।।

সংসারেতে অনাসক্ত তীব্রবৈরাগ্যব্রত
গৃহ ছাড়ি পুন সে চলিলা।
বহুতীর্থভ্রমণ করি ক্রমে এল নীলাচলপুরী
শ্রীজগন্নাথ দরশন কৈলা।।

আসি ঝাঁজপীটা মঠে রহিলেন অনুরাগে
(শ্রী) রামদাস বাবাজী সঙ্গ তরে।
দুই জনা দোঁহারে হেরি দু নয়নে বহে বারি
দোঁহে ভাসে আনন্দ অন্তরে।।

"To obtain the eternal substance
by means of this impermanent body
worship Nitāi and Gaura
under a blessed guru's guidance.

"The religious norm for the Age of Kali
is *saṅkīrtana* of the names most holy
and the age's descent is Śrī Gaurāṅga Hari.

"Finding shelter with a blessed guru
recite the names filling your breath;
don't rely on breathing.

"Wife, sons, and family,
whom you call *yours* again and again,
on the last day will bind you and have you burned.

"This material life is impermanent;
though you see it, you seem not to believe it.
All of you, brothers, worship day and night."

By giving this kind of instruction
how many folks, wretched and poor,
did he give shelter to at his feet?

By giving the Gaura and Kṛṣṇa *mantras*
he intoxicated them with love of the holy names.
Hundreds and hundreds took shelter with him.

Not attached to household life
and dedicated to intense renunciation,
he left home again and went traveling.

Visiting many holy places,
eventually he arrived in Nīlācala
and had a holy sight of Śrī Jagannātha.

He came to Jhāñjapīṭā Maṭha
and stayed there with great enthusiasm
to associate with Bābājī Śrī Rāmadāsa.

When the two men saw each other,
tears of joy flowed from their eyes
and bliss flooded their two hearts.

শ্রীরামদাস বাবাজী সঙ্গে গৌরলীলা কীর্তন রঙ্গে
ঝালি অর্পণ কীর্তন শুনিলা।
রথাগ্রে গৌরাঙ্গলীলা শুনিয়া ব্যাকুল হিয়া
কিছু দিন তথা বাস কৈলা।।

গৌরগুণ সঙরিয়ে গৌরহরি দেখবে বলে
নীলাচল হইতে চলিলা।
হা নিতাই গৌর বলে কাঁদিয়া কাঁদিয়া চলে
নবদ্বীপধামে প্রবেশিলা।।

সেই নবদ্বীপ ধামে ফলাহারী বাবা নামে
শ্রী গৌর গোপীদাস বাবাজী রহে তাতে।
(বিগ্রহ) নিমাইচাঁদ সেবা দরশনে মনোলোভা
সেবা সমর্পণ কৈলা হাতে।

উপযুক্ত পাত্র দেখে
নিমাইচাঁদ সেবা সমর্পিল উপযুক্ত পাত্র দেখে

সেই সেবা ভার লয়ে অতি আনন্দ হৃদয়ে।
শ্রী তিনকড়ি গোসাঞি আমার।
প্রাচীন রাধাবল্লভ সেবা এক গোস্বামী হইতে পাই তাহা
সেই আশ্রমে স্থাপন কৈল তার।।

যত সেবা অচল দেখে মেগে লয় মন দুঃখে
পরিপাটী সেবা করয় তার।
এই মত কত সেবা উদ্ধার করিল যে বা
একে একে শুন পরিচয়।।

In Śrī Rāma Dāsa Bābājī's company,
while enjoying muscial praise of Gaura's sports,
he heard the song of the swing festival offering.
And hearing of Gaurāṅga's deeds before the chariot
most perturbed became his heart.
And there he stayed a few days more.

Remembering Gaura's many merits
and saying he will see Gaurahari,
he departed from Nīlācala.
Saying, "O, Nitāi! O, Gaura!"
he wept and wept as he traveled
and at last arrived in Navadvīpa.

In that holy town of Navadvīpa,
lived Śrī Gauragopī Dāsa Bābā
known also as Phalāhārī Bābā.[142]
He served Nimāicānda;[143]
his heart's desire was to see [the holy land].
He handed his service into Tinkaḍi Gosvāmī's hands.

Finding such a suitable recipient
he offered him Nimāicānda's service,
finding such a suitable recipient.

He took responsiblity for that service
with a most gladdened heart
my Tinkaḍi Gosvāmī.
The service of old Rādhāvallabha images
he received from a Gosvāmi there
and established them in his *āśrama*.

All the services he saw that were not current
he asked for with a saddened heart.
His service he performed with skill.
In this way he saved so many services.
Hear an introduction to them one by one.

---

[142]i.e., Carpophagous (fruit-eating) Bābā.
[143]The name of his sacred image of Śrī Caitanya.

বৃন্দাবনে তপোবনে গুঞ্জনবিহারী নামে
সুচারু সেবা করাইলা।
অক্ষয়বটে রামসীতা দেবী অটল যুগল তার
(বৃন্দাবনে) মুরারিমোহনে সেবা লইলা।।

গোবর্ধন শ্যামসুন্দর রাধাকুণ্ডে গিরিধর
রাধাবল্লভ মনোহরপুরে।
স্থানে স্থানে সেবা লইল সুচারু সেবা করাইল
সেবা দেখে আনন্দ অন্তরে।।

নীলাচল ধাম যাইয়া টোটাগোপীনাথে চাহিয়া
প্রেমাবেশে বিভোর হইল।
গদাধর সেবিত গৌরহরি প্রতিষ্ঠিত
যাঁর অঙ্গে গৌর প্রবেশিল।।

সেই টোটা গোপীনাথে রহিলেন সে টোটাতে
চটের বসন পরিয়া।
তালপাতার কুটির করি রহিলেন মৌন ধরি
নাম জপে কাঁদিয়া কাঁদিয়া।।

গৌর-গোপীনাথের লীলা- ভোগেতে হল বিভোলা
দিনরাত ভেদ জ্ঞান গেল।
আশ্রিতগণ তাহা হেরি সবার নয়নে বারি
গুরু-গৌর প্রেমেতে মাতিল।।

সেই গোপীনাথের সেবা নানাবিঘ্ন দেখি তাহা
সেবাভার গ্রহণ করিল।
গোস্বামীদের বুঝাইয়া সেবা পরিপাটী কৈল
আনন্দেতে হৃদয় ভরিল।।

In Tapovana in Vṛndāvana
for an image named Guñjanavihārī
he created a service most pleasing.
In Akṣayabaṭa is Rāmasītā Devī,
unshakable Divine Loving Couple of his.
(In Vṛndāvana) he took on
the service of Murārimohan.

In Govardhana is Śyāmasundara,
in Rādhākuṇḍa is Giridhara,
and Rādhāvallabha is in Manoharpur.
In various places he took on service
and set it up most pleasingly.
Seeing that service, joy fills one's heart.

Going to Nīlācala, he gazed at Ṭoṭāgopīnātha
and became lost in a trance of love.
Served by Gadādhara and established by Gaurahari,
into Ṭoṭāgopīnātha's body Gaura entered.

With Ṭoṭāgopīnātha he stayed in that garden,
wearing burlap as his cloth.
Building a cottage of palm leaves,
he stayed there observing silence
and weeping as he chanted the holy names.

Enjoying the sports of Gaura and Gopīnātha,
he was lost in trance, not distinguishing day or night.
His disciples watching that, everyone filling up their eyes,
became maddened by love of Śrī Guru and Gaura.

Seeing many obstacles in the service of Gopīnātha
he accepted the responsibility of that service.
Making the Gosvāmīs understand,
he created order in the service
and his heart was filled with joy.

যে যে স্থানে ভজন কৈল মহাতীর্থ স্থান হৈল
অদ্যাবধি স্থান বিদ্যমান।
রাধাকুণ্ড শ্যাম সরোবর বর্ষাণা পাবনসরোবর
গোবর্ধন আর কোকিলাবন।
রতনকুণ্ড চন্দোরী বড় বৈঠান রাসস্থলী
পাণ্ডৰগন সেরগড় স্থান।।

দুর্বাসাকুণ্ড পাণ্ডৰবন হরিয়াল চামেলিবন
বিলাসগড় আর নন্দগ্রাম।
পরমাদ্বয় ব্রহ্মাণ্ডঘাটে আদিবদ্রী শ্যামঘাটে
বিলাসকুণ্ড উনানী পেষাই গ্রাম।।

কদম্বখাটী আদি স্থান বৃন্দাবন ভজনস্থান
(আর) নবদ্বীপ ভজনস্থান।
মণিপুর ঘাটস্থিত রাধবল্লভ আশ্রম বিরাজিত
গঙ্গাতীরে প্রাচীন মাযাপুর স্থান।।

এই সব স্থানে ঘুরি সাধনভজন করি
কলিজীবে শিক্ষা কৈল দান।
সাধন ভজন বিনা সাধ্যবস্তু তো মিলে না
আচরণ করি শিক্ষা দিল।
তীব্র বৈরাগ্য করি অষ্টকাল লীলা স্মরি
ভাব-প্রেমে বিভোর হইল।
শত শত জীবগণে বিকাইল শ্রীচরণে
স্নেহভালবাসার মুগ্ধ হইয়া।
সবা প্রতি সমভাব নাহি ভেদাভেদ ভাব
নাম দিল করুণা করিয়া।

Those places in which he did private worship
have now become great holy places
and even today those places exist.
Rādhākuṇḍa, Śyāmasarovara,
Barṣāṇa, Pābanasarovara,
Govardhana and Kokilavana, Ratnakuṇḍa
Candorī, Baḍa Baithāna, Rāsathalī,
the place called Pāṇḍava Seragaṛa,

Durvāsākuṇḍa, Pāṇḍavavana,
Hariyāla, Cāmelivana, Vilāsagaṛa,
Paramādvaya, Brahmāṇḍaghāṭa,
Ādibadrī, Śyāmaghāṭa,
Vilāsakuṇḍa, Unānī, Peṣāi Grāma,

Kadambakhāṭī and so forth
are places where he did private worship in Vṛndāvana.
His private worship places in Navadvīpa are
the Rādhāvallabha *āśrama*
situated at Maṇipura Ghāṭa
and on the bank of the Gaṅgā, Old Māyāpura.

In all these places he performed private worship
and gave instruction to Kali's living beings.
"Without practice and private worship
the objective cannot be reached," [he said.]
Performing it himself, he gave instruction.
Practicing intense renunciation
and remembering the sports of the eight periods,
he become lost in divine love and deep emotion.
Hundreds and hundreds of living beings
he accepted at his blessed feet,
engrossed in affection and love for them.
Towards all he was equally disposed;
he had no discriminatory feelings.
He bestowed the holy names with compassion.

কিবা ধনী কিবা কাঙ্গাল সবারে করিয়া কোল
(বলে) ভাই পেয়েছ মানব জনম।
চৌরাশী লক্ষ যোনি ভ্রমণ করিয়া তুমি
পাইয়াছো ভজ শ্রীকৃষ্ণচরণ।
জীব নিত্য কৃষ্ণ দাস তাঁহার চরণে আশ
তাহা বিনা বিগলে জনম।।

এবার না ভজ তবে পুনঃ চৌরাশী যে ভ্রমিবে
পশুপক্ষী কীট হীন জনম।।

ভজ ভজ ওহে ভাই প্রাণের গৌর নিতাই
পতিতপাবন দয়াময়।
ব্রজের কৃষ্ণ বলাই নদীয়াতে গৌর নিতাই
মার খেয়ে নাম প্রেম বিলায।
শ্রী গুরু চরণে রতি সেই সে উত্তমা গতি
শ্রী গুরু পদাশ্রিত হইয়া।
আশ্রয় লইয়া ভজে তারে কৃষ্ণ নাহি ত্যজে
ভবসিন্ধু যায় সে তরিয়া।।

এইমত উপদেশ কত কলিহত জীবে
প্রেমধনে ধনী করাইল।
সাতাত্তর বৎসর ধরে ভারত ভ্রমণ করে
আনন্দেতে মাটি মাতাইল।।

Whether rich or whether destitute,
he embraced one and all, saying:
"Brother, you have attained a human birth.
You gained it after wandering through
eighty-four hundred thousand wombs
Now, worship Śrī Kṛṣṇa's feet.
The living being is Kṛṣṇa's eternal servant.
All it wants is at his feet. Without that this birth is wasted.

"If this time you do not worship,
you will wander the eight-four again,
in lesser births like animals, birds and bugs.

"Worship, worship, O brother mine,
your life-breath's Gaura and Nitāi,
uplifters of the fallen, most compassionate.
Vraja's Kṛṣṇa and Balāi
are in Nadīyā Gaura and Nitāi.
Even when struck[144] they spread holy name and love.
Attachment to the blessed guru's lotus feet
is the ultimate goal, for one who is sheltered there.
One who seeks that shelter and worships,
Śrī Kṛṣṇa does not reject. Such a one
crosses over the ocean of becoming."

With the kind of instruction above
how many Kali-troubled living beings
did he enrich with the treasure of love?
For seventy-eight years he roamed Bhārata
and made the earth drunk with joy.

---

[144]Nitāi was attacked and struck by the two brothers, Jagāi and Mādhāi.

আরো অপরূপ কথা দুই মহাপুরুষের এক কথা
সাতাত্তর বর্ষ ধরাধামে।
নামপ্রেম দান কৈল কলিজীবে উদ্ধারিল
বাবাজী রামদাস তিনকড়ি দুজনে।।

শেষে নীলাচলে যাইয়া হরিদাস মঠে রইলা
ভক্তবাৎসল্য লীলা সঙরিয়া।
হরিদাস ঠাকুরের প্রতিজ্ঞা কাজীর শাসন কথা
(যদি) খণ্ড খণ্ড প্রাণ যায় চলিয়া।।

এইসব লীলাকথা হৃদয়ে বাড়য়ে ব্যথা
গৌর গৌর বলে বুক ভাসে।
মনে মনে আর্তি বাড়ে গৌরলীলা মনে পড়
প্রার্থনা করয়ে অভিলাষে।।

হা গৌর প্রভু নিতাই করুণা করহ এই
আর দূরে না রাখিবে ফেলে।
কত যে করুণা কৈলা কত মত নাচাইলে
এ বার চরণ নিকটে লেহ তুলি।।

এই মত বিরহ বাড়িল নীলাচল হৈতে চলিল
নবদ্বীপধামে উপনীত।
মণিপুর ঘাট স্থিত রাধাবল্লভ বিরাজিত
নিজাশ্রমে করিলেন স্থিতি।।

There is another amazing part of this saga:
the same story for two great saints.
Seventy-eight years in this earthly abode,
they gave love for the holy name
and uplifted the living beings of Kali,
Bābājī Rāmadāsa and Tinkaḍi.

In the final days he went to Nīlācala
and stayed at the Haridāsa Maṭha,
recalling those sports of affection to *bhaktas*.
The pledge of Haridāsa Ṭhākura,
the story of the Kazi's punishment;[145]
in case his life, broken into pieces, departs.

All of those stories of divine sports
increased the pain in his heart.
Saying, "Gaura, Gaura," his chest he drenched with tears.
In his heart of hearts his distress increased;
Gaura's deeds came to his mind
and he prayed with intense desire:

"O Gaura, O Prabhu Nitāi, show this one your grace.
Don't cast me far away any more.
How much compassion you have shown me
and how many the ways you've made me dance!
Now lift me up close to your feet."

This kind of torment of separation increased
and from Nīlācala he departed.
To Navadvīpa he was taken.
There at Maṇipura Ghāṭa,
where Rādhāvallabha shines bright,
in his own *āśrama* he stayed.

---

[145]This refers to the punishment given to Haridāsa Ṭhākura by a Muslim ruler for taking up Vaiṣṇava practices.

সদা বিরহে গরগর মুখে নিতাই গৌরকিশোর
রাধবল্লভ বদন হেরিয়া।
আর ধৈর্য্য নাহি ধরে নিত্যলীলায় যাবার তরে
রহিলেন মৌন হইয়া।।

তেরশত নব্বুই সনে বারোই ফাল্গুন শনি দিনে
প্রভাতে যাহার আকর্ষণে।
শ্রীবাস অঙ্গন হইতে শ্রীজীব গোস্বামী নামেতে
উপনীত প্রভুর দরশনে।।

তেঁহ তিনকড়ি প্রভুরে মনে গুরু বুদ্ধি করে
তে কারেণে নিকট আসিল।
দেখেন অন্তিম কাল ব্যাকুল হইল প্রাণে
অর্ত্তিতে অঙ্গ স্পর্শ কইল।।

প্রভু আমার তিনকড়ি শ্রীজীব গোস্বামী হেরি
মনে বড় আনন্দ হইল।
যেন প্রাণের নিতাই আমার যাইবার লাগে তার
প্রিয়জনে পাঠাইয়া দিল।।

নিত্য লীলাস্থলী শ্রীবাস অঙ্গন সদা রাস সংস্কীর্তন
প্রাণ গৌর নিত্যানন্দ লইয়া।
কৈলেন রাস সংকীর্তন সঙ্গে সব প্রিয়জন
ব্রজভাবে বিভোর হইয়া।।]

He was always overwhelmed in separation;
on his lips was "Nitāi, Gaurakiśora,"
gazing on Rādhāvallabha's face.
He no longer could maintain patience
to enter into that eternal sport;
he kept himself in silence.

In the year thirteen hundred and ninety,
the twelth of Phālguna, Saturday,[146]
being drawn by him in the morning,
from Śrīvāsa Aṅgana Śrījīva Gosvāmī
came to visit the Master Tinkaḍi.

Master Tinkaḍi he thought of as his *guru*
and for that reason he came to him.
Seeing that the end was near
his life-breath became agitated.
In distress he touched Tinkaḍi's body.

My Master Tinkaḍi,
seeing Śrījīva Gosvāmī,
felt great joy in his heart:
"It was as if my life-breath Nitāi
to start me on my way to him
has sent me one of his own dear friends."

Śrīvāsa Aṅgana is an eternal place of sport.
There is always singing about the Circle Dance (Rāsa)
along with our life-breaths, Gaura and Nityānanda.
There, all of their dear friends together
perform congregational singing about the Circle Dance
becoming lost in the feelings of Vraja.

---

[146]The English year was 1984. Phālguna is the eleventh Indic month lasting from about the middle of February to the middle of March.

(ব্রজের) নিভৃত কুঞ্জের নিভৃত কুঞ্জ নবদ্বীপ রূপে ব্যক্ত
যোগপীঠ শ্রীবাস অঙ্গন।
বৃন্দাবন রাস কেলী নদীয়ায় কীর্তন কেলী
নন্দ নন্দন শচীর নন্দন।।

কিছু ভিন্ন ভেদ নাই
তারাই এরা, এরাই তারা কিছু ভিন্ন ভেদ নাই।।

নন্দনন্দন শচীনন্দন
পারিষদ গোপীগণ নন্দনন্দন শচীনন্দন।।

বৃন্দাবনে রাস কেলী
নদীয়ায় সংকীর্তন কেলী বৃন্দাবনে রাস কেলী।।

বৃন্দাবনে বংশীধ্বনি
নদীয়ায় সে নামের ধ্বনি বৃন্দাবন বংশীধ্বনি।।

তাই আনন্দ আর ধরে না
আমার প্রভু গুণমণির তাই আনন্দ আর ধরে না
আমায় নিতে এসেছে বলে তাই আনন্দ আর ধরে না।।

জীব গোসাঞির পানে প্রভু দেখেন নয়নে
ধারা বয়ে যায় দু নয়নে।
শ্রীজীব গোসাঞি দেখি ব্যাকুল হইল অতি
নামসুধায় চাহি মুখ পানে।।

The hidden bower of the hidden bowers (of Vraja)
is manifest in the form of Navadvīpa.
Its sacred center is Śrīvāsa Aṅgana.
The sport of the Circle Dance of Vṛndavana
is in Nadīyā the sport of sacred singing (*kīrtana*).
The Son of Nanda is the Son of Śacī.

There is not the slightest difference;
they are these and these are they.
There is not the slightest difference.

The Son of Nanda is the Son of Śacī;
their companions are the cowherd girls.
The Son of Nanda is the Son of Śacī.

In Vṛndāvana is the sport of the Circle Dance.
In Nadīyā is the sport of congregational singing.
In Vṛndāvana is the sport of the Circle Dance.

The sound of the flute in Vṛndāvana
is in Nadīyā the sound of the holy name,
the sound of the flute in Vṛndāvana.

Therefore, he could no longer control his joy,
my master a jewel of merit;
he could no longer control his joy.
Saying "he has come to take me,"
he could no longer control his joy.

On Śrījīva Gosvāmī Master gazed,
streams of tears flowed from his eyes.
Śrījīva Gosvāmī seeing that
became extremely distressed,
gazing upon his face with the nectar of holy name.

আশ্রিতজনে নাম করে ভসিয়া নয়ন জলে
সেই নাম শ্রবণ করিয়া।
জয় নিত্যানন্দ রাম তিন বার করি উচ্চারণ
চলিলেন জগৎ ত্যজিয়া।।

নামের সহিত গেল রে
জয় নিত্যানন্দ রাম বলে নামের সহিত গেল রে (মাতন)

অনুভব কর ভাই রে
আমার প্রভুর প্রাপ্তি রহস্য অনুভব কর ভাই রে

সারা জীবন কৈলেন স্মরণ
শ্রীগৌর যুগল চরণ সারা জীবন কৈলেন স্মরণ

জয় নিত্যানন্দ রাম বলে ছড়িল জীবন

বড় অপরূপ কথা ভাই রে
আশ্রয় বিষয় তত্ত্বময় বড় অপরূপ কথা ভাই রে

বলেছেন ঠাকুর নরোত্তম
রাধাকৃষ্ণ পাইতে নাই
নিতাই কৃপা বিনে ভাই রাধাকৃষ্ণ পাইতে নাই

রাধাকৃষ্ণ মিলিত তনু
সে যে রাসবিলাসের পরিণতি
আমার গৌরাঙ্গ মূর্তি সে যে রাসবিলাসের পরিণতি

সে মূরতি পেতে গেলে
নিতাই আশ্রয় নিতে হবে সে মূরতি পেতে গেলে

A disciple began to chant the holy names.
While his eyes were aflood with tears
and the holy names rang in his ears,
he proclaimed out loud three times:
"Victory to Nityānanda Rāma!"
and leaving aside the world, he went on.

O, with the holy names he went
Victory to Nityānanda Rāma!
O with the holy names he went.

Realize it, O brother!
The secret of my Master's attainment.
Realize it, O brother!

All of his life he practiced remembering
Śrī Gaura and the Divine Couple.
All of his life he practiced remembering.

Saying, "Victory to Nityānanda Rāma," he left life.

This is a most amazing story, O brother!
the subject and object are full of truth.
This is a most amazing story, O brother!

Said our Ṭhākura Narottama:
"One cannot reach Rādhā and Kṛṣṇa
without the grace of Nityānanda.
One cannot reach Rādhā and Kṛṣṇa."

The combined body of Rādhā and Kṛṣṇa,
the ultimate stage of the Circle Dance,
is our Gaurāṅga's holy image,
the ultimate stage of the Circle Dance.

If one wants to reach that image,
one has seek shelter with Nitāi,
If one wants to reach that image.

ব্রজে রাধিকা আশ্রয় কৃষ্ণ বিষয়
মধুর শ্রী নবদ্বীপে
নিতাই আশ্রয় গৌর বিষয়　　মধুর শ্রী নবদ্বীপে

তাই নিতাই বলে ছড়িল পরাণ
পাইবার লাগি গৌর যুগল চরণ, তাই নিতাই বলে ছড়িল পরাণ

শ্রীগৌরহরি শ্রীমুখবাক্য
শ্রীমুখে বলেছেন গৌরহরি
পানিহাটির রাঘবের কাছে　　শ্রীমুখে বলেছেন গৌরহরি

শুন শুন ওহে রাঘব তোমায় গোপ্য কই।
আমার দ্বিতীয় নাই নিত্যানন্দ বই।।
তিলার্দ্ধ নিত্যানন্দে দ্বেষ যার রহে।
সে জন ভজিলেও কভু আমার প্রিয় নহে।।

গান ১

আজ তোমা শারাইয়া　　বিদরিয়া যায় হিয়া
আর কিগো পাবো দরশন।
তোমার সেই ভাল বাসা　　সমরিলে সেই কথা
প্রাণমন করে আনচান।।

তোমার আশ্রিত গণে　　ব্যাকুলিত হয় প্রাণে
একবার দেখিবার তরে।
একবার দেখা দিয়া　　দাও প্রাণ জুড়াইয়া
আশীর্বাদ কর কৃপা করে।।

In Vraja Rādhikā is love's container;
Kṛṣṇa is the object of her love.

In honeyed Śrī Navadvīpa
Nitāi is container; Gaura's the object,
in honeyed Śrī Navadvīpa.

Saying "Nitāi" he departed from life
to attain the two lotus feet of Gaura,
saying "Nitāi" he departed from life.

Words from the blessed lips of Śrī Gaurahari,
With his blessed lips said Gaurahari
to Rāghava of Pāṇihāṭi
with his blessed lips said Gaurahari:

"Hear me, O Rāghava, hear!
To you I speak a secret truth.
I have no second but for Nitāi.
One with even an iota
of hatred for Nityānanda,
though that person may worship me,
can never become someone dear."

Song One

Today you have departed
leaving me broken-hearted.
Will I ever see you again?

The love that you had for me
when it comes to my memory
makes my heart-mind nostalgic.

Those whom you have protected
are in our vital cores anxious
to have your vision one more time.

Give us one more glimpse of you
and ease our troubled life-breaths.
Show us your grace and give us your blessing.

মায়া বন্দন ঘুচাইয়া নিতাই গৌর ভজাইয়া
শ্রী নামে নিষ্ঠা রুচি দান কর।
এ জন্ম বিফলে গেল গুরু গৌর সেবা না হইল
এই নিবেদন যে আমার।।

আমার অন্তিম কালে জয় গুরু শ্রী গুরু বলে
যেন আমার প্রাণ বাহিরয়।
যদি জন্ম হয় পুনঃ শ্রী গুরু সঙ্গ পাই যেন
তবে ধন্য এ দীন হৃদয়।।

গান ২

জয় জয় তিনকড়ি গোস্বামী দয়াময়।
হেন প্রভু কোথা গেলে হইয়া নির্দয়।।
হেন প্রভু কোথা গেলে না দেখিয়ে আর।
কি হবে মোদের, দশা করহ বিচার।।
কার মুখে নিতাই গৌর কথা বা শুনিব।
শ্রী ব্রজধামে নীলাচলে কার সঙ্গে যাবো।।
শ্রীনবদ্বীপে কার সঙ্গে বাস বা করিব।
শ্রীগুরু গৌর তত্ত্ব কথা কোথা বা শুণিব।।
সবে যদি চলে গেলে আঁধার করিয়া।
মোদের কি দশা হবে দেখ বিচারিয়া।।
কাল কলির পীড়নে পীড়িত সদাই।
জুড়াইবার স্থান নাই কারে বা জানাই।।
এই বার দয়া কর করুণা করিয়া।
অপরাধি বলে যেন না দেহ ফেলিয়া।।

Unravel our bondage to *māyā,*
make us worship Nitāi and Gaura,
give us firmness and taste for the holy names.

This birth has passed without result.
I've not served Guru and Gaura.
Here is my desparate and humble plea:

In the final moment of my life,
saying, "Glory Guru, Blessed Guru,"
let my vital breath exit and depart.

If I must take another birth,
let me have my Guru's company.
Then this poor heart will be happy.

Song Two

Glory, glory! Compassionate Tinkaḍi Gosvāmī.
Where has such a great Master
gone, becoming merciless?
Where has such a great Master
gone, not showing himself any more?
What will be our condition now?
Please give this some consideration.
From whose lips will we hear now
those stories about Nitāi and Gaura?
In Śrī Vraja and Nīlācala,
whose association will we seek out?
In the dear company of whom
will we stay at Navadvīpa?
From whom will we now hear truths
about Śrī Guru and Gaura?
If everyone has gone, creating gloom,
consider what our state will be.
Always pained by the torments of Kali
with no place for relief nor anyone to inform.
This time compassionately show us grace
and don't cast us away as offenders.

এ জন্ম বিফলে গেল রিপুর সেবায়।
নিরন্তর জ্বলে হিয়া না দেখি উপায়।।
সবে মিলে কর দয়া গৌর ভক্ত গণে।
প্রাণে যেন যায় গুরুদত্ত নাম গানে।।
এ বার মরিয়া যেন পাই গুরু ধনে।
তবে এ হৃদয আপনাকে ধন্য মানে।।

সমাপ্ত

শ্রী হৃদয়ানন্দ দাস বাবাজী মহারাজ

This birth has passed without fruit
in the service of the enemies.
Our hearts are burning without rest
and no means of escape do we see.
All together shower your grace
on the *bhaktas* of Śrī Gaura,
so that our lives are spent singing
holy names given by our gurus,
and so that this time we will attain
our guru's fortune after we pass away.
Then this heart[147] will think itself fortunate.

The End

Śrī Hṛdayānanda Dāsa Bābājī Mahārāja

[147]Pun on the author's name: Hṛdayānanda or Hṛdaya for short. "Hṛdaya" means "heart."

Part IV

Appendices

Glossary of Terms and Names

bhajana *Bhajana* comes from the Sanskrit root $\sqrt{bhaj}$ which means "to pursue, practice, cultivate; to serve, honour, revere, love, adore; to experience, incur, undergo, feel." *Bhaj* is the root for the words *bhakti* and *bhakta* as well. Thus a *bhakta* performs *bhajana* and develops *bhakti*. In this work, *bhajana* is translated as "private worship." Private worship refers to various religious practices performed by an individual alone, in that individual's solitude, apart from participation in group or communal practices and rites. In the Caitanya community, private worship consists primarily of repetition of the names of Rādhā and Kṛṣṇa, called *nāma-japa*, and remembering or meditating on one's *mantras* (*mantra-smaraṇa*). *Nāma-japa* has three levels of recitation: vocal, whispered, and mental. Vocal *japa* is loud enough to be heard by others nearby and is thus sometimes considered to be a form of *kīrtana* (See *japa* and *kīrtana* below). Whispered *japa* is loud enough for only the chanter to hear. The mental form of *japa*, also known as remembering (*smaraṇa*) the holy names, is performed only in the mind without moving one's lips. Some practitioners combine repetition of the holy names with a practice called remembering the daily sports (*līlā-smaraṇa*) of Rādhā and Kṛṣṇa as they are described in some of the meditation/visualization texts of the tradition. Others, however, focus entirely on repeating the holy names in the belief that when the time is right, the sports of Rādhā and Kṛṣṇa will appear before them without any extra effort. These two forms of practice are referred to as multiple-form and single-form *bhakti* cultivation, respectively. The division is derived from the discussion of *bhakti* in Rūpa Gosvāmin's *Bhakti-rasāmṛta-sindhu* (1.2.264-8) and is discussed in greater detail in Manindranath Guha's work, *Nectar of the Holy Name.* Refer to those works for more detail.

Private worship is performed on a daily basis by practicing members of the Caitanya tradition and is dependent on the instructions of the practitioner's gurus (both initiating and instructing). It also often includes simplified ritual for the worship of private images of the practitioner's desired deities (in this case, Caitanya and Nityānanda, Giridhārī, and Rādhā and Kṛṣṇa).

An example of group practice as distinct from private worship is *saṅkīrtana,* the festive singing of the holy names and songs about the qualities and sports of Rādhā and Kṛṣṇa to the accompaniment of musical instruments (see below). Though generally performed in a group, it can be performed by an individual alone. Another example of a communal or group practice would be the worship of sacred images of Rādha and Kṛṣṇa in an established temple. Such worship is performed by one individual on behalf of a group or community of believers who look on and participate by singing or dancing or contributing money or materials to the worship.

bhajana-kuṭīra A *bhajana-kuṭīra* is a small hut or cottage meant for private worship. It may also be the place where a practitioner lives, but it is thought of as having its main purpose fulfilled in allowing the practitioner to concentrate on his or her private worship without being adversely affected by the weather or other outside conditions. *Bhajana kuṭīras* are generally built in secluded places preferably in one of the places considered holy or sacred by the tradition. One can then sit quietly apart in one's *kuṭīra* and concentrate on the performance of private worhip.

bhakti *Bhakti* is the main term in Indic religion for the recognition of one's dependence on and desire to cultivate love for the supreme being. *Bhakti,* as mentioned above, comes from the Sanskrit root $\sqrt{\textit{bhaj}}$ which means "to partake in," "to divide or share with," "to resort to," "to honor or worship." While *bhakti* can be felt for and practiced towards one's parents, other elders, and teachers, it has come to refer primarily to the cultivation and eventual experience of powerful feelings of love for a given deity. In the case of *bhakti* directed to Kṛṣṇa, it is connected with the development of a particular kind of intimate relationship with Kṛṣṇa and with all the complex feelings that go with that relationship.[148] A multivalent term, *bhakti* is applied to the set of practices that are undertaken as part of the cultivation, to the end result of that cultivation, also called *preman* or love, and in the form of *bhakti-rasa*, to the tasting or enjoyment of the "flavors" of that love. Thus, the path of *bhakti* usually begins with a set of practices like hearing the sacred texts and singing or chanting the names of Kṛṣṇa, say, undertaken out of a desire to gain intimacy with him and his dear companions; it then passes through the appearance of genuine feeling for or attraction (called *rati*) to the deity in the heart of the practitioner, and culminates in the experience of sacred rapture (*bhakti-rasa* or *preman*). This last stage is the point at which the love that previously appeared in the heart rises fully into consciousness and becomes relished by the one who possesses it. All of these stages (practice, appearance, and tasting) are referred to as *bhakti* and one who has it in any of its forms is called a *bhakta*.

Gaura(hari) "Golden Hari," Hari or Viṣṇu with a golden complexion. This is one of the many names of Śrī Caitanya. Sometimes he is called Gaura, "Golden," Gaurāṅga, "Golden-limbed," and Gauracandra, "Golden Moon."

Goloka/Gokula World of Cows/Herd of Cows. This is Kṛṣṇa's paradisal world located far beyond the reaches of the material realm. There he lives with his loving companions as an eternal cowherd boy. The Caitanya tradition believes this cowherd form to be Kṛṣṇa's highest form and cowherding his eternal activity. The pastoral planet on which this takes place for all eternity is called Goloka. The basis for these ideas is probably the *Brahma-saṃhitā*, the fifth chapter of which Śrī Caitanya is said to have found and copied during his tour of South India. The second verse of that text reads:

> Like a lotus with a thousand petals
> is the great abode called Gokula.
> Its pericarp is his residence
> produced by a portion of his Ananta.[149]

---

[148] There are five recognized relationships according to Rūpa Gosvāmin: peaceful appreciation (*śānta*), servitude (*dāsya*), friendship (*sakhya*), parental affection (*vātsalya*), and erotic attraction (*madhura*, lit. sweet). The degree of intimacy increases with each successive form.

[149] *Brahma-saṃhitā*, 5.2:

Gokula is practically synonymous with Goloka. There might be a slight distinction made in some texts, but in the *Brahma-saṃhitā* the two seem to be the same. Later, in verses 46 and 52, the name Goloka is used instead of Gokula. Gokula means a herd of cows or a village of cowherds with a herd of cows.

Govinda A name of Kṛṣṇa: "Possessor of cows." *Go* can have a number of meanings. Cow is the most common meaning and the word "cow" is in fact etymologically related to the Sanskrit word *go*. *Go* has also been used to mean the senses and the rays of the sun. The *vinda* part of the name is said to come from the root √*vid*, "to find, acquire, procure, possess." Interestingly, some scholars think the name Govinda may have been brought back into Sanskrit from Prakrit where is was a corrupted form of Gopendra, King of the Cowherds.

Hari A name of Viṣṇu or Kṛṣṇa. The name probably comes from the root √*hṛ*, "to take, bear, carry in or on, carry off or away, steal." Thus, it is often thought to mean the one who carries away one's sins or who steals one's heart. It also means the color yellow or green and might be a reference to the color of the complexion of Viṣṇu or Kṛṣṇa. See the entry for Kṛṣṇa for more details. The root √*hṛ* also means "to master, overpower, subdue, conquer, win, win over" and thus the qualities of victory and mastery are applied to Hari. It might be from this set of meanings that *hari* also came to mean "lion," thus also suggesting that Viṣṇu/Kṛṣṇa occupies the same place among gods and men as lions do in the animal world. A last set of meanings center around ideas like "to enrapture, charm, and fascinate." These powers of fascination too are attributed to the great god Viṣṇu/Kṛṣṇa.

japa Muttering, whispering, repeating. *Japa* is from the root √*jap* which means "to utter in a low voice." It is one of the ways in which the holy name and the usual way in which other mantras are recited. It

---

सहस्रपत्रं कमलं गोकुलाख्यं महत्पदम्।
तत्कर्णिकारं तद्धाम तदनन्तांशसम्भवम्॥

Ananta is, according to Śrī Jīva, Baladeva, Kṛṣṇa's brother, who on the higher plane is the first expansion of Kṛṣṇa, often depicted as a huge snake with unlimited heads called Ananta or Śeṣa, and who acts as the facilitating force, manifesting and arranging Kṛṣṇa's eternal abode for Kṛṣṇa's sport. The portion out of which this abode is produced is light, says Jīva.

is said to be of three types: silent or mental (*mānasika*), whispered (*upāṃśu*), and vocal (*vācika*. In actuality, however, only the second one is really *japa*. The first falls under the scope of "remembering" (*smaraṇa*) and the third is part of *kīrtana*. See Sanātana Gosvāmin's commentary on the *Hari-bhakti-vilāsa* (Play of Devotion to Hari) (11.472).

Kali-yuga This is the last of the four ages that make up a complete cycle in the Hindu conception of time. It lasts 432,000 years according to later Hindu calculations (originally it was only 1200 years) of which approximately 5,000 years have already passed. The complete cycle begins with the Kṛta-yuga or "Age of Fours." It is also called the Satya-yuga, the Age of Truth or "the Golden Age" and represents a time when the world is new and fresh. Peace, prosperity, and religious practice are found in full measure. Life is long and people are good and happy. The Kṛta-yuga lasts four times as long as the Kali-yuga. The next age after Kṛta is the Tretā-yuga, the "Age of Triads." It is three times as long as the Kali-yuga and contains three-fourths of the goodness and truth of the Kṛta-yuga. Then comes the Dvāpara-yuga, the "Age of Deuces." It has half of the goodness and truth of the Kṛta-yuga and is twice as long as the Kali-yuga. The Kali-yuga, the "Age of Ones," is the last and the worst of the four ages. When it is over the world will be partially destroyed and remade and the cycle will start over again at the top. All together these ages last ten units of time ($4 + 3 + 2 + 1 = 10$), a unit being equal to the duration of the Kali-yuga. Thus, the whole cycle is 4,320,000 years long. The names of the ages come from the Indian game of dice, the best throw being *kṛta* (four dots), the next best *tretā* (three dots), then *dvāpara* (two dots), and last *kali* (one dot), the losing die. Kali is not to be confused with Kālī, the dark, ferocious goddess of death and protection popular in Bengal and other parts of India, the anger-manifestation of the goddess Durgā.

kīrtana "Mentioning, repeating, saying, telling, praising." It comes from the root $\sqrt{\textit{kīrt}}$, "to mention, make mention of, tell, name, call, recite, repeat, relate, declare, communicate, commemorate, celebrate, praise, glorify," and is related to the word *kīrti*, which means "fame." Thus, it means to make famous or spread the fame of someone. Mentioning, repeating, saying, telling, etc. are all ways of doing this. In the context of Vaiṣṇava practice it means to mention, repeat, say, tell of, or praise Kṛṣṇa's names, qualities, forms, and activities. As *saṅkīrtana*, or "complete telling," it means to sing of those things to musical accompaniment and according to the Gosvāmins, in groups. Śrī Jīva says that among all the forms of *kīrtana*, loud *kīrtana* of Kṛṣṇa's names is the best.[150] About *saṅkīrtana* he says: "*kīrtana* performed by many people gathered together is called *saṅkīrtana*. And because it leads to a special, astonishing delight it is better than the former (ie. *kīrtana*)."[151] The musical connection is made by Sanātana Gosvāmin when he says that *saṅkīrtana* means the complete or sweet-sounding, loud singing of the names of the enjoyer of the Rāsa dance (Kṛṣṇa) with melody, rhythm, and so forth.[152] Thus, for the purposes of this text *kīrtana* is the loud repeating or telling of Kṛṣṇa's names, qualities, forms, and activities and *saṅkīrtana* is the loud and musical repeating or telling of Kṛṣṇa's names, qualities, forms, and activities as part of a group.

Kṛṣṇa Kṛṣṇa is the primary name of the god worshipped in the Caitanya tradition. The word *kṛṣṇa* is quite ancient. It is found many times in the oldest of the Vedas, the Rig Veda (15th-10th cents. BCE), but it rarely occurs there as a name. There it means "black, dark, dark-blue" and is often found in opposition to *śukla* and *śveta* which mean "white." It may come from the root $\sqrt{kṛṣ}$ which means "to draw, draw to one's self, drag, pull, drag away, tear; to lead or conduct; to draw into one's power, become master of, overpower." Thus, Kṛṣṇa is often invested with a power of attraction. Kṛṣṇa draws the hearts and minds of all beings away from all else and brings them to himself. The word *kṛṣṇa* may be from another root, however, the root $\sqrt{kṛś}$ which means "to become lean or thin, emaciated; to cause the moon to wane." This would fit better with the word's meaning as "dark" and its common usage in referring to the dark half of the lunar month (*kṛṣṇa-pakṣa*) when the moon wanes.

Śrī Jīva in his commentary on the *Brahma-saṃhitā* discusses the meaning of the name "kṛṣṇa" after demonstrating on the basis of

[150]Śrī Jīva Gosvāmin, *Bhakti-sandarbha*, para 265: नामसङ्कीर्तनञ्चेदमुच्चैरेव प्रशस्तम्

[151]ibid., para 269: अत्र च बहुभिर्मिलित्वा कीर्तनं सङ्कीर्तनमित्युच्यते। तत्तु चमत्कारविशेषपोषात्पूर्वतोऽप्यधिकमिति ज्ञेयम्।

[152]Śrī Sanātana Gosvīmin, comm. on Bb, 2.1.21: संकीर्तयन्तीति। तस्य श्रीरासरसिकस्य नाम ये सम्यक् सुस्वरं गाथाबन्धादिनोच्चैर्गायन्तीत्यर्थः।

the construction of certain passages of the *Bhāgavata Purāṇa* that it is the predominant or primary name of the supreme being. Predominance means that all other names are included in it and that it refers to the primary and highest agent of all divine actions and expansions. He cites a verse of unknown origin that gives a meaning of the name as follows:

> 'Kṛṣ' is a word that means 'being' (*bhū*) and 'ṇa' means delight (*nirvṛti*). The oneness of those two is the supreme *brahman* conveyed by the word *kṛṣṇa*.[153]

Jīva then quotes another, verse from the *Gautamīya Tantra* that has almost the same meaning:

> The word 'kṛṣ' means existence (*sattā*) and 'ṇa' has the nature of joy (*ānanda*). Therefore, happy is the self that consists of being and joy.[154]

After dwelling on some hermeneutic issues, Jīva provides the following explanatory summary:

> The verse from the *Gautamīya* should be explained in this way. In the first half [of the verse] Kṛṣṇa is [defined as] joy that has the power of attracting all. In the second half [it is said that] since he is the joy that attracts all therefore the self [the supreme self, *paramātman*] and the living being find pleasure in him. The reason for that is that the self [both the supreme self and the living being self] consists of the joy of *bhāva* [being, feeling] which is divine love (*preman*). Therefore, the word *kṛṣṇa* refers to the greatest joy of all that attracts all by its beauty and qualities. And that word applies by convention only to the son of Devakī [Devakīnandana]. His ability to give

---

[153]Śrī Jīva's comm. on *Brahma-saṃhitā.*, 5.1:

> कृषिर्भूवाचकः शब्दो णश्च निर्वृतिवाचकः।
> तयोरैक्यं परं ब्रह्म कृष्ण इत्यभिधीयते॥

[154]ibid.:

> कृष्शब्दस्य सत्तार्थो णश्चानन्दस्वरूपकः।
> सुखरूपो भवेदात्मा भावानन्दमयस्ततः॥

joy to all is seen in the *Vāsudeva Upaniṣad*: "the son of Devakī gives pleasure to all."[155]

Thus, according to this argument, the fundemental nature pointed to by the name Kṛṣṇa is pleasure or joy that attracts all.

madhukarī *Madhukarī* means the "maker of honey," in other words, the honey bee. In this context *madhukarī* means going from house to house, the way a honey bee moves from flower to flower, collecting alms-food for one's meals. This is the way that most renunciants in modern Caitanya Vaiṣṇavism get the food on which they live. They depend on the charity of others which they regard as an avenue of Kṛṣṇa's grace on them. What they get varies from day to day depending on the houses they go to. Some days they get enough food and some days they do not. In both cases it is regarded as the grace of Rādhā and Kṛṣṇa.

mañjarī *Mañjarī* means "cluster of blossoms, flower, bud" and is the word applied to what is envisioned in the Caitanya tradition as the eternal, feminine identity of those followers who seek to become the servants of Rādhā and assist her in her amorous love affair with Kṛṣṇa. A *mañjarī* is a young cowherd girl (12-13 years old) who is both a friend and a servant of Rādhā and who favors Rādhā even over Kṛṣṇa. It is not known who first used the term in this special sense, but it may have been Rūpa Gosvāmin. There is a description of such a female cowherd identity in the *Padma Purāṇa*,[156] but it is not known how early or authentic that passage is. The *mañjarī* identity was later picked up and used extensively by Raghunātha Das Gosvāmin, Kavikarṇapūra, Gopālaguru Gosvāmin, and Kṛṣṇadāsa Kavirāja.

One might view the *mañjarī* metaphorically as a "bud" or "sprout" on the vine of Rādhā. A verse from the great poem of Kṛṣṇadāsa Kavirāja, the *Govinda-līlāmṛta* (Ambrosia of the Sports of Govinda), suggests that there is such a symbiotic relationship between Rādhā

[155] ibid.: गौतमीयपद्यञ्चैवं व्याख्येयम्। पूर्वार्द्धे सर्वाकर्षणशक्तिविशिष्ट आनन्दः कृष्ण इत्यर्थः। उत्तरार्द्धे यस्मादेवं सर्वाकर्षकसुखरूपोऽसौ तस्मादात्मा जीवश्च तत्र सुखरूपो भवेत्। तत्र हेतुः। भावः प्रेमा तन्मयानन्दत्वादिति। तदेवं रूपगुणाभ्यां परमबृहत्तमः सर्वाकर्षक आनन्दः कृष्णशब्दवाच्य इति ज्ञेयम्। स च शब्दं श्रीदेवकीननन्द एव रूढः। अस्यैव सर्वानन्दकत्वं वासुदेवोपनिषदि दृष्टम्। देवकीनन्दनो निखिलमानन्दयेदिति।

[156] *Padma Purāṇa*, 5 (Pātāla-khaṇḍa), Chapter 83.

and her friends. Kṛṣṇa embraces Rādhā and shivers and goose-bumps appear on the bodies of her *mañjarī* friends.[157] As both a friend and a servant, the *mañjarī* enjoys a certain degree of intimacy with Rādhā that the other girlfriends (*sakhīs*), who are just friends of Rādhā, don't. The *mañjarī* is also typically a year or so younger than Rādhā and the other *sakhīs* (who are eternally 14-15 years) and thus is able to play a subservient role to them.

The kind of love that a *mañjarī* feels for Rādhā and Kṛṣṇa is defined by Rūpa as *tat-tad-bhāvollāsa-rati*, a love that rejoices in their (Rādhā and Kṛṣṇa's) feelings for each other and pleasures derived from each other. Rūpa defines it in his *Bhakti-rasāmṛta-sindh* (Ocean of the Ambrosia of the Rasa of Bhakti).[158] See also *preman*.

Niyama-sevā Niyama-sevā is a month-long observation of special austerities and practices that begins on the bright Ekādaśī (the eleventh day of the waxing moon) of the lunar month of Āśvina (September-October) and lasts until the day after the bright Ekādaśī of the lunar month of Kārtika (October-November). One can begin the vow either on that Ekādaśī day of Āśvina or on the full moon day or at the Autumnal Equinox according to the *Hari-bhakti-vilāsa*.[159]

According to Śrī Svarūpa Dāsa Bābājī's little pamphlet, *Niyamasevā o Dāmodara Māsa* (*Niyama-sevā and the Month of Dāmodara*), there are ten rules or recommendations to observe during Niyama-sevā:

1. One should not eat fish, honey, meat, kidney beans, other kinds of beans, a vegetable called *kalamī*, another called *paṭal*, eggplant, wine, food given in charity, oil, raw or white pepper, ordinary salt and other things.
2. One should not have oil massages, use beds, eat off of bell-metal plates, accept things not offered to the sacred image, or use a razor.
3. One should not harm any living creature with one's body, mind, or words.

[157] Kṛṣṇa Dāsa Kavirāja, *Govinda-līlāmṛta*, 10.12-3.
[158] Śrī Rūpa Gosvāmin, *Bhakti-rasāmṛta-sindhu*, 2.5.128.
[159] Gopāla Bhaṭṭa Gosvāmin, *Hari-bhakti-vilāsa*, 16.183:

आश्विने शुक्लपक्षस्य प्रारम्भो हरिवासरे।
अथवा पौर्णमासीते संक्रान्तौ वा तुलागमे॥

4. One must associate with the good and holy, read scriptures like the *Bhāgavata Purāṇa* and other texts, and perform hearing and singing.
5. One should not bring into one's heart any evil ideas or bad thoughts.
6. One should recite hymns like the *Śrī Dāmodarāṣṭaka, Śrī Gopāla-sahasra-nāma, Śrī Viṣṇu-sahasra-nāma, Śrī Rādhā-kṛpā-kaṭākṣa-stotra,* Śrī Dāmodara-līlā *kīrtanas, Śrī Govardhanāṣṭaka,* and so forth.
7. For those who are incapable [of reciting the other hymns], the chanting or *japa* of the Mahāmantra is the best of all.
8. One should rise two hours and twenty-four minutes before sunrise and after going to the toilet, take one's bath or perform *ācamana.* After this one should spend one's days attending, participating in, or performing the awakening of the sacred images of Śrī Hari and *kīrtanas* of his end-of-the-night sports, the auspicious greeting (*maṅgalārati*), early morning bath, the service of Tulasī, the service of the sacred images, the honoring of grace-food, the laying down of the images for naps, their awakening later, the auditing of sacred texts in the afternoon, the evening greeting ceremony, honoring grace-food, and finally the putting of the sacred images to bed at night.
9. Performing Niyama-sevā at Rādhākuṇḍa is especially praised. There are a number of practices and celebrations throughout the month for those spending this period at Rādhākuṇḍa.
10. At the end of Niyama-sevā many go from Rādhākuṇḍa to Vṛndāvana on the full moon day to view the Rāsa-līlā.

preman Sacred or divine love, *preman* or *prīti,* is considered in the Caitanya tradition to be the fifth and highest goal of human life, beyond even liberation from rebirth (the fourth).[160] *Preman* is defined by Rūpa Gosvāmin in this way: Attraction (ie. delighting in Kṛṣṇa, *kṛṣṇa-rati*), when it becomes condensed or intensified such that it completely melts the heart of its possessor and creates in that person a strong sense of possessiveness towards Kṛṣṇa, is called

[160]Hindu tradition recognizes four goals of human life (*puruṣārtha*): wealth, pleasure, piety, and liberation. Caitanya Vaiṣṇavism has added to those four a fifth, divine or sacred love.

sacred love. It is a selfless love that is concerned more for the welfare and pleasure of the one loved than for the pleasure of the one loving. It, thus, stands in opposition to lust or selfish love (*kāma*) which seeks self-gratification.

Rādhā Rādhā is Kṛṣṇa's divine lover. She is the highest example of sacred love (*preman*). She among all the cowherd women pleases Kṛṣṇa the most and though not wishing it, she derives the greatest pleasure from loving him. Theologically, she is Kṛṣṇa's pleasure power (*hlādinī-śakti*) in person. By connecting with her as her friends and servants (i.e. as *mañjarīs*, see above), others also become capable of pleasing Kṛṣṇa and, through her, of deriving pleasure from loving Kṛṣṇa. Though not mentioned explicitly in the 10th Canto of the *Bhāgavata Purāṇa* she is considered to be the one *special* cowherd woman Kṛṣṇa took with him when he disappeared from the rest of the cowherd women who had come to dance with him in the forest of Vṛndāvana during the episode of the circle dance.

Rādhākuṇḍa Rādhākuṇḍa is the pond of Rādhā. It is the pond in which she likes to bathe and at which Rādhā and Kṛṣṇa meet during the middle of the day. There is a famous verse about Rādhā and Rādhākuṇḍa from the *Padma Purāṇa*:

> Just as Rādhā is dear to Viṣṇu, so is her pond dear to him. Among all the cowherd ladies, she alone is the most extremely beloved to Viṣṇu.[161]

The pond in the District of Mathura that is currently recognized as Rādhākuṇḍa was discovered by Śrī Caitanya at the village of Āriṭa during his visit to Vṛndāvana. That is described by Kṛṣṇadāsa Kavirāja in his *Caitanya-caritāmṛta* (18.1-11). The land around the pond was later acquired by Śrī Jīva Gosvāmin and since then Rādhākuṇḍa has remained one of the most important sacred sites in the Caitanya tradition.

---

[161] *Padma Purāṇa*, cited in Rūpa's *Ujjvala-nīlamaṇi*, 3.5:

यथा राधा प्रिया विष्णोस्तस्याः कुण्डं प्रियं तथा।
सर्वगोपीषु सैवैका विष्णोरत्यन्तवल्लभा॥

Rādhā-ramaṇa The "enjoyer of Rādhā," a name of Kṛṣṇa that indicates his special erotic relationship with the cowherd woman Rādhā. The Rādhāramaṇa Mandira is one of the temples in Rādhākuṇḍa.

rāgānugā-bhakti "Passion-pursuing" or "passion-following," specially as an adjective for the kind of *bhakti* taught by Śrī Caitanya according to his followers. *Rāgānugā-bhakti* is a form of *bhakti* cultivation that receives its impetus from a different source than the "rule-motivated" *bhakti* or *vaidhī-bhakti* of older forms of Vaiṣṇavism. Passion-pursuing *bhakti* is motived by a desire to develop the same kind of passionate love for Kṛṣṇa that his beloved servants, friends, parents, and lovers have. It is impelled, therefore, by a strong desire or greediness (*lobha*) to love Kṛṣṇa the way they do. For this kind of *bhakti* Kṛṣṇa's dear servants, friends, parents, and lovers become the models. Their actions motivated by their love for Kṛṣṇa become the sources of the practices adopted by the practitioner in the cultivation of their kind of *bhakti*.

Rule-motivated *vaidhi-bhakti*, on the other hand, is performed out of a sense of duty, duty instilled by respect for the accepted scriptures or by one's family traditions and other social institutions. One worships Kṛṣṇa because one's father or mother or earlier ancestors did or because the scriptures one trusts say one should. It is almost the opposite of passionate *bhakti* in which one worships or undertakes practice because one has a strong desire to do so.

rasa Aesthetic rapture. In this text *rasa* is used as shorthand for *bhakti-rasa*, sacred rapture. *Rasa* was a concept developed in Sanskrit aesthetics to describe the aesthetic experience of the connoiseur in enjoying plays and poetry. Though first discussed in the *Nāṭya-śāstra* of Bharata Muni (4-5th cents. C.E.), Abhinavagupta (10th cent. C.E.) is probably most responsible for bringing the idea of *rasa* to its highest level of sophistication in his commentaries on the *Dhvanyāloka* and on the *rasa-sūtra* of the *Nāṭya-śāstra*. Bhojarāja (11th cent. C.E.), king of Dhārā, developed the idea of *rasa* independently and in a different way. Each writer has his distinct areas of influence, but Abhinavagupta's understanding of *rasa* came to be regarded as the mainstream tradition. Rūpa Gosvāmin, following the lead of several predecesors, took the idea of *rasa* and applied it to religious experience, surprisingly relying more on Bhojarāja's understanding than on Abhinavagupta's. The result was his version of the idea of *bhakti-rasa*, sacred rapture, which became dominantly influential in the later Caitanya Vaiṣṇava tradition and in other Vaiṣṇava traditions as well.

One experiences sacred rapture when one's feeling (*bhāva*), that is, delight in Kṛṣṇa (*kṛṣṇa-rati*), is brought to the level of enjoyment or tastiness by means of the excitants (*vibhāvas*), consequents (*anubhāvas*), and transient emotions (*vyabhicāribhāvas*). The feeling of delight in Kṛṣṇa is, according to the Caitanya tradition, outside the natural world (*alaukika*), and it consists of pure being or goodness (*śuddha-sattva-viśeṣātmā*) that appears in the mind of a practitioner at some point in his or her development in *bhakti* and becomes part of the mind. Then when the practitioner encounters the excitants, consequents, and transients in literature, drama, or song, that delight is transformed into full-fledged joy or bliss. Since *preman* is an intensified or condensed form of delight in Kṛṣṇa, the threshold for the transition of delight into joy becomes dramatically lowered in *preman*. Then the mere sight of a peacock feather or a bluish rain cloud can send a person with *preman* into the throes of sacred rapture.

saṅkīrtana See *kīrtana*.

smaraṇa Remembering or recollecting. This refers to a Caitanya Vaiṣṇava practice that is more of a form of meditation or visualization than it is a "remembering," as remembering is commonly understood. The practitioners have never really experienced what they are "remembering." So, for them, it is not remembering at all. What they are really doing is focused or guided thinking about Kṛṣṇa and what he and his various companions are doing at any particular moment of the day. Thus, remembering is based on the idea that Kṛṣṇa is engaged in an eternal series of actions or sports which is taking place daily in Kṛṣṇa's otherworldly paradise, Goloka. The day is divided into eight periods and Kṛṣṇa's activities in each of those periods is "remembered" in the corresponding period of the practitioner's day. Thus, when Kṛṣṇa is in the forest bower with Rādhā at the end of the night and must be awakened and returned to his home before his mother and other elders discover he is missing, the practitioner "remembers" or visualizes it, placing himself or herself in the action in a mentally conceived or imagined body (usually but not always that of a *mañjarī*) given to him or her by the guru. A number of poetic works have been composed by followers of Caitanya to help the practitioner in this process of creative envisioning or remembering. The longest and most detailed is the *Govinda-līlāmṛta* (Ambrosia of the Sports of Govinda) by Kṛṣṇa Dāsa Kavirāja.

sāttvika-bhāvas The *sāttvika-bhāvas* are a group of eight autonomous, physical reactions or conditions. They are regarded as outward physical manifestations of powerful, inner religious emotions. Those emotions, called *bhāva*, when heightened, enhanced, and relished, become known as *bhakti-rasa*, or sacred rapture. (See above)

Rūpa gives the standard list of physical reactions from the tradition of Sanskrit aesthetics:

> They are becoming stunned [immobilized], sweating [profusely], standing of hair on end, cracking of the voice, violent trembling, losing or changing color, tears, and fainting.[162]

The members of the Caitanya tradition generally regard the presence of some of the *sāttvika* reactions as indications of a high level of religious development in a particular practitioner. The manifestation of all eight simultaneously or at various times is considered a sign that the practitioner has reached the highest level of spiritual attainment, the level of feeling or tasting divine love (*preman*). This need not necessarily be so, however. One of the great Chaitanyite aesthetician-theologians, Śrī Rūpa Gosvāmin, devotes a whole chapter to the eight *sāttvikas* in his work on the nature and expressions of *bhakti* towards Kṛṣṇa.[163] Śrī Rūpa is not the inventor of the eight *sāttvika* conditions. He adapted them from the older tradition of Sanskrit aesthetics and dramaturgy.[164]. There, they are understood as part of the actor's craft. In other words, good actors are able to fake them, to incorporate them into their acting in

---

[162]ibid., 2.3.16:

ते स्तम्भस्वेदरोमाञ्चाः स्वरभेदोऽथ वेपथुः ।
वैवर्ण्यमश्रु प्रलय इत्यष्टौ सात्त्विकाः स्मृताः ॥

[163]The *Bhakti-rasāmṛta-sindhu* (The Ocean of the Nectar of the Flavors [Raptures] of Bhakti)

[164]They are mentioned for the first time in the *Nāṭya-śāstra* (Treatise on Drama) (4th-5th cents. C.E.) attributed to Bharata Muni

order to bestow the aura of reality on whatever part they are playing. In Rūpa's adaptation they are understood to be produced autonomously out of one's powerful feelings of love for Kṛṣṇa. Rūpa says:

> The mind when overrun by feelings connected with Kṛṣṇa, either directly or somewhat indirectly, is called the *sattva* by the wise. And those conditions that are produced from that *sattva* are called the *sāttvikas*. They are of three varieties: moist, anointed, and dry.[165]

The word *sattva*, therefore, refers to the mind when it is overrun by or overcome with emotion relating to Kṛṣṇa.[166] Those emotions are felt either in direct connection with Kṛṣṇa or indirectly. The physical conditions or reactions that are produced from the *sattva* are called the *sāttvika*, that is, conditions born out of the *sattva*. Thus, the physical conditions called *sāttvika* are produced when the mind (or heart) of a person is overrun by emotions relating to Kṛṣṇa. They are the external manifestations of powerful inner emotional experiences relating to Kṛṣṇa. Rūpa divides them into three varieties not by the kind of condition they are (i.e. tears, trembling, etc), but by how they are produced. He gives them names indicating a decreasing order of "moistness" or affection (*sneha*). The first, the *snigdha*, are the "moist ones." This group refers to the physical reactions of a person who has developed feelings of love for Kṛṣṇa and who experiences or tastes those feelings in direct connection with Kṛṣṇa. They have two sub-varieties depending on whether they arise from the five main forms of love for Krishna[167] or the seven minor forms of love for Kṛṣṇa.[168]

---

[165] Brs., 2.3.1-2:

कृष्णसम्बन्धिभिः साक्षात्किञ्चिद्वा व्यवधानतः ।
भावैश्चित्तमिहाक्रान्तं सत्त्वमित्युच्यते बुधैः ॥
सत्त्वादस्मात्समुत्पन्ना ये ये भावास्ते तु सात्त्विकाः ।
स्निग्धा दिग्धास्तथा रुक्षा इत्य् अमी त्रिविधा मताः ॥

[166] The word *sattva* which ordinarily means "being, existence, entity" is used in a technical sense here to mean mind in a special state of emotional arousal. This idea, too, is borrowed from the earlier Sanskrit aesthetic tradition.

[167] Peacefulness, servitude, friendship, parental love, and erotic love. These are the five main forms of *kṛṣṇa-rati*, attraction or love for Kṛṣṇa.

[168] The seven minor forms of attraction for Kṛṣṇa are: the comic, wonder, the heroic, com-

The second group, the "anointed ones" or *digdha*, are the physical reactions of a person who also has developed feelings of love for Krishna, but whose reactions do not occur in direct connection with Kṛṣṇa. In other words, they occur in situations influenced by that person's love for Kṛṣṇa but not in direct connection with Kṛṣṇa himself. The example Rūpa gives is that of Mother Yaśodā, Kṛṣṇa's foster mother in Vraja, who hears in a dream the demon Pūtanā, the ogress who tried to kill Kṛṣṇa by smearing poison on her beasts. Yaśodā wakes up twisting about in her bed and trembling like a leaf. Immediately, she goes to look for her son. Yaśodā's trembling is, according to Rūpa, a *sāttvika* reaction that results from her love for Kṛṣṇa, but it is aroused by a nightmarish vision, not the direct perception or presence of her son. Her reaction, as a result of her love for Kṛṣṇa, derives its moistness or affection from that love and thus it is considered "anointed."

The last type is the dry or arid (*rukṣa*) group of *sāttvikas*. Arid *sāttvikas* occur sometimes in those who seem like they are true *bhaktas* who have developed love for Kṛṣṇa but who actually have not yet reached the level of having developed love for Kṛṣṇa. Those *sāttvikas* appear as a result of the joy or wonder or other powerful emotions that is produced by hearing stories about Kṛṣṇa's sweetness or his amazing acts and so forth. Thus, it sometimes happens that even those who have not yet developed genuine love for Kṛṣṇa may exhibit some of the *sāttvika* physical reactions. While these *rukṣa-sāttvikas* are considered genuine, they demonstrate that it is unreliable to judge a person's spiritual advancement on the basis of the presence or absence of the *sāttvikas*.

shravan (śravaṇa) Hearing or listening. Hearing is the first stage in the practice of *bhakti*. It means hearing from the guru, the scriptures, and other Vaiṣṇava about Kṛṣṇa, his names, his qualities, his forms, and his activities. Hearing if done well, it is said, will destroy the impurities or diseases of the heart and mind and clear the way for the descent of *bhakti* into them.

vaidhī bhakti See *rāgānugā* above.

Vaikuṇṭha Kṛṣṇa's lower heaven. Vaikuṇṭha is the place where Kṛṣṇa's

---

passion, fury, terror, and disgust. These are minor or secondary because, though blended with love for Kṛṣṇa, that love contracts itself and takes a secondary place, allowing the other emotions to be dominant. In the main forms, it is love for Kṛṣṇa that dominates.

majestic aspect is manifested. Vaikuṇṭha is from the word *vikuṇṭha* which means " sharp, keen, penetrating, irresistible." Complementing his majesty is his sweetness (*mādhurya*) or intimate aspect which is manifest in his higher heaven called Goloka (see above). In Vaikuṇṭha Kṛṣṇa reigns as Viṣṇu with four arms and possesses all the majesty and opulence of a super-cosmic king. Those who worship Kṛṣṇa by means of rule-motivated *bhakti* (*vaidhi-bhakti*) are said to go to Vaikuṇṭha after gaining success. Those who worship by passion-motivated *bhakti* (*rāgānuga-bhakti*) instead go to Goloka.

Vrajendranandana The son of the king of Vraja, another name of Kṛṣṇa. The king of Vraja, the pasture lands, is Nanda the cowherd and Yaśodā is his wife. Kṛṣṇa is referred to as Nanda's son, though according to the story of his birth, Kṛṣṇa was actually born as the son of Vasudeva because of which he was known as Vāsudeva. To protect him from the evil king Kaṃsa, Vasudeva carried him on the night of his birth to the village of Nanda and swapped him for Nanda's new-born daughter. Along these same lines, Kṛṣṇa is also often called Nandanandana and Yaśodānandana.

Introduction to the Author (by Jagadish Das)

Binode Bihari Das Bābājī was born in Barisal, Bangladesh, in 1947. In 1950 he and his parents, losing all their property and in poverty, went to West Bengal and settled in the district of 24 Parganas. Both his parents passed away when he was still quite young, his father when he was eight years old and his mother two years later.[169]

Binode studied only up to the fifth class of primary school, then left and joined a troop of dancers and singers. He learned to sing and dance as he traveled with them, suffering sometimes from much exposure and hunger. At the age of eighteen he found work with the government and studied with a private tutor until he passed the tenth class level. Eventually he was promoted in his department to supervisor. He lived a solitary life, continuing his study of music which included the study of tabla, harmonium, and sitar. As a result he became a certified radio artist as well.

Binode lived the modern life in Kolkata and did not consider a spiritual life until 1974 when, at the age of twenty-seven, a neighboring lady gave him a book on the life and teachings of Śrī Rāmakṛṣṇa Paramahaṃsa Deva.

While reading this book, Binode realized that his life was not fulfilling. Seeing modern social life to be a lie, he thought to himself that he needed to develop a peaceful, spiritual life instead. To do this, though, what should he do?

[169]This account was given to Jagadish Das by Binode Bihari Das Bābājī during Jagadish's stay in Vraja over the months of September to February in 2006-7.

After only one day, Binode decided he needed to change his life. He transferred to another job and moved to another place (Konagar) where he lived alone and reflected. He changed his eating habits, as well, eating only pure foods, and began to practice silence and other things to improve his spiritual life. He often went to a local library and borrowed books on spiritual life; he read anything that might give him some understanding about how to lead such a life. This went on for awhile, until he realized that having a guru was important, along with associating with saintly persons (*sādhu-saṅga*) and repeating the holy names (*harināma*). Then for the next five years he traveled around to many holy places in search of a guru.

Feeling unsatisfied and sad at not yet finding a genuine guru, one night Binode dreamed that he should to go to Giri Govardhana [Mount Govardhana in the District of Mathurā, Uttar Pradesh]. He had never heard of this holy place before and after asking around, he found out that it was near Vrindaban.

Binode went to Giri Govardhana and chanced upon Prabhupāda Tinkaḍi Goswami's *āśrama*; he was deeply impressed with it—but Prabhupāda was not there at the time. He returned home and later came back, going this time to nearby Radhakund where he questioned a local *sādhu*. He was told that an accomplished saint (*siddha-puruṣa*) was there at Rāsh Bāri. Binode went there and then met Bābā. Bābā was very kind to him and Binode was deeply impressed. For a time, Binode went back and forth from home to visit Bābā. Then in 1980 while doing the eighty-four square mile circumambulation (*parikramā*) of Vraja, he again met Bābā—who told him to come back and see him after the holy circumambulation was over.

When Binode went to see Bābā, Bābā asked him to put on neck beads and take holy name initiation, but he refused. Bābā insisted, however, and told him that he would give it to him the next day. Bābā then instructed Vanamali Das Bābā to prepare him. Thus, he received the holy name and when he did he thought to himself, "now that I have a true guru, why should I go home? Why should I leave?"

Feeling troubled about leaving, Binode went to Bābā as if swept along by some force and with tears in his eyes, he prayed to Bābā to let him stay with him and not leave, "I don't want to go back to work," he told Bābā. Bābā became very pleased and laughing out loud said, "Very good! Very good! Then you should stay." Binode never went back to his home again.

From that time on Binode lived with Bābā and his group of *sādhus*. He became one of Bābā's personal servants and traveled with Bābā and his group to many of the holy places of Vraja, Purī, and Navadvīpa. It was in Navadvīpa in 1984 that his blessed gurudev entered into eternal life with Bhagavān Śrī Kṛṣṇa (*nitya-līlā-praveśa*).

Before his gurudev passed away he asked Binode to go to Chandari in Vraja to practice private worship (*bhajana*). Feeling very lonely after the departure of his guru Binode was unable to decide where to live, where to settle down for engagement in private worship. After visiting many *āśramas* and temples and staying in each for a few days, he understood that those places were filled with too much activity and conflict and thus were not good places for him to settle in for private worship. He felt mentally disturbed in those places.

Binode realized that he should live alone in seclusion if he wanted to progress in private worship, but since he had never lived completely alone he was worried about whether or not he could do it. Thinking like this, he wept often, unsure of where to go. Traveling about in this way, one day he arrived in Barsāna. A *sādhu* there gave him a little hut for private worship. He lived there for four years doing private worship under difficult conditions, leading an austere life of poverty. While living there he collected information on the life of his blessed gurudev and wrote this book.

At this time a *sādhu* settled nearby who constantly disturbed Binode. Thus, he decided it was time to leave. He went to a nearby forested area called Premasarovara [Lake of Love] and settled into an empty hut there. There he stayed for the next eight years. After that, many people, having heard of his reputation, started coming to that area inquiring about him.

As a result Binode went to Chandrasarovara [Lake of the Moon] near Govardhana and other places to practice private worship. Finally, he went to the small village of Lekhi and settled down there for the next nine years. After that he returned to Barsāna, because a devotee had purchased land and built a large hut for him to live undisturbed in the execution of his private worship. That is where he lives at present. He uses this place as a base and continues to travel about India as a *sādhu mahātmā* (great-souled holy man).

His Other Book

Binode Bihari Das Bābājī has written one other book in Bengali: *Obstacles to the Gradual Unfolding of Bhakti* (*Bhakti-krama-vikāśer Antarāya*). It is a guide for practitioners on the path of Caitanya Vaiṣṇavism. As the name implies it is directed at helping practitioners overcome the common obstacles and pitfalls on the path of cultivation of divine love or *kṛṣṇa-prema*. It is written in the form of a dialogue between a disciple and his guru. Currently, it is being translated into English by Madhumati Dasi under the name *Road-blocks in Bhakti*. Parts of the rough draft of the translation can be found at ¡www.freewebs.com/babajimaharaj/¿.

My Recollections — Neal Delmonico

The first time I saw Bābā Tinkaḍi Gosvāmī was in a picture. I was more than a little surprised at what I saw. He did not look like a Caitanyite renunciant at all, at least none that I was familiar with. My first impression was that he was some sort of Śaivite or Nātha-panthī *sādhu*. The long hair and beard, the huge beads circling his neck, his near-nakedness, huge dark *tilaka* (markings on head, chest and arms), the coarse loincloth and upper cloth; all this added up to a very strange holy man, not one I usually associated with the followers of Śrī Caitanya. I had just been to visit another famous Caitanya Vaiṣṇava, one of the great writers and theologians of the twentieth century, Śrī Kanupriya Gosvāmī. During our conversation I had asked him where I might purchase some of his books. I was interested in collecting as many as I could for later study. He sent me to a small shop in the market area of the West Bengal town of Navadvīpa where his house was located. After our meeting I went directly to the shop and asked for the books. The shopkeeper pulled out all the books he had of Kanupriya Gosvāmī and then he pulled out some pictures of Bābā Tinkaḍi, some of which are published in this volume, in which he thought I might also have an interest. I looked at the pictures and scratched my head. Finally, I thanked the shopkeeper, paid for Kanupriya's books and returned the Tinkaṭi Bābā pictures. Little did I know that in a year or two I would meet that *bābājī* personally and eventually become one of his first non-Indian (*videśī*) disciples.

When I first saw those pictures of Bābā, I had been a member of another religious organization for almost five years. It was under the influence and auspices of that organization that I first traveled to India and stayed there for a number of years. During that period I had learned with reasonable facility Sanskrit, the classical language of India and the language most of the Caitanya tradition's religious texts were written in, and I had learned high or literary Bengali (*sādhu-bhāṣā*) as well. Eventually, I discovered with the help of an elder friend and mentor certain inconsistencies and anomalies in the background of that organization and I lost my faith in it and its leader. At the same time I developed a strong desire to find a more authentic and traditional approach to Kṛṣṇa-centric *bhakti*. At that time, I was sent by that same friend, Dr. O. B. L. Kapoor, to meet a great, accomplished (*siddha*) practitioner of mainstream Caitanya Vaiṣṇavism. Guess who that great practitioner turned out to be? When I first visited him he was staying at his *āśrama* at Chakleswar on the bank of the Mānasa-sarovara lake at the foot of Mount Govardhana. At that time Bābā was around 70 years of age. My first visit happened to be on a festival day and Bābā was overseeing a special Caitanya Vaiṣṇava rite called the Chauśatī Mahānta Bhoga (Feast for the Sixty-four Saints), a feast honoring sixty-four great saints of the Caitanya tradition. Festival foods were offered to the sacred images of Rādhā and Kṛṣṇa and then served to the sixty-four saints on sixty-four leaf plates laid out in rows along with cups for drinks and leaf bowls for sweets. After the saints have "eaten," the food is collected and offered to the guests in attendance.

Bābā was walking around among his busy disciples who were laying out the feast in the courtyard of the *āśrama*, giving them directions. He looked much like he did in those pictures I had seen earlier: longish hair and a beard, huge *tulasī* beads around his neck, his hand always in his bead bag, and wearing nothing but a loincloth and an upper cloth over his shoulders. I could see that the coarse cloth I had noticed in the pictures was a kind of burlap or gunny sack cloth. He walked with a limp and his left hand remained curled up by his side, paralyzed as a result of a stroke he had suffered a few years earlier. His sonant, trombone-like voice gave orders and directions in rapid Bengali which was very hard for me, with my mostly theoretical knowledge of high Bengali, to understand. He seemed also to speak with a slight slur, perhaps also the result of that stroke. He radiated a kind of sweetness, gentility, and humility that were palpable and heart-warming. He seemed to me at that time the diametrical opposite of the guru whom I was considering leaving.

I was introduced to him by one of my companions, another of his disciples named Parimal Bishwas. Parimal and his grandmother Binaparni had been instrumental in telling me about Bābā and helping me to find my way into his presence. He asked me a few questions which I was unable to understand and had to depend on Parimal to translate for me. He was especially pleased when he heard my name, Nitai Das. Nitai or Nityānanda Prabhu was one of Śrī Caitanya's dearest companions and a powerful force, along with his wife Jāhnavā or Jāhnavī Mātā, in the establishment and spread of the early Caitanya movement. Bābā was born in a Gosvāmī family that traced its ancestry back to one of the close followers and disciples of Nityānanda Prabhu, Śrī Guṇanidhi Gosvāmī. Therefore, his face lit up when Parimal told him my name. He ordered Parimal to be sure I got sufficient grace-food, the food that had been offered to and sanctified by the sacred images and then by the sixty-four saints. I watched the ceremony that was being performed and sang along with the disciples as they performed *kīrtana* (responsorial singing with drums and cymbals) while the saints ate. Later I was given a generous plate of grace-food and as I was about done eating, Parimal came along with a little bit of food from Bābā's own plate for me.[170]

Towards evening I was called in to Bābā's room and asked if I had any questions for him. Through Parimal I asked him about the thing foremost in my mind at the time, the importance of initiation in the Caitanya tradition. That had been one of my most shocking discoveries about the organization I was considering leaving. Caitanya Vaiṣṇavism, being a tradition based on or at least heavily influenced by a body of religious texts called *tantras*, places great importance on empowerment through initiation (*dīkṣā*).[171] My organization appeared to lack any connection with the Caitanya tradition through initiation, a lack which led to a number of oddities and anomalies in teaching and practice. Bābā responded to my question by saying that proper initiation was extremely important in the tradition of Śrī Caitanya. He used a modern and rather simple example to make his point. Bābā compared proper initiation to electrical sockets in houses. An electrical outlet that is connected to the powerhouse will provide all the power one needs. An outlet that is not connected to the powerhouse will be dead and useless. Thus it is important to receive initiation from someone connected with the

[170]This is considered a special honor in the Caitanya tradition.

[171]Gavin Flood has noted in a recent study: "The idea that to worship a god one must become a god is a notable feature of all tantric traditions, even ones which maintain a dualist metaphysics." And, "Empowerment of the body, which means its divinisation, is arguably the most important quality in tantric traditions, but a quality that is only specified within particular traditions and texts." Gavin Flood, *The Tantric Body*, 11. (London: I. B. Tauris, 2006)

powerhouse—Śrī Caitanya or one of his close companions—through a lineage of transmission of mantra (*guru-paramparā*). This made sense to me at the time and, whether he intended it or not, helped me make up my mind on whether or not to leave the organization I was in at the time. Their electrical outlet was dead, I felt, their connection with Śrī Caitanya nonexistent or at best imaginary. Many of the anomalies in teaching and practice of that organization stemmed, so it seemed, from that absence of meaningful connection. The institution of initiation (*dīkṣā*) had been operating for centuries in traditional Caitanya Vaiṣṇavism to prevent the adulteration or unwarranted mutation of the tradition.

It seemed like Bābā was always on the move. Over the few months following that first meeting with Bābā I visited him several times but generally never in the same place and again usually in the company of Parimal and Parimal's grandmother, Binaparni Debi. They seemed to be able to keep track of his mysterious movements. During those visits I learned more about Bābā's background and his mode of practice, both by observing him and by talking to those around him. I discovered quite early the degree of respect and pride with which he was viewed by those around him and by members of the mainstream community of Caitanya Vaiṣṇavas. Bābā was from one of the high caste families of Gosvāmins refered to as *ācāryas*, "most respected or universal teacher," by the rest of the community. It was not common for people of his status to renounce household life and take to the path of intense private worship and austerity. Ordinary members of the community spoke of his sacrifice with wonder and pride. Moreover, the degree of self-privation that he practiced was considered remarkable. He gave up all comforts so that he could concentrate fully on the worship of Śrī Rādhā and Kṛṣṇa. He preferred to stay in lonely, isolated places, away from populated areas and often infested with snakes and other dangerous animals. As several of the stories collected here suggest, dangerous animals did not seem to harm him. Binaparni Debi once told me that he had a hard time keeping servants and companions with him because they were afraid of the places he liked to perform his worship in. Servants, I wondered? What does an austere renunciant need with servants? I was told that when Bābā was younger he did everything for himself, but as he grew older and physically weaker, especially after the stroke, he depended on helpers more and more. When I met him his servant was Sītānātha Dāsa Bābājī. Sītānātha Bābā cooked for Bābā and helped him take care of his physical needs (cleaning, washing clothes, taking medicine, etc.). Some of the others who stayed with him, either his disciples or friends, would also help out from time to time.

About six months after that first meeting, I decided to leave the organization I had been in, go live with Bābā and ask for his guidance. It was a difficult decision to make since I had achieved a certain amount of recognition, status, and comfort in the old organization. I was also close to the founder-teacher of that organization since I had traveled with him as a personal secretary for a couple of years. I thought of him as a father and he treated me like a son. What lay ahead in the snake-infested wilds of Vraja was uncertain. My mentor suggested that I take initiation secretly from Bābā and remain in the organization I was in, but that did not feel right to me. Besides, I did not like certain of my old organization's behaviors and attitudes towards members of other traditions and of the Vaiṣṇava community at large. I found those attitudes arrogant and offensive, and giving offense to such good people (*sādhus*) was warned against in the texts of the tradition as a major impediment to advancement in spiritual life. So, I remained divided for several months, increasingly uncomfortable. And, when the opportunity arose, I vanished into thin air, or so it must have seemed to my former colleagues.

When I vanished I was traveling back from Bombay to the Vrindaban temple I had been residing in. Instead of returning to the temple I went to Parimal's house in Vrindaban, dropped the baggage I didn't want to take with me, found out where Bābā was and how to get there, and set out.

At that time Bābā was staying at a little pond called Ratan-kuṇḍ, a few miles from a town called Chata on the main highway between Mathura and New Delhi. I got off the bus at Chata with a shoulder bag stuffed with books and a few other things, asked directions to a village near the kuṇḍ, and set off down a dirt road through agricultural fields. It was near the end of the rainy season and it was sprinkling lightly off and on. I could see that many of the fields around me were flooded from the heavy rains of the days before. By the time I reached the village closest to Ratan-kuṇḍ it was twilight and as I walked down the path that ran through the center of the village I came upon a group of men sitting on village beds having a smoke and chatting after the labors of the day. In my broken Hindi I informed them of my destination and asked for directions.

One of the elders informed me that Ratan-kuṇḍ was about a mile and a half away and advised me to spend the night in the village and go on early the next day. I was insistent, however, and when it looked like I was ready to go on anyway, one of the young men in the group stood up and offered to guide me there. The young villager was tall and very muscular. He was about a head taller than me though I was six feet tall. He grabbed my bag full of books, hoisted it on his shoulder and led the way. We hadn't gone very far outside the village before we were wading through water, first only knee deep and then waist deep. It would have been deeper except that he was guiding me along the raised ridges that bordered all the fields in that area, ridges that he seemed to be able to feel with his feet, but I could not. More than once my foot slipped and he had to reach back and keep me from going completely under. It was a very eerie scene. As I looked around me in the dying glow of the day all I saw was water in all directions with twisted, half-submerged trees scattered here and there looking very much like sinking swimmers reaching up in a last desperate effort to grab hold of something. It was silent except for the water swishing around our waists and the occasional squawking of a disturbed bird. It would be a lie to say that I wasn't afraid. I was petrified. The calmness and confidence of my guide was the only reassurance I had. Over the years I have often wondered if my enormous guide had not been Balarāma, Kṛṣṇa's super strong brother, himself.

After what seemed an interminable time, we abruptly turned off of the ridge we were following and started crossing through the flooded middle of a field. The water was then chest deep. It was by then nearly dark and I could not see much of anything except for my guide in front of me leading me on. As we progressed across the field the depth of the water began to lessen and before too long we were walking through knee deep water. In the distance I began to hear the sounds of drums and cymbals and the faint high tenors of human voices. As we walked, a denser darkness loomed up in front of us, a darkness that seemed to have patches here and there of flickering, weak yellow-orange light. The sounds of drums and music became louder. When we drew close I saw a stone house sitting up on a little knoll, the light of candles and lanterns in its windows and the strains of sacred music floating. We worked our way up to the house and went around a corner where we found two or three steps and a door on which the young Vrajavāsī began to pound. The door swung open and there in the reflected light of the lanterns were the astonished faces of a half a dozen *bābājīs*. Soon the cry went up: "Nitai Das eṣeche! Nitai Das eṣeche, e rakam rāte, e rakam bṛṣṭite, Nitai Das eṣeche! Ki adbhut!"[172] My Bengali was good enough to understand

[172] "Nitai Das has come; Nitai Das has come. At this time of night and in this kind of rain! How astonishing!"

that. This experience seemed like a suitable transition from my old life to my new one, a dramatic rite of passage through water and darkness, a symbolic death and rebirth.

The *bābājīs* ushered us into the house. We were soaked from the waist down and wet from the waist up. One of the younger *bābās* took the bag of books from the young man and placed it in a corner. Surprisingly enough, the books inside the bag, riding on the shoulder of the young Vrajavāsī, remained relatively dry and safe even in the midst of the constant drizzle and flooded fields through which we waded. Another older bābā began to talk to my guide in Hindi, or probably more correctly Braj Bhasha. The young Vrajavāsī told him of my arrival at his village and our trek through the deepening night to the house. Meanwhile, another *bābājī* tried to talk with me as best he could. This was the first time I was without someone to translate for me. I told him as clearly as I could that I had come to stay with Bābā for a while this time and that I wished to learn from him and become his disciple. We had interrupted their evening *kīrtana*. Bābā who had been sitting in the back room of the house listening to the *kīrtana*, and singing along, came out to see what had stopped it. When I saw him emerge from the darkness of the neighboring room I bowed down at his feet and touched them. This was the proper etiquette in the Caitanya Vaiṣṇava world for greeting one's guru or any great saint or practitioner. He reached down and patted me on the head with his right hand, gave me his blessing, and then had me rise up and sit near the lantern. The young Vrajavāsī also bowed down and touched his feet. When the young man rose up again, Bābā asked him a number of questions and invited him to stay the night, since it was still raining and the village was far away. The young man respectfully declined and Bābā ordered that he be given some grace food before he went. There was a lot of concern about the flooding and that was one of the topics the *bābājīs* discussed with the young Vrajavāsī. The *bābājīs* were afraid that the water would keep rising and flood the house. It had already surrounded it on all sides and caused Ratan-kuṇḍ, which was a small pond. to expand beyond its banks. After the young man had eaten and rested a bit, I thanked him for his help and he took our leave, heading out the door into the drizzle and dark. As soon as he was gone the *kīrtana* began again.

And so began my life with Bābā. Over the next several months many things happened, but this is not the time or place to recount them all. I will just highlight some of the events that give some sense of what it was like to live with Bābā out in the lonely reaches of Vraja in those days. After *kīrtana* that first night we ate. This usually took place outside, but since the flood waters were everywhere outside, we ate inside. All of the *bābājīs* were seated in a line in the room we had done *kīrtana* in. I was put in another room to the side of that room and opening on to it. It was my first taste of the kind of food the *bābājīs* ate in Bābā's entourage out in the remote areas. Our meal consisted of a curried vegetable dish and *roti*, a large, thick flat-bread made of wheat. One broke pieces off of the bread and used them to pick up and eat with the vegetable. Drinking water was also provided. It was a good thing, because the vegetable was quite spicy and the flat-bread required a good deal of chewing. Everything we ate had been begged from the local villagers. Every day a small group of the younger *bābājīs* went out begging for alms, a process called *madhukarī*. *Madhukarī* means "honey-maker" and refers to the way the honey bee moves from flower to flower gathering a little pollen and nectar from each as it makes honey. Like the honey bee, the bābājīs went from house to house begging for alms. Whatever they received was what we ate that day.

That first night, after *kīrtana* and after the night-time meal, I was shown a sleeping spot on the floor in a room off the main room and right outside of Bābā's room. It was an eerie first night. I spread my blanket out and stowed my books and other belongings near my head against the wall. As I was falling asleep I could hear the rain still falling outside the window. I felt pleasantly peaceful and at ease as I drifted into the second state of consciousness, dream. I don't remember what I dreamt that night but at some point, perhaps around midnight or one in the morning, I woke up. The house was dark except for the dim light of the lantern from the next room which had been turned down to low. I could hear the soft breathing of the other *bābājīs* and an occasional snore from some distant corner of the house. Then I heard what sounded like an animated conversation coming out of Bābā's room. Bābā was talking softly and very quickly, punctuating his speech with chuckles and laughs. Besides his voice I heard no other. I wanted to get up and peek in, but I was afraid of disturbing him and the one other *bābā* who was stretched out across the doorway to Bābā's room. I would have had to step over him to poke my head into Bābā's room. I listened quietly for a while as Bābā's talking went on, punctuated with chuckles here and there. I don't know how long I listened there quietly trying to catch some phrase or group of words that I might recognize, but eventually sleep took me over again. In the morning I asked Banamālī Dāsa Bābā, one of the *bābājīs* I recognized from my previous visits, about Bābā's talking that night. He chuckled as he said loudly (because everyone reacted to my weak understanding of spoken Bengali by assuming or acting as though I was deaf) that Bābā talked like that often in the wee hours of the morning, and that he was talking with Śrī Rādhā and Kṛṣṇa. I stared at him for a moment in disbelief. He seemed entirely sincere about what he was saying.

The next few days were difficult. The rain had stopped and the rising water, too, had stopped right at the jam of the door of the house. There were seven of us staying in that house. We were surrounded by water on three sides. The fourth had an open space that rose slightly to another small, one-room house on one side, and the steps leading down to the small pond called Ratan-kuṇḍ, the "pond of the jewel," on the other. The rest of the pond, of course, had overrun its banks and its water was mixed with that of the flooded fields surrounding it. For the first few days, one had to wade through some flood water to get from the door of the house we were in to that open space. The upshot is that we were housebound for several days. I don't remember exactly what we did for those next few days. Bābā instructed me to spend all my time chanting, that is, repeating the holy names of Kṛṣṇa. He wanted me to complete three *lakhs* (300,000 or a hundred and ninety-two times around a Vaṣṇava string of beads)[173] of holy names a day and didn't want me to take part in any of the chores like the others of his entourage had to. For me it was just sitting and chanting. Bābā himself chanted at least three *lakhs* a day and practiced a vow of silence each day until he had completed them. He was usually finished by around two or three in the afternoon. Since he started around one or two in the morning, it took him ten to twelve hours to finish three *lakhs*. Completing that practice was enormously difficult for me. I had never chanted so many rounds before. The organization I had just left only required sixteen rounds, or twenty-seven thousand repetitions, of the holy names, which generally took me about two hours. Bābā wanted me to do twelve times that many. At the speed I was accustomed to chanting it would have taken me twenty-fours to do three *lakhs*. I chanted pretty much all the time except during our early morning *ārati* (about 4:30 A.M.), meals (1:00-1:30 P.M., 9:00-9:30 P.M.), our afternoon scriptural readings (3:30-5:30 P.M.), evening *kīrtanas* (6:30-8:30 P.M.) and sleep (10:00-4:00 A.M.). Of course, none of this was exact; we were not on a daconian schedule. Beginnings varied a little bit each day. At first I wasn't able to complete even one

[173]It actually comes out to 331,776 because there are sixteen names in the Mahāmantra and one hundred and eight beads on a Vaiṣṇava garland of beads. 16 x 108 x 192 = 331,776.

lakh. Eventually, as I became more focused and faster at chanting, I came close to completing two *lakhs*, but I never reached the goal that Bābā set for me during that stay. Till today I have not been able to complete three *lakhs* in a single day.

From the second night of my stay I was assigned the roof as my sleeping place, since the rain had stopped and the sun had dried it out. That night was one of the most miserable nights of my life. The mosquitos were as thick as clouds. I tried to wrap myself up in my woolen blanket, even though it was a hot night and the woolen blanket made me extremely uncomfortable, but that did nothing more than draw their interest. By morning I was covered with bites. Another member of Bābā's entourage slept up on the roof with me, a young Bengali man named Śyāmānanda Dāsa. He had a mosquito net and seemed surprised that I didn't have one, too. In the morning he informed the other *bābājīs* that I had no net and Banamālī Dāsa, was immediately dispatched through the mud and flood to a village five miles away to purchase one for me. That night Śyāmānanda helped me figure out how to set it up securely on the roof and what had been one of the most hellish experiences I have ever had was transformed into one of the most heavenly. There I laid safe within the confines of my net, on top of my blanket instead of wrapped up in it, with thousands of mosquitos buzzing around outside the net, not one of them able to reach me. On top of that, a cool night breeze blew though the cotton openings of the net and cooled me. It was an extremely pleasant experience. Needless to say, I slept wonderfully. Unfortunately, however, in a couple of weeks, I came down with a malarial fever, which was quickly recognized by Bābā and the other *bābājīs* when I complained of headaches, aching body parts, and chills. Poor Banamālī Dāsa Bābā was sent out again to that same village, this time to purchase some chloro-quinine tablets. I was immediately moved from the roof of the main house to the small one-room house nearby which I shared with Śyāmānanda. I spent the next week or so in bed, inside my mosquito net, miserable, headachy and feverish. With the medicine, the rest, and the care of the *bābājīs*, I was soon back to normal. Still, life with Bābā had not started off easily.

Over the next several months I had many great opportunities to observe Bābā and the religious life that he led and that surrounded him. When the paths to the nearest villages became less treacherous, parties of two or three were sent out each day to perform *madhukarī*, begging for alms. Sometimes they came back with a respectable supply of fresh vegetables and coarsely ground wheat flour, occasionally some fresh buttermilk. Sometimes they came back with nothing. The average farming household in that area was relatively poor. Still, when the villagers had a little something extra they shared it. That was the way bābājīs lived. I don't recall missing any meals. We always seemed to have enough flour for those big, thick *rotis* which I found so hard to digest, even if all we had with it was a kind of gravy-like sauce made from chick-pea flour, water and spices. I remember watching one day as Sītānātha Dāsa Bābājī, who did most of the cooking during that period, looked among the bushes that grew behind the house for at least some edible leaves to mix in with that sauce. Everything, no matter how poor, was always offered to the sacred images whose service was the heart of the community. Only after it was offered to them did we get to honor it as grace-food (*prasāda*).

Since I was busy chanting rounds all day and Bābā, too, stayed mostly in his room chanting and maintaining his vow of silence, I rarely saw him before midafternoon when he came out of his room and walked about until the readings began. During the readings he became like an eager child, expressing excitement and wonder at the stories being read. At that time, the text being read was the *Śrī Gopāla-campū*, "The Story of Gopāla," of Śrī Jīva Gosvāmin.[174] Vanamālī Dāsa Bābājī generally did the readings. Bābā would walk back and forth as he listened, chuckling from time to time or making little exclamations of wonder at something in the reading. Sometimes he would stop and comment on a passage or ask a question of Banamālī Dāsa Bābājī. Occasionally, he would turn to me and speak in Bengali, giving me some instruction that the reading put him in mind of. When he saw that I wasn't following very well he would switch to Hindi. When he saw that I was still not following, he would sometimes try to say what he meant in English, a language which he knew a little of, but was not in the habit of speaking. Gradually I began to understand parts of what he said to me. I remember his stressing the importance something called *sadācāra*, ritual purity. That was one of my biggest challenges during those early days and months, learning how to maintain a high level of ritual purity. When one remembered one's *mantras* (not that I had been given them yet) or performed ritual worship of sacred images (for me then my worship was directed just to pictures, but later I was given a sacred stone from Mount Giriraja), one had to be in a state of ritual purity.

---

[174] A *campū* is a special kind of poetic composition that mixes prose and verse.

Ritual purity (*sadācāra*) is different from simple cleanliness. After all, we were bathing, brushing our teeth, and washing our clothes in the flood waters. We were pooping and urinating out in the surrounding fields and to cleanse ourselves we rubbed ourselves with mud with our left hands and bathed in the nearby muddy pond (Ratan-kuṇḍ). Cleanliness and ritual purity often overlap, but they do not coincide. The behaviors that make up *sadācāra* more or less coincide with typical behaviors discussed in historians of religion such as Mircea Eliade and others.[175] One has to be in a state of ritual purity when one comes into contact with the sacred; otherwise one runs the risk of being harmed.[176] In addition, the extreme purity of the sacred is often indistinguishable from extreme impurity. In fact the word we often used to refer to impurity was *prasādī*, "full of grace!" Anything that came into contact with something that was *prasādī*, like an article of clothing, had to be cleaned before it could be used again. For me the challenge was learning how to do important things, like eating, for instance, with only my right hand. The left hand, used for cleaning purposes, was considered permanently impure. My ritual purity was so much under suspicion that I was never allowed to enter the room where the sacred images were kept, or the kitchen where the food for the images was prepared.

One of the things I remember most vividly was the frequent fasting we did. We fasted at least twice a month for the days called Ekādaśī, the eleventh day after the full and new moons. On those days we fasted not only from food but also from water. In addition, we performed *kīrtana* of the holy names all night beginning after our usual evening *kīrtana* and singing until the early morning *ārati* at 4:30 A.M., the time when the sacred images were awakened and greeted. To my surprise, I sometimes found that as the night wore on, fewer and fewer singers remained in the *kīrtana* until eventually I was the only one remaining. I had sometimes to carry both lead and responsorial parts for the last couple of hours. When the others disappeared and how, I never knew. The chanting kind of puts one in a trance especially after a day long fast. All I know is that at some point in the night I would look up and find everyone else had crawled off to bed leaving me alone with the karatals (hand cymbals). Perhaps it was the first time I observed Ekādaśī out with the *bābājīs* that,

[175]"The ambivalence of the sacred is not only in the psychological order (in that it attracts or repels), but also in the order of values; the sacred is at once 'sacred' and 'defiled.'" Eliade, *Structure and Morphology of the Sacred*, 14-15. See also Mary Douglas' *Purity and Danger*.

[176]ibid., 15. "It is dangerous to come near any defiled or consecrated object in a profane state—without, that is, the proper ritual preparation."

when the others began to stir from their blankets, Bābā came out of his room and asked Banamālī Dāsa Bābājī who had done *kīrtana* all night. Banamālī, looking a little shame-faced, nodded in my direction and said: "o" (him). It may have been my imagination, but it seemed to me that Bābā looked at me a little differently after that.

Observing Ekādaśī twice a month was certainly challenging. But usually in addition to the two monthly fasts there were fasts in honor of a holiday or two. There is a saying among Bengalis: "Twelve months, thirteen holidays." Among the Vaiṣṇavas there are certainly a lot more holidays than that, and they are all observed in pretty much the same way: a twenty-four hour fast and *kīrtana* of the holy names all night.

On the days after the Ekādaśīs and the holidays it was considered important to break one's fast before a certain time. We usually broke our fasts with a drink made of ground black pepper and solidified molasses or *guḍa*. It was supposed to be good for an empty stomach. After that we would have some grace food. I generally felt extraordinarily contented after these day-long fasts, though rather tired because of staying up all night long. One is not supposed to sleep while the sun is up unless one is ill. So climbing into bed the night after a fast was especially pleasant.

Occasionally, people came to visit Bābā, often from as far as Calcutta. They would appear out of the deepening dusk, spend the night, and then vanish before the sun was very high in the sky. We had a famous singer of *kīrtana*, who was one of Bābā's disciples, appear that way one evening. He was a heavy-set man and I was told by one of the *bābājīs* that he was famous in Bengal for singing beautiful *kīrtana*. That night after our usual evening *kīrtana* he sang some songs for us. He really was stupendous. He voice was rich and deep and when he sang half the *bābājīs* shivered in delight. I did, too, by association. Though I could not yet follow the meaning of the songs I recognized their beauty and feeling. Bābā sat back in the shadows where his physical responses to the *rasas* of the songs would be not be obtrusive or even noticeable except to those who were watching. It never occurred to me to watch. Instead, I watched our singer as he gently and with deep emotion teased the *rasa* out of a song and built to its overwhelming climax. It was a sublime experience.

On another occasion, two middle-aged women arrived, seemingly out of nowhere, at our house at Ratan-kuṇḍ. It was Ekādaśī and so we were all fasting. On Ekādaśīs the sacred images do not fast, so Bābā ordered that the women be offered grace-food from the offerings to the images. The women were disciples of Bābā's from Calcutta and had come for a short visit to see him and receive his blessing. Who knows what they must have gone through to get to us. They did not seem particularly well off, so it is not likely that they had a driver waiting for them on the main road five miles away. They probably rode the train from Calcutta, took a bus from Mathura, and walked those last five dusty miles. The women were welcomed warmly by the *bābājīs* and treated respectfully. They had their audience with Bābā, bowing before him and touching his feet. That night the Ekādaśī *kīrtana* started up right after our regular evening *kīrtana*, and as usual as the night wore on *bābājī* after *bābājī* disappeared into the shadows. Eventually, it was just me and the women carrying the *kīrtana*. At various points in the early morning, half in a trance, I altered the tune to which we were singing the Mahāmantra. I didn't mean to; it just came out oddly. This usually happened when I was singing by myself in those early morning hours, but no one ever was there to notice. This time, however, each time it happened the women immediately changed back to way it was before and we continued on. I felt a little embarrassed, but overall I was grateful for the company. None of the *bābājīs* complained about having to listen to female voices as sometimes happens in other renunciant companies. When daylight came, we broke our fasts and off the women went, after receiving grace food and breaking their fasts, to retrace their steps back to their homes.

After the flood waters had fully receded and the fields around us more or less dried out, we were sometimes joined in the afternoons for our readings by several other *bābājīs* who lived by themselves in isolated huts scattered around the neighboring area. One *bābājī* took a special interest in me. At this point I sadly can no longer remember his name. I remember, though, one afternoon after our reading he asked Bābā if he had given me initiation (*dīkṣā*) yet. Bābā replied that he hadn't. The *bābājī* then entreated him to give me full initiation. Bābā replied that he was waiting for a transformation to occur in me before he would give me initiation. Then I understood why I had been set apart and was required to do nothing but the chanting of the holy names (and the other group activities, of course) while the others had other services and duties to perform. Bābā had spotted something in me that he did not like and wanted changed before he would bestow the grace of initiation on me. I don't know what it was that Bābā saw in me that he didn't like. Bābā's requiring me to chant a huge number of holy names was meant to purify me of whatever that flaw in my character was. He remained adamant, however, and in spite of the repeated entreaties of that *bābājī* benefactor of mine, which he delivered every time he visited us, Bābā withheld initiation from me for quite some time. Eventually, as my number of daily repetitions of the holy names moved beyond the one *lakh* (100,000) marker and came close to two *lakhs* (200,000) Bābā partially gave in. As we shall see later he gave me partial initiation, not all of the mantras that are ordinarily given in a full initiation, but some of them. Perhaps he began to see some of that transformation he had been waiting for in me, or perhaps he became worried when he saw me fall ill, as I did several times during my stay with him, or perhaps, after I eventually decided to return to the USA, he worried that I might miss out on the opportunity for initiation altogether and die without it. I guess I will never know.

I observed a few more interesting aspects of Bābā while I was living with him. One day a villager from the local area came to see him. Everyone could see from his flushed look and somewhat listless movements that he was not feeling well. He asked Bābā for some medicine. Much to my surprise Bābā asked one of the other *bābājīs* to go get his box. The *bābājī* came back in a few minutes with a wooden box about two feet tall and a foot and a half wide with numerous drawers filled with small glass bottles. The box was a portable homeopathic pharmacy! When and where Bābā learned homeopathy, I haven't the slightest idea. Binode Bihārī Dāsa Bābājī says nothing of it in his account. He asked the young man a number of questions, felt his head, and took his pulse. Then he ordered one of the *bābājīs* who were looking on to wrap up in a small piece of paper some tiny pills of a particular type for the visitor. The man thanked him, touched his feet, and departed. This was another of the ways in which Bābā served the local communities. I only saw this happen once during my stay with Bābā, however. So I don't know how common an occurrence it was. Just the presence of Bābā and other holy men like him was considered auspicious by the local villagers, good for the welfare of the village. As I learned during my stay with him, far from being put out by the presence of Bābā and his small band of companions, the local people were happy to have him nearby and to share with him their meager food. They felt he and others like him bring them good luck, made their lives better.

Another activity that Bābā was enthusiastic about was organizing seven day readings of the *Bhāgavata Purāṇa*. Towards the end of our stay at Ratan-kuṇḍ, he began making arrangements for the performance of a *Bhāgavata-saptāha* at a village a few miles away where he intended to move next in his constant circumambulation of the sacred realm of Vraja.

I saw Bābā meet with somebody during the planning stages of that rite and hand over a fairly substantial amount of money. Then, a week or two later, one of Bābā's local (Vrajavāsī) disciples arrived at Ratan-kuṇḍ with a tractor hauling a large open trailer. This disciple was a farmer in the vicinity and was often called upon to help Bābā and his party move from one place to another. Because of the paralysis left by his stroke some years earlier, Bābā could no longer walk far distances. We had been warned to have our things ready, and when the tractor arrived, we all piled on to the trailer with all of our belongings. Bābā sat up near the front and one of the *bābājīs* pulled out a *mṛdaṅga* (clay drum), others some *karatals* (hand cymbals). We started *kīrtana* as the tractor started off across the fields. We rode like that for about an hour doing *kīrtana* as we passed through fields, down dirt roads and through small villages. Eventually, we came to a village that had on its outskirts an L-shaped building consisting of a number of rooms joined together side by side and enclosing on two sides a wide open space that stood between it and the village. The tractor pulled up in front of the building and we all climbed off of its trailer. This was to be our home for the next few weeks. Unfortunately for me, my stomach could not seem to adjust to the thick coarse flat-breads we were eating. So I spent much of my time running for the fields behind the buildings we were staying in and then to the town well to take a quick bath and wash my clothes.

A significant portion of the open space in this new home was eventually covered by a tent, which was open at the sides and had a raised platform, backed by a tent wall, at one end. This was where the *Bhāgavata-saptāha* was to be performed. The ceremony started a few days later at an auspicious time on an auspicious day and was punctuated with numerous *kīrtanas* and *pūjās* and much distribution of food. It was reasonably well attended by people from the nearby village and other surrounding villages. Three *bābājīs* had been brought in to recite the *Bhāgavata Purāṇa* over the seven day period. Two of them recited the Sanskrit verses of the text very rapidly, seated on the raised platform, for several hours during the days of ritual. Naturally, few people were present during the morning and afternoon. The recitation was not actually meant for an audience, since it was recited rapidly and without amplification. In the evenings the audience area of the tent, which was spread with a large thick, faded red rug, filled up and there was a lecture on the *Bhāgavata* in Hindi given by the third *bābājī* and a *kīrtana* and *ārati* were performed afterwards. The lecture generally focused on some particular passage or story and did not attempt to cover all that had been recited during that day. After the *kīrtana* grace-food was distributed to all those who had come for the festivities. I, of course, understood very little of the proceedings. I was just getting accustomed to spoken Bengali and everything in the ritual seemed to be in Hindi. As many of the *bābājīs* informed me, the rite was considered very powerful and just being in the vicinity of the recitation was purifying to one and all. I, of course, participated in the *kīrtanas* and *āratis* and helped out wherever else I could.

As the number of rounds I did increased, strange things began to happen to me. Perhaps I was influenced by all the talk about transformation or purification, but it seemed as if memories buried deep in my mind began to bubble to the surface, like the impurities buried in butter do when making ghee. They aroused in me strange emotions of loss, separation, and nostalgia. Things and people that I literally had not thought of for years began to appear vividly before my eyes, almost as fresh and clear as the day I first experienced them. I had the feeling that something indeed was beginning to happen to me because of all the chanting, and frankly it began to frighten me. I suspected that if I continued with that intense *sādhana*, all those for whom I had love and affection would be lost to me, would in effect become strangers, and that my world would become forever changed. Home would no longer be home; parents, family, and friends would no longer be familiar to me. I felt deeply uneasy about entering a world in which all of my values had been shuffled and inverted. Years later I found a passage in a book by Carlos Castaneda that captured something of what the transformation I felt approaching was about to do to me. Towards the end of his third book, *Journey to Ixtlan*, Don Genaro describes his own meeting with his ally:

> "What happened when you grabbed your ally, don Genaro?" I asked.
>
> "It was a powerful jolt," don Genaro said after a moment's hesitation. He seemed to have been putting his thoughts in order.
>
> "Never would I have imagined it was going to be like that," he went on. "It was something, something, something ... like nothing I can tell. After I grabbed it we began to spin. The ally made me twirl, but I didn't let go. We spun through the air with such speed and force that I couldn't see any more.

Everything was foggy. The spinning went on, and on, and on. Suddenly I felt that I was standing on the ground again. I looked at myself. The ally had not killed me. I was in one piece. I was myself! I knew then that I had succeeded. At long last I had an ally. I jumped up and down with delight. What a feeling! What a feeling it was!

"Then I looked around to find out where I was. The surroundings were unknown to me. I thought that the ally must have taken me through the air and dumped me somewhere very far from the place where we started to spin. I oriented myself. I thought that my home must be towards the east, so I began to walk in that direction. It was still early. The encounter with the ally had not taken too long. Very soon I found a trail and then I saw a bunch of men and women coming towards me. They were Indians. I thought they were Mazatec Indians. They surrounded me and asked me where I was going. 'I'm going home to Ixtlan,' I said to them. 'Are you lost?' someone asked. 'I am,' I said. 'Why?' 'Because lxtlan is not that way. Ixtlan is in the opposite direction. We ourselves are going there,' someone else said. 'Join us!' they all said. 'We have food!'"

Don Genaro stopped talking and looked at me as if he were waiting for me to ask a question.

"Well, what happened?" I asked. "Did you join them?"

"No.I didn't," he said. "Because they were not real. I knew it right away, the minute they came to me. There was something in their voices, in their friendliness that gave them away, especially when they asked me to join them. So I ran away. They called me and begged me to come back. Their pleas became haunting, but I kept on running away from them."

"Who were they?" I asked.

"People," don Genaro replied cuttingly. "Except that they were not real."

"They were like apparitions," don Juan explained. "Like phantoms."[177]

Don Genaro concludes his account of meeting and wrestling with

[177] Carlos Castaneda, *Journey to Ixtlan*, 306-7. (New York: Simon and Schuster, 1972)

his ally by saying: "I will never reach Ixtlan."[178] Ixtlan which was his home and the people of his former life became like phantoms to him. His encounter with his ally had thrown him out of his old world into another, separate reality. As he says a little earlier in the narrative: "After my encounter with the ally nothing was real any more."[179] Though I had not read Castaneda when I was staying with Bābā, I was afraid that something dramatic was about to happen to me if I continued as I was. So, I hatched a plan to return home to the USA and finish my education.

Bābā was not pleased. About the time I was making up my mind to return to the United States, several of the others who were not yet *bābājīs* decided to take the formal vows of entry into the state of being a *bābājī*, a rite called *veśa*, change of habit (way of dressing). Bābā wanted me to do that, too. He was disappointed when he learned that I had other plans and that I would be leaving soon. I often have wondered what my life would have been like if I had stayed and taken *veśa* as Bābā had wanted me to. It is very hard to tell, but since the life of a bābājī is very hard, there is a high likelihood that I would not have lived very long. I had already had malaria and was also cultivating a fine case of amoebic dysentery. Though generally of sturdy disposition, I have a sense that India would have worn me down. Bābā himself passed on, or "entered into eternal sport (*nitya-līlā*)," as we in the Vaiṣṇava tradition like to say, only about eight years later. On the other hand, several of the *bābājīs* who were with Bābā when I lived with him lived for quite a long time. Śrī Sītānātha Dāsa Bābājī who was Bābā's cook passed away only quite recently and Śrī Banamālī Dāsa Bābājī who saved me so many times and in so many ways, walking miles through flooded landscape to get me a mosquito net and then more miles to get me chloro-quinine, is still alive in Rādhākuṇḍa, though his health is very fragile. From the point of the view of the Caitanya tradition, if I had stayed I would have passed through that transformation that Bābā was waiting for and made tremendous advancement towards the goal of cultivating divine love for Kṛṣṇa, especially in the company of one such as Bābā. And if I had died before achieving that, dying in Vraja or Navadvīpa or Jagannātha Purī would have insured my entry into the eternal sport. But I was too timid.

When Bābā learned that I planned to return to the United States he relented in his determination to make me wait for initiation. Perhaps he thought he might not see me again or that he had been too hard on me.

---

[178] ibid., 311.
[179] ibid.

It is impossible to tell. At any rate, before I departed I was called in to his room and he gave me half of the mantras usually given in initiation: the *guru-mantra* and *gāyatrī*, the *gaurāṅga-mantra* and *gāyatrī*, the *nityānanda-mantra* and *gāyatrī*, and the *advaita-mantra* and *gāyatrī*. He withheld the core mantras from me: the *gopāla-mantra* and the *kāma-gāyatrī* and a few others. Nevertheless, the meditative avenues to himself as my guru, to Śrī Caitanya, Śrī Nityānanda, and Śrī Advaita were opened up for me.

As I packed my bags, several of the *bābājīs* came to me asking for my belongings. My warm wool blanket went, as did my mosquito net, and several of the other items I had accumulated over the preceding months. My load seriously lightened, I stretched myself out on the ground before Bābā to offer my last obeisance to him for a while, and touched his feet for blessing. Then, with a heavy heart I headed out for Parimal's house in Vrindaban and from there to Delhi and from Delhi back to the USA.

I saw Bābā several times over the next few years. When I returned to India as part of the University of Wisconsin Year-in-India program in 1978 to study Sanskrit with a Pāṇinian scholar, J. Prabhakara Sastry, in Vishakhapatanam, I visited Bābā in Vraja during our breaks. The first time I visited him he was at Rādhākuṇḍa. I stayed with him for about a week before I had to return to Vaizag. During that visit Bābā gave me the rest of the initiation *mantras*. Later in the year I returned again after my studies had ended, this time with my wife at the time, Josephine. She had come to India for the second half of my nine month stay there. Bābā gave her initiation during our stay with him, once again at Rādhākuṇḍa.

After that, I was not able to visit India until 1983 when I was given a grant to study Bengali through the American Institute of Indian Studies. Calcutta was my home base for that nine month period. At my earliest opportunity, I went to visit Bābā who was then staying in Jagannātha Purī in Orissa. He was living as an honored guest at the Haridāsa Ṭhākura Maṭha at that time, surrounded by several of his disciples. I was shocked when I first saw him. His health had greatly declined in the five years since my last visit. He was no longer able to straighten out his back and as a result he sat and walked slumped forward, his head almost parallel with the ground. In order to make eye contact with him one had to bend over and look up into his face. In spite of this condition, which must have been very painful, his right hand was constantly in his bead bag and an endless murmured stream of holy names issued from his lips. Though his body was thus contorted, he was mentally alert and recognized me immediately. He did not speak to me much but passed a comment on to me through someone, that I had some *saṃskāras*. *Saṃskāras* are, in traditional Indian psychology, deeply embedded impressions of past experiences that affect our current ways of thinking and actions by either creating attractions or repulsions to certain types of objects or activities. These are the bearers of *karma*, the results of one's past actions, according to Indian philosophy. I do not know what exactly Bābā meant, but I was reminded of his concern eight years earlier, when I was living with him, about the need for some kind of transformation in me, and the fear I felt when certain psychological changes seemed to be ready to occur in me. This was his final judgment on my life and the choices I had made.

After this visit to Bābā, I never saw him again alive.

When I went to visit Bābā again in the following February at his *āśrama* in Navadvīpa, I arrived a day too late. Bābā had entered eternal sport the day before. When I arrived, the *āśrama* was jam-packed with people and I was completely without a clue as to what had happened. I soon learned the reason for the big crowd. It was the day nearly the whole of the Vaiṣṇava community of Navadvīpa had gathered at Bābā's *āśrama* to say goodbye and to celebrate his entry into eternal sport. Many Vaiṣṇavas came from much further, as well. Just like on the first day when I visited Bābā, his disciples and members of the community were performing the feast of the sixty-four saints, this time in his honor, and huge amounts of food were being prepared as offerings to the saints and afterwards to feed the crowds of visitors and guests. The festivities lasted all day long. There were *kīrtanas* sung by some of the finest singers in West Bengal. Food was distributed and there were rites and ceremonies for the sacred images in the temple and before the picture of Bābā draped in fragrant garlands and fine cloth. It stood in the little hut in the courtyard of the temple where he stayed and performed his private worship when he came to the *āśrama*. It may sound strange to a western audience, but there was not a wet eye in the whole assembly. It was a joyous occasion. We all believed that Bābā had rejoined the close company of Śrī Rādhā and Kṛṣṇa, which was not a cause for sadness. Many of us, to be sure, felt a sense of loss and deep feelings of separation from him, but those feelings were generally pushed to the back of our minds, to be recalled and suffered later in our solitudes after the festivities. To many of us Bābā's passing was the end of an era. We knew of no one else who matched Bābā's sincerity and fervent enthusiasm for private worship. He was the last of the old school of renunciant Vaiṣṇava practitioner, and as far as I can tell no new school has yet formed.

It has been nearly a quarter of a century since Bābā passed on. I have changed a great deal since then and indeed the whole world has changed. I still think back on him with great fondness and more than a small twinge of sadness, sadness that I did not, could not, go as far in the training as he wanted me to. Whatever the reality of the world may be at any given time, we all to a degree perceive it differently according to our trainings. The world I perceive today as the mostly unregistered backdrop of my life and moments of consciousness is very different from the world he inhabited, which, as I have imagined it, was one of sweetness and joy, a world in which Rādhā and Kṛṣṇa and their friends walked the earth and visited him for humorous and loving chats. The training he wanted me to undergo would have opened that world to me, but I only went part way. Now I am some sort of a hybrid being, like a centaur or satyr. The world I mostly inhabit is that of a trained scholar of the history of religions, but sometimes when my rationality is relaxed and when just the right light shines I catch a glimpse of that neighboring world of Bābā's, a world full of magic and sweetness just beyond my reach. Who can say with certainty that it is not as real as the worlds we occupy with other trainings? My hope is that others reading this account of the life of Bābā will be able to catch a glimpse of the delightful world he occupied as well.

My Recollections — Joseph Knapp

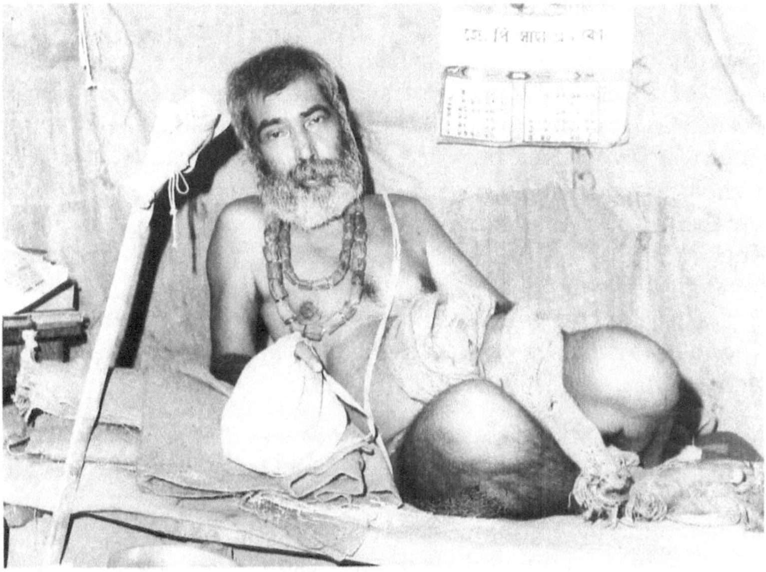

Śrī Gurudeva!

In writing this tribute I will try to present many of the things I remember about the extremely transcendent, extraordinary nature and yet complete humanness of a truly loving, compassionate, illuminated and transmuted holy man who lived simultaneously in two separate worlds—the internal spiritual world and the external spiritual world!

The *rasika* tradition is known for its *siddhas* or accomplished saints, who, while living in the holy places of the tradition, are thought to have direct visions of and interactions with God. These events occur while in both meditative absorption (*samādhi*) and normal consciousness, or in other words, while in both the inner and the outer worlds. Śrī Śrī 1008 Kiśorīkiśorānanda Bābā, Tinkaḍi Gosvāmī, was accepted by the *sādhu* community as *siddha*—perfected or fully accomplished in the realization of the *rasika* tradition, a truly inconceivable state of attainment and being! And apart from that he is my dear most, loving *bābā* (spiritual father).

Dear reader, kindly excuse me, for in my writing of my blessed *gurudeva*, I will be writing to some extent about myself. Still, the important parts of this reminiscence are about him—the blessed *gurudeva*—since he has showered his compassionate grace upon all those connected with him.

I was living in the mountains north of Santa Cruz in the fourth month of a vow of silence and several years into daily practice of hours of spiritual exercises (*sādhana*), under the guidance of a great, realized Vaiṣṇava Aṣṭāṅga Yogī who lived only a few miles up the road from the yogic household in which I lived. Being also influenced by Śrī Rāmakṛṣṇa Paramahaṃsa and Ānandamayīi Mā (both famous Bengali saints), I was mixing my *sādhana* with their influences and thinking sadly how unfortunate it was that there was no one on the planet doing what I was doing. Then by chance I heard about an American who had recently moved into town and who was giving classes on the Hindu classic, the *Bhagavad-gītā*.

I went to listen to his lectures and to meet this young man. I was then seventeen or eighteen years old. We met and as he talked about his tradition and his blessed *gurudeva*, I was enthralled and came to realize that I had found my tradition—the one I thought did not exist! Over the next few months (and more) we became exquisite friends. He gave me hours and hours of his time translating sacred texts from this wonderful tradition, teaching me proper etiquette (*sadācāra*) so that I could live with his *gurudeva* and the group of *bābājī*s that surrounded him.

He also gave me Bengali self-study books and I began to teach myself the Bengali language. He gave me his *gurudeva*'s photograph, as well as pictures of two other great *siddhas* (perfected ones) of the tradition, which I took home and worshiped. As the days turned into weeks and the weeks into months, I found myself delighted, fulfilled and illuminated. I will explain this a little more—I spent the afternoons and evenings with my new friend, whose name was Jagadānanda dās (Bābā's first *dīkṣā*-receiving western disciple), absorbing from him what I could of the teachings, practices, loving-compassion, and endearing worship ceremonies. Then I would go home to sleep. As I lay there waiting for sleep, my eyes closed, I could swear that someone was shining a powerful flash-light on the area of my forehead associated with the third eye. When I opened my eyes I found no one there and certainly no flash-light. This happened every night for many months.

After spending that time with Jagadānanda Dāsji, I went off to get a job to raise money for a trip to India so that I could live with his *guru*. I wanted his *guru* to become my blessed *guru*!

When I arrived in India, at the holy place where Bābā lived, I inquired about his whereabouts. The next morning I was guided to an *āśrama* in the small town where Bābā was staying at the time [Bābā was known to stay at one place for only one to three months at a time and then move to another place for private worship (*bhajana*)]. I saw him just as I came in from the street, across a small field where he was standing. I could not believe my eyes—he looked like an ancient *ṛṣi* (seer) of a time centuries past. I was brought before him and introduced through a letter Jagadānanda Dās had written on my behalf. I cannot rightly describe him—he was the very form of luminous, compassionate, divine love.

I was accepted immediately by Bābā with love, and by the group of *sādhus* who surrounded him. I sincerely offer my deepest, heart-felt thanks to Jagadānanda Dāsji for his help in instructing me in proper etiquette when living with such holy men. Otherwise, I would have caused much anguish among them. I also thank him for the precious time he spent with me translating the many holy writings of our tradition so that I might swim in their sacred meanings.

A typical day for us with Bābā started with waking up at 3:30 am, (although he and one advanced *bābājī*, a very dear older guru brother named Vanamālī Dās Bābājī) would rise by 2:00 am). After taking care of one's bathroom needs and then bathing in a nearby holy river or *kuṇḍa* (water tank or pond) we would put holy markings (*tilaka*) on twelve places on the upper parts of our bodies. Then we would all sit together for prayers and *kīrtana* (singing and chanting the holy names of God) for two to three hours. This included the performance of an *ārati* ceremony (a ritual greeting the sacred images with offerings of lights, incense, flowers, and such). At sunrise we would finish the *kīrtana* with the circumambulation of the holy temple, the holy basil plant (Tūlasā Devī), and so forth. Each of us then went off to our own rooms or corners of the temple to do our two to eight hours of private meditation and worship practice (called *bhajana-sādhana*). Different functions have to be performed by the *sādhus* of any given temple or *āśrama*. Some are cooks, one, the *pūjārī* serves and worships the sacred images (*ṭhākura*, some buy groceries, and some wash the temple floors, etc. Everyone, including the head of the monastery (the abbot or *mahānta*), helped with the chores. At noon was the first meal or honoring of sacred or grace food (*prasāda*)—food that had been prepared following specific codes and observances and then offered to the sacred images. After the offerings, all of us partook of the holy remnants, considering them compassionate blessings from our most holy and sweet, loving God.

I want now to recall several special occasions in the company of Baba that show something of his extraordinary attainment. Some of the following incidents occurred before the author of this book, Binode Bihari Dāsjī, met Bābā.

One sunny day at about ten in the morning I was sitting outside with some of the other *bābājīs* when I saw that Sītānāth Dās Bābājī (Baba's personal attendant) was working on a project. I went over to help him. The project was to level the ground where Bābā took his afternoon walks. The pathway was uneven because of large ruts from water erosion. Sītānāth Dādā (older brother) was digging from an available source of dirt nearby to fill in the ruts and even out the walkway. The only problem was that the place he was digging from was used as a trash area where all the used, partially fired clay cups were thrown and broken and the place where the neighborhood toddlers would pee. Digging and spreading this particularly dirty dirt was an atrocious job. It smelled horrible and had many fired clay fragments mixed in it. When we were done the pathway was raised and even, but smelled of months and maybe years of piss, and one could see broken shards of clay sticking up in many places.

As I said, it was a bright, sunny day with no clouds in the sky at all. Sītānāth Dāsjī and I went to the local lake, bathed to clean ourselves, and went to honor grace-food, for it was by then noon. After that we went outside again to sit for more casual meditation. That was when I observed clouds roll in. Rain clouds came rolling in and poured down their load of water for a good five minutes. Then, as quickly as they appeared, they departed and the sun came out again shining brilliantly. I realized that that brief rain had accomplished two things: (1) it smoothed out all the broken shards of clay that had been sticking up, and (2) it took away the horrible smell! Over the next few hours before Bābā came out for his walk the ground dried just perfectly, so when he walked, he walked on a firm, even, sweet-smelling ground. This is an example of how nature serves the *siddha-avadhūta-mahātmā* (perfected, purified, great-souled one)!

On another occasion I noticed that living creatures never harmed Bābā. I was at his *kuṭir* (a small room or hut for private worship) which in this case was made of earth. It was just after a rain and large ants were out roaming around hunting for food. They were all around and had the nasty habit of biting people. I found it difficult to sit there with so many of them crawling around me and biting me, but Bābā was unaffected. I thought to myself, "Wow, this is difficult for me. I want to see why is Bābā so unaffected." One simple reason was that he was just not being bitten! I watched closely for a long time and noticed that not very many of them would even crawl onto his body, but even when they did none of them bit him. Bābā was a friend to all and was completely cleansed of any trace of worldy qualities. Being saturated with divine love, compassion, and joy, all around him felt it, even the ants! Why would they be any different from the thousands and thousands of other living beings who came to Bābā to feel his Illuminated brilliance and be blessed by it?

There is another story about Bābā that occurred before I came to live with him. It was witnessed by his long-time attendant Sītānāth Dās Bābājī. One day Sītānāth came around to the *kuṭir* bringing Bābā his meal of grace-food. He suddenly became frightened and was taken aback. He stood motionlessly and quietly, watching as a deadly cobra climbed up Bābā's body. He watched it as it stayed a while wrapped around Bābā's shoulders and then, in its own time, slithered off and away into the jungle.

Though this next event seems more about myself, it really is not. After months of living in the holy land with Siddha Mauni Bābā (another name of Tinkaḍi Goswami) and other *sādhus* and saints, doing private worship eighteen hours a day, I noticed that during the nighttime gathering for the singing of prayers and *kīrtana*, many sacred feelings of love would rise in my heart—and with such intensity that I had to get up, walk over to Bābā and bow at his feet. This happened many times during the three to four hour period. I felt so grateful to him for what he was giving to me—this divine love rising in my heart. This experience continued for a number of weeks.

One of my main forms of service for Bābā was to be alone with him from about 7:00 am to 11:30 am. I was to help him with anything he needed during that time. Since he hardly needed anything then, I often used that time while sitting with him for meditation. What I loved to do was remain very quiet and meditate with him, hoping no-one would come for his blessings and bring him out of *samādhi* (meditative trance). He was in *samādhi* most of the time. If he was given five or ten minutes of undisturbed quiet, he would enter into *samādhi* and soon he would start giggling and talking to someone in a voice so sweet only poetry can describe it. He entered into the sacred time and space of Rādhā and Kṛṣṇa and interacted with them and the cowherd girls. This is the *samādhi* of the *rasik* practitioner—participating in the activities of God and his beloved family and friends who are pure, loving beings. Among them are the realized *rasik* saints and *siddhas*!

Then perhaps someone might come for his blessings and he would come out of his meditative trance for awhile. But sure enough, within five or ten minutes of their leaving, he was back laughing and talking in transcendent sweetness!

Out of many things I noticed while living with Bābā over the years was his distinctly other-worldly energy—an aura of transcendent love of God—an energy field that extended around and through him. This divine love *śakti* (power) was always consistent—whether he was tired from traveling or refreshed from a recent bath. Whether I was happy with him or felt troubled inside, frustrated with him or angry, whenever it came time to bow at his feet (the standard way of showing respect in the Caitanya tradition) I would experience the same transcendent, love-of-God energy as I had at other times. His level of illuminated realization was extraordinary. One of the reasons for this was that he was personally and directly blessed by Śrī Rādhā, the veritable Queen of Vraja, the divine love power of *svayam bhagavān* (God himself), Śrī Kṛṣṇa.

Bābā used to smile at me and shake his head with the comment I was a lucky person. He often did this when I went out for the circumambulation or a respectful walk around the holy mountain of Govardhana (fourteen miles around) and would bring him home very special kinds of grace-food from our tradition's famous sacred images hundreds of miles away! How did I do this? While on the holy walk I would visit with three or four different guru-uncles (guru-brothers of my own blessed *gurudeva*), who would always smile at me and bless me. They all loved Bābā very much and one in particular, Śrī Satyahari Bābā, would give me that rare grace-food to deliver to his beloved guru-brother—my own Tinkaḍi Bābā! You can imagine what wonderful *sevā* (service) this was for me. Even now, I shiver with great love and feeling as I think about it. Satyahari Bābā had great love and affection for everyone he met, but he specially loved my Bābā. For him his love was multiplied by the power of ten.

I remember one day in a particular holy site where we were living. During Bābā's afternoon walk some of us would circumambulate him as a act of respect and affection. After doing so I remember standing in front and to the side of him, but quite a distance away to observe him and the *sādhus* and devotees who were gathered around him. I was standing there gazing at him when I found myself seeing a beautiful blue disk over his heart, the heart of my *gurudeva*! I saw this with my naked eyes. It was fascinating and actually rather unbelievable to me. I rubbed my eyes, opened and closed them, yet the disk was still there. I pinched myself several times and yet it was still there. It was visible for three or four minutes. Later, I talked with a guru-brother about it and he said it was a *darśana* (a holy vision) of Kṛṣṇa. It was the sacred manifestation of God in the heart of a realized guru. I consider myself lucky to have seen it.

I remember the first day the author of this book, Binode Bihari Dāsji, came to see Bābā. He was a very friendly and sincere man; we became friends right away. He commented to me about how happy I was and how good it was of me to greet people and make them feel comfortable. I feel he saw qualities in me that he possessed himself. He later came to live with Bābā and became one of his personal attendants.

During an especially sacred month, the month of Dāmodara or Kārtika (October-November) that comes each year there are special observances (Niyama-sevā) and increased practice for us to do. During this time of year we lived in a holy place called Rādhākuṇḍa (the holy pond of Śrī Rādhā). There Bābā would host great saints like Śrī Jīv Gosvāmī and practitioner-scholars like Manīndranāth Guha. I remember one year in particular when Manīndranāth Bābu gave *pāṭha* (a reading and elucidation of a sacred text). The text he read was the *Ānanda-vṛindāvana Campū* ("Blissful Vṛndāvana"). During the afternoon readings Bābā would walk up and down listening, sometimes with tears running down from his eyes during parts of the reading. At other times he would laugh out and make joyous comments related to the text. It was indeed a special time!

After a number of years *gurudeva* started getting sick and several disciples from West Bengal came to take him to Jagannath Puri. I followed and stayed with him awhile there and in Bengal. While in Puri I could not help but notice one day Bābā's reaction to a particular man who came to him for spiritual blessings. Bābā exclaimed "Sādhu, Sādhu" and pointed to him. When I looked closer to see to who it was, I noticed it was the same person Bābā had said the same thing about a few years before when he visited him in Vraja. This is the only person I heard Bābā say this about in all the years I was with him. It was extraordinary to me and so this time I made sure to meet him in order to try to understand what Bābā was talking about, what Bābā meant by *sādhu*. He turned out to be a very gentle, unassuming and honest man, in other words a *sādhu*!

One more thing happened during this time that is worthy of mention. While living in the holy city of Jagannath Puri I began to get sick. Due to the high salt content in the water I had developed problems digesting food. After several months of this I became weaker and weaker until I got so ill I lost a lot of weight and could not keep my balance while walking. The blessed *mahānta* of the Haridās Ṭhākur Maṭha where we were being hosted, Śrī Nitaipada Dās Bābājī Mahārāj, was concerned for my life and reported to my *gurudeva* that he thought I was dying. As for me, I was in so much bliss all the time that I did not notice how close to death I had come. Bābā called me into his presence and raised his hand in front of me as a blessing. This he held for one or two minutes. I fell into a state of God-awareness and felt something shift physically inside of me. From that moment I was cured of my physical problems. Although it took a few weeks to gain my strength back, from the moment of his blessing I was cured. I am very thankful for his blessing.

There is an understanding that the guru never dies; he is always in the hearts of his disciples. This is a true statement and begs a few comments. A *siddha* guru is skilled and always ready to grace the world through his chosen disciples. He will manifest in different ways and through different avenues, but he is present none the less. Whether he communicates through dreams, is present in dream-time or manifests directly, it is the disciple who needs to become worthy of his grace. If it is fantasy or even inflated experience, then the ego will prevail and lead the disciple to an unworthy end, but if there is a true, selfless, loving, humble connection with the *siddha* guru—then there will be grace and spiritual progress for the disciple and for everyone with whom the disciple comes into contact. This is the compassionate grace-magic of this powerful tradition.

How can I end this recollection? How can I properly express the qualities of a person so loving, so wise, so deeply surrendered to God—in love with God and in loving interaction with God? He was completely and powerfully blessed by God and able similarly to bless others with the holy name of God. He gave everything to God and his devotees so thoroughly and powerfully that God gave back to him, protected him, took away any inconveniences from his life and showered him with love divine. How can I share him—such a precious jewel—with you, dear readers, in such a way that you too might receive his blessings as I and so many others have? I am always anxious to find ways of doing this. I think the greatest blessing is to be able to share him with you. Kindly bless me and forgive my excesses in this most personal of confessions.

My Recollections — Mark Tinghino

I did not spend nearly enough time with Bābā while he was on the planet. That was mainly because of my residing in America and only being able to visit India for relatively short periods of time. The first time I met Bābā in January of 1980 he was seated on a mat in his room at our temple in the village of Govardhana, which was dimly lit. The first thing I noticed was that his face was glowing like hot coals and shifting hues from pink to yellow to white to blue. It was not a physical phenomenon with physiological causes. It was an otherworldly glow. Given his reputation as a *siddha bhajanānandī* (a person accomplished in private worship), I was not amazed by that manifestation. Communication between us was impeded by my lack of fluency in conversational Bengali, which differed in many respects from the medieval Bengali texts that I had studied up to that point in time. I don't recall any exchange of words between us at that first meeting. If there were, it was very brief. I had made my intentions known upon my arrival at the temple. I had come to apply for *mantra dīkṣā*[180] from Bābā. This was communicated to him via his other disciples. He was sizing me up as a potential initiate.

I was scolded soon after arriving for making too high a donation to a local Śiva-liṅga temple nearby on my way from New Delhi and for not hiding my camera inside my steel trunk. The *sādhus* were apprehensive, because the dacoits in surrounding villages had spies that would report back to those criminal enterprises whenever foreign tourists with valuables were seen in the area. It was the first time I had stayed in that

[180]A form of initiation in which one receives through one's right ear the sacred verbal formulae called *mantra* from one's guru.

remote a region, although I had made daytime excursions there when living in Vrindaban, which is a fairly large settlement, more of a small city than a village.

I was able to converse with some of the Bengali devotees at the temple to some extent, although I wished I were more fluent in modern Bengali. The first evening of my stay at Govardhana was my first experience of the type of *kīrtana* practiced by the *bābājīs*. I had taken part in many group *kīirtanas* in India, America and Europe throughout the 1970s, but the *bābājīs'* slightly different agenda was far more intense and entrancing. I would have to attribute that to the many years of practice and the dedicated renunciation of the various participants. Bābā came out of his room when he heard the banging of the clay drums and clanging of the hand cymbals. He stood off to one side smiling, leaning on his wooden staff and enjoying the chanting as he counted his *mantras* on his beads. I was part of a group of Westerners from the post World War II baby boom counter-culture who had taken to the *bhakti* movement founded by Śrī Caitanya Mahāprabhu in the 16th Century. A few of us studied the Sanskrit and Bengali languages and sought to cultivate *rasa* (devotional rapture) via our newfound discipline that included *pūjā* (image worship), *mantra-japa* (repetition of mantras) and *kīrtana* (singing the names and sports of the Divine Couple). Now I was surrounded by those who had been born into a culture steeped in those traditions and who were some of the foremost *rasikas* (experiencers of *rasa*) of their generation. That made all the difference.

In the several weeks of my living at the temple, Bābā stayed in his room much of the time performing his *bhajana* (private worship), only emerging for short periods of time to meet with visitors in the afternoon or late morning or to listen to the evening *kīrtana* program. I took every opportunity to ask him questions. After a few days of sleeping on the dusty temple room floor, I requested for other accommodations to be arranged for me, since I had been suffering from allergies (a common problem for me in rural India with its ubiquitous dust and its cumulative smoke from wood fires burning in homes and temples). It is not that the temple room was not swept regularly. It was just the nature of the dry and arid terrain and the rustic construction of the temple, which was not an opulent marble palace like many of the larger Indian temples.

After a few weeks I was summoned to go out with Bābā one afternoon. He mounted a bicycle rikshaw with his wooden staff and I was handed his water pot to carry as I accompanied him on foot. We headed out to a deserted area alongside the hill of Govardhana. The rikshaw driver and I helped Bābā climb down from the carriage. Bābā and I proceeded down a path into a dense thicket of dried brush. Within the thicket was a small, one room, brick hut that had been hidden from view. It had a thatched roof with an overhang in front supported by vertical wooden columns at the two corners that formed a sort of open porch providing shade from the hot desert sun. We sat down under the overhang with our hands on our chanting beads. After several minutes I attempted to make some light conversation regarding the idyllic setting. He then said something to me in Bengali, but I could not follow his dialect. After repeating himself a couple of times with no response from me, he then stood up and pointed to inside the brick hut, indicating that I should enter.

After sitting on the floor of the hut for awhile, I heard a couple of other men speaking with Bābā in Bengali. Eventually one of them came to get me, and several people soon arrived for a reading of the *Caitanya-caritāmṛta* followed by a short *kīrtana*. After we arrived back at the temple, I was informed by Advaita Das Bābājī that Bābā had decided to bestow *dīkṣā* upon me and that I was to make a small donation towards a feast as part of an upcoming festival featuring a seven day long reading of the *Śrīmad Bhāgavata Mahāpurāṇa*. I was then taken into Bābā's room where he had first had me sit on a floor mat and water a *tulasī* plant in a clay pot on the floor. He then recited to me the set of initiation *mantras*, and he had me repeat those out loud. (I had received a powerless set of those *mantras* in a prior initiation; now I was finally getting an empowered set in the line of succession from Śrī Nityānanda Prabhu).

After the seven day festival of reciting the *Bhāgavata*, I went to stay at a Keśīghāṭa *āśrama* in Vrindaban, which was headed by the late Śrī Paṇḍita Kṛṣṇacaraṇa Dāsa Bābājī. Bābā requested that I come to visit him at our Rādhākuṇḍa temple once a week while staying in Vrindaban, so I purchased a bicycle to make that trip, which was about a two hour ride each way. Binapani Biswas, one of the elderly Bengali widows who lived near the Keśīghāṭa *āśrama* always knew where Bābā was traveling. So, I would need to check with her first before heading out. Although he was staying at Rādhākuṇḍa most of the time, he would sometimes move out to another locale in the surrounding countryside. When it was a place too far to reach by bike, I would have to take a bus or horse carriage.

On one of my visits to our Rādhākuṇḍa temple, I was sitting out in the sunny courtyard on the banks of the famous pond with Bābā. A couple of monkeys were cavorting on a tall tree overhead, and while wrestling with each other they lost their footing and fell on the ground screaming a few feet away from us. The ruckus caused Bābā to slip out of his trance of *japa* meditation. As he looked over at the two monkeys, he started laughing. It was infectious, and I had to break out laughing with him, although I had not immediately seen the humor in the situation.

After a few months my three month tourist visa, which I had extended for the customary six-month limit, was almost expired, so I went to stay at our temple in Navadwip, West Bengal. I then had to return to America.

My next trip to India was in December of 1982. I was working on a master's degree at the University of Chicago at the time, so I could only make that trip during the four week winter break between quarters. Bābā was living at the Haridās Maṭha in Puri, Orissa, at the time. It was a two room suite on the upper level, with a small bedroom where Bābā slept and a fairly large outer drawing room where I slept on my camping mattress on the floor with a few of Bābā's entourage. The drawing room was also used for Bābā's reception of visitors in the morning and lectures in the afternoon.

Bābā at that time was in a very weakened condition due to his declining health. He spent much of his time reclining in his bedroom and chanting. Sometimes he would have several of us gather around his bed and perform *kīrtana*. On that trip I had brought a handheld super 8 millimeter movie camera with me. I filmed Bābā answering questions in his bedroom, and I filmed a lecture and *kīrtana* in the outer drawing room. Unfortunately, the quality of the cheap microphone that came with the camera left much to be desired, and it is virtually impossible to make out the conversation in the segment in Bābā's bedroom. Still, it is a rare record of the life of a renowned figure in Caitanyaism, and hopefully someday we can recover that conversation via sound enhancement.

Although my time with Bābā was brief, they are moments to be treasured. He was engaged in *bhajana* most of the time, which was extremely inspirational to those of us with far less dedication. My own practice was taken to a new level while residing with him. Whenever I asked him about my course of action, such as whether I should finish my formal college education and pursue graduate studies, he would always say that the most important thing was maintaining the daily *bhajana*, and that as long as that was carried out, everything would be fine.

Bibliography

Bābā, Ananta Dāsa, *Śrī Guru Tattva Vijñāna & Śrī Bhakta Tattva Vijñāna*, 1st edn., Two essays by Paṇḍita Ananta Dāsa Bābājī Mahārāja. English translation by Advaita Das. (Rādhākuṇḍa, India: Śrī Ananta Dāsa Bābājī Mahārāja, 2003).

Bharati, Premananda, *Sri Krsna: the Lord of Love*, 2nd edn., New edition with introductions and scholarly apparatus and appendices of the 1912 edition published by William Ryder and Son, Ltd. (Kirksville, MO, USA: Blazing Sapphire Press, 2007).

Callewaert, Winand M. & Snell, Rupert eds., *According to Tradition: Hagiographical Writing in India*, 1st edn., A collection of essays with introduction by Rupert Snell on hagiography in different Indic traditions. (Wiesbaden, Germany: Harrassowitz Verlag, 1994).

Dāsa, Haridāsa, *Śrī Śrī Gauḍīya Vaiṣṇava Jīvana, Dvitīya Khaṇḍa*, 3rd edn. (Navadvīpa, India: Haribol Kuṭīra, 489 GA [1975]).

Dāsa, Vinoda Vihārī, *Bhakti-krama-vikāśer Antarāya*, 1st edn., In Bengli. Binode Bihari Das Bābājī's earlier book on the obstacles to the development of *bhakti*. (Vṛndāvana, India: Śrī Murārī Dāsa, 1995).

Dāsa, Vinoda Vihārī, *Prabhupāda Śrī Śrī 108 Kiśorīkiśorānanda Bābā, Tinkaḍi Bābā*, 1st edn., In Bengali. The source text for this translation. (Keśīghāṭa, Vṛndāvana, India: Śrī Murārī Dāsa Bābājī, 1999).

Ṭhākura, Narottama Dāsa, *Sri Sri Prema Bhakti Candrika*, 1st edn., With the commentaries of Vishvanatha Chakravartipada and Srila Ananta Dasa Babaji Maharaja. Translated into English by Advaita Dasa. (Rādhākuṇḍa, India: Śrī Ananta Dāsa Bābājī Mahārāja, [n.d.]).

Ghose, Shishir Kumar, *Lord Gauranga or Salvation for All*, vol. 1-2, 3rd edn. (Calcutta, India: Piyush Kanti Ghose, 1923).

Gosvāmin, Gopāla Bhaṭṭa, *Śrī Hari-bhakti-vilāsaḥ*, 1st edn., Edited by Purīdāsa Mahāśaya with the commentary of Sanātana Gosvāmin. In Sanskrit. (Mayamanasiṃha (now in Bangla Desh): Śacīnātharāya-caturdhurīṇa, 1946).

Gosvāmin, Jīva, *Śrībhakti-Śrīprīti-nāmaka-sandarbha-dvayam*, 1st edn., Edited by Purīdāsa Mahāśaya. In Sanskrit. (Vṛndāvana, India: Haridāsa Śarmā, 1951).

Gosvāmin, Raghunātha Dāsa, *Stavāvalī*, 2nd edn., In Sanskrit with the commentary of Vaṅgeśvara Vidyābhūṣaṇa and a Bengali translation. (Mūrśidābād (West Bengal, India): Rādhāramaṇa Yantra, 1329 [1923]).

Gosvāmin, Rūpa, *Ujjvala-nīla-maṇi*, reprint edn., Edited with the commentaries of Jīvagosvāmin and Viśvanātha Chakravarty by M. M. Pandit Durga Prasad & Vasudev Lakshaman Shastri Panashikar. In Sanskrit. (Varanasi, India: Chaukhamba Sanskrit Pratishthan, 1985).

Gosvāmin, Rūpa, *The Bhakti-rasāmṛta-sindhu of Rūpa Gosvāmin*, 1st edn., Translated with introduction and notes by David L. Haberman. (New Delhi, India: Indira Gandhi Center for the Arts, 2003).

Gosvāmin, Rūpa, *Śrī Śrī Bhakti-rasāmṛtra-sindhuḥ*, 3rd edn., Edited with the commentaries of Śrī Jīva, Mukundadāsa, and Viśvanātha Cakravartin and a Bengali translation by Haridāsa Dāsa. In Sanskrit and Bengali. (Mathurā, India: Śrī Kṛṣṇajanmasthāna, 495 [1981]).

Gosvāmin, Rūpa, *Ujjvala-nīla-maṇiḥ*, 2nd edn., Edited with the commentary of Viṣṇudāsa Gosvāmin by Haridāsa Dāsa, In Sanskrit with a Bengali translation. (Navadvīpa, West Bengal, India: Mukundadāsa, Ga. 478 [1964]).

Gosvāmin, Sanātana, *Bṛhad-bhāgavatāmṛta*, 1st edn., Edited with the author's own commentary by Purīdāsa. In Sanskrit. (Mayamanasiṃha (now in Bangla Desh): Śacīnātharāya, G458 [1944]).

Guha, Manindranath, *Nectar of the Holy Name*, 1st edn., An English translation of the author's Bengali work, *Śrīman-nāmāmṛta-sindhu-bindu*. (Kirksville, MO, USA: Blazing Sapphire Press, 2006).

Hawley, John Stratton, 'Morality Beyond Morality in the Lives of Three Hindu Saints', in Hawley, John Stratton ed., *Saints and Virtues*, 1st edn., chap. four, pp. 52–72 (Berkeley: University of California Press, 1987).

Jackson, William J., *Tyāgarāja: Life and Lyrics*, 1st edn. (Madras: Oxford University Press, 1991).

Jackson, William J., 'A Life Becomes a Legend: Śrī Tyāgarāja as Exemplar', *Journal of the American Academy of Religion*, vol. LX, no. Four, 717–736 (1992).

Jackson, William J., *Songs of Three Great South Indian Saints*, 1st edn. (Delhi: Oxford University Press, 1998).

Kapoor, Dr. O. B. L., *The Saints of Bengal*, 1st edn. (Radhakunda, India: Srila Badrinarayana Bhagavata Bhushana Prabhu, 1995).

Kapoor, Dr. O. B. L., *The Companions of Sri Chaitanya Mahaprabhu*, 1st edn. (Radhakunda, India: Srila Badrinarayana Bhagavata Bhushana Prabhu, 1997).

Kapoor, Dr. O. B. L., *Experiences in Bhakti: the Science Celestial*, 2nd edn. (Kirksville, MO, USA: Blazing Sapphire Press, 2006).

Kapoor, O. B. L., *The Saints of Vraja*, 2nd edn. (New Delhi, India: Aravali Books International (P) LTD, 1999).

Kavirāja, Kṛṣṇadāsa, *Caitanya-caritāmṛta*, vol. 1-6, 4th edn., Edited with commentary by Dr. Rādhāgovinda Nātha. In Bengali and Sanskrit. (Kalikātā: Sādhanā Prakāśanī, [1963]).

Kavirāja, Kṛṣṇadāsa, *The Caitanya Caritāmṛta of Kṛṣṇadāsa Kaviraja*, 1st edn., A translation and commentary by Edward C. Dimock, Jr. Edited by Tony K. Stewart (Cambridge, MA: Department of Sanskrit and Indian Studies, Harvard University, 1999).

Mahāprabhu, Śrī Caitanya, *Śrī Śrī Śikṣāṣṭakam*, 1st edn., With the commentary of Śrī Ananta Dāsa Bābājī Mahārāja. Translated into English by Advaita Das. (Rādhākuṇḍa, India: Śrī Ananta Dāsa Bābājī Mahārāja, 2003).

Nāth, Nīradprasād, *Narottama o Tāñhār Racanāvalī*, 1st edn., In Bengali. On the life and works of Narottama Dāsa Ṭhākura. Contains editions of all his major works and many attributed to Narottama Dāsa. (Kalikātā (Kolkata), India: Kalikātā Viśvavidyālaya, 1975).

Purīdāsa ed., *Śrīmad-bhāgavatam*, vol. 1-3, 1st edn., In Sanskrit. No commentaries. (Mayamanasiṃha, Bangla Desh: Śacīnātharāyacaturdhurīṇa, 1945).

www.ingramcontent.com/pod-product-compliance
Lightning Source LLC
Chambersburg PA
CBHW031236290426
44109CB00012B/311
* 9 7 8 0 9 7 4 7 9 6 8 8 8 *